D1426717

IN THE BEGINNING
Personal Recollections
of Software Pioneers

ROBERT L. GLASS

IEEE
COMPUTER
SOCIETY

Los Alamitos, California

Washington ● Brussels ● Tokyo

Library of Congress Cataloging-in-Publication Data

Glass, Robert L., 1932–
    In the beginning: personal recollections of software pioneers /
Robert L. Glass.
        p.   cm.
    Includes bibliographical references.
    ISBN 0-8186-7999-9
    1. Computer software—Development—History.   2. Electronic
data processing personnel.   I. Title.
QA76.76.D47G565   1998
005.1 ' 092—dc21
[B]   97-11391
                                            CIP

Copyright © 1998 by The Institute of Electrical and Electronics Engineers, Inc. All rights reserved.

Copyright and Reprint Permissions: Abstracting is permitted with credit to the source. Libraries are permitted to photocopy isolated pages beyond the limits of US copyright law, for private use of their patrons. Other copying, reprint, or republication requests should be addressed to: IEEE Copyrights Manager, IEEE Service Center, 445 Hoes Lane, P.O. Box 1331, Piscataway, NJ 08855-1331.

IEEE Computer Society Press Order Number BP07999
Library of Congress Number 97-11391
ISBN 0-8186-7999-9

Additional copies may be ordered from:

IEEE Computer Society Press	IEEE Service Center	IEEE Computer Society	IEEE Computer Society
Customer Service Center	445 Hoes Lane	13, Avenue de l'Aquilon	Ooshima Building
10662 Los Vaqueros Circle	P.O. Box 1331	B-1200 Brussels	2-19-1 Minami-Aoyama
P.O. Box 3014	Piscataway, NJ 08855-1331	BELGIUM	Minato-ku, Tokyo 107
Los Alamitos, CA 90720-1314	Tel: +1-908-981-1393	Tel: +32-2-770-2198	JAPAN
Tel: +1-714-821-8380	Fax: +1-908-981-9667	Fax: +32-2-770-8505	Tel: +81-3-3408-3118
Fax: +1-714-821-4641	mis.custserv@computer.org	euro.ofc@computer.org	Fax: +81-3-3408-3553
Email: cs.books@computer.org			tokyo.ofc@computer.org

Publisher: Matt Loeb
Developmental Editor: Cheryl Baltes
Advertising/Promotions: Tom Fink
Production Editor: Lisa O'Conner
Cover photograph: Ornithopod dinosaur tracks in the Cretaceous Dakota Group of Colorado,
by Anthony J. Martin.
Cartoon artist: P. Edward Presson
Printed in the United States of America by Edwards Brothers, Incorporated

IEEE
COMPUTER
SOCIETY
IEEE

PREFACE

When history passes judgment on the change-filled time in which we now live, one thing seems fairly certain—this will be called the "computer age."

Beginning around the middle of the twentieth century, and extending far enough into the future that few of us can imagine its ending, the computer age is the period of time during which computer power has dramatically changed, and continues to change, how the world functions. Few aspects of our lives are not touched by—and often, heavily influenced by—computers.

Was the computer's arrival a cosmic accident, an invention whose time simply came? Did the population explosion and the resulting social complexity make the computer a necessary tool to subdue that complexity inevitable? These questions are unanswerable, of course, but interesting to ponder.

The purpose of this book is not so much to address unanswerable questions as to capture concrete realities. The computer age, as any other, was made possible by the people who built it. The reality this book captures is that of the software pioneers of the field, the people who wrote the programs that made that complicated but very dumb product called a computer perform the magic that we have come to understand so well. Software, most would agree, makes the computer hardware world go 'round. But who are the pioneers who made the software world go 'round? And what were their experiences?

The time is right for such a book. In fact, the time is probably now or never. Given that the use of software to solve the world's problems began in the 1950s, those pioneers who began their professional careers at that time—perhaps then in their 20s—are now well into their 60s. Many of software's early innovators have already retired from the field, and some have died. Capturing the personal recollections of these pioneers now is essential, or they will be lost forever.

But is that enough of a reason for anyone to be interested in reading this book? Could not such a book simply be a compilation of dry-as-dust information written by old fogies who are out of touch with today and can only vaguely recall those past days?

There are several important reasons why I believe this material is worth reading:

1. Professionals in our field are surprisingly misinformed about its history. As the editor of a professional journal, I frequently see papers cross my desk that describe computing's past as prologue to some new idea they are presenting—and they get that past totally wrong. It is time to record the truth of that prologue, if only to enable tomorrow's professionals to build more solidly on the realities of the past.

2. The old truism "everything old is new again" is just as true in computing as it is in other fields, especially in software. The stories in this book clearly show us that such modern concepts as data abstraction, modularity, and structured approaches date much earlier in the field than their appearance in the academic literature. In many fields of endeavor, practice often precedes theory (for example, the steam engine and human flight pre-dated the theories of thermodynamics and aerodynamics), and the software field is no exception. These stories help to capture the field's true evolution.

3. Written history has a tendency to be cold and austere, full of too many dates and "major" events and too few human experiences and true turning points. In this book, we capture those human experiences and clues to those turning points through the personal recollections of those who lived them. This book is as alive as the people whose stories it contains.

There you have it. If you have read this far, perhaps your curiosity has at least been piqued by what we are trying to do here. So let me step aside and let you read on.

Welcome to the world of computing's past!

Robert L. Glass
At the end of the twentieth century

CONTENTS

1

INTRODUCTION

If this is the Computing Age, where do we stand in its evolution? Especially in the software development portion of the Computing Age, how far along are we on the road to maturity?

There are those who would say that the software development field is flawed and, perhaps, even failed. They are the ones who cry "software crisis" (claiming that software is always over budget, behind schedule, and unreliable) and who thereby imply that the field has made little progress since its early days.

But look around you. You probably bought this book in a bookstore that used a bar code system to track price, inventory, and sales. You probably paid for this book with a credit card and fully expect the charge to be correctly reflected in your monthly statement. You may be reading this book on an airplane that was designed with the help of a computerized system, is being flown in part by a real-time system, and for which your reservations were made by yet another system. In your computer-produced newspaper you read about electronic warfare or some new space flight that would simply be impossible without successful computing. And all of those things that we label "computing" or "system" are enabled by software. In short, there is ample empirical evidence in the lives of all of us that we have progressed well beyond the early, flawed phase of the software development field.

We are currently in the "Emerging Era" of the software portion of the Computing Age. We have had dramatic successes in software development over the past 40 years, but we are only a little more than a couple of human generations into the field, and we know there is lots more to be learned. In the corresponding era of the automobile age, for example, we would still have seen primitive things like mechanical brakes and tunable carburetors and wooden-spoked wheels and manual chokes. Our software products and enterprises of today include the (eventually failed) Nashes and Studebakers and Hudsons, as well as the (successful) Chevrolets and Lincolns and Dodges. And we cannot tell, at this point, which will emerge as the winners.

Past is prologue. To better understand where we are today, it helps to consider our yesterdays. This book is about the experiences of those who were instrumental in a preceding era, which I call software's "Pioneering Era" (1955–1965). They are the people who struggled with hardware that frequently failed, computing systems that filled huge rooms, computers so costly that we optimized machine instead of human time, and rudimentary software tools that may or may not have included a compiler, and probably did not include a generalized operating system. The people of this era were pioneers in every sense of the word.

As I began to put together this book, I contacted many of the pioneers of the software field, asking for their personal recollections. I made a deliberate effort to pursue not just the recollections of the Very Visible people in the field, but the recollections of the Less Visible people as well. Truth in history, as we well know, is elusive. What I remember about the 1950s may or may not match what others remember. And because history is often written by the visible members of the field simply because they are visible, I made a special effort to capture the recollections of those less visible but just as real. From the stories in this book, I hope you will be able to form an accurate picture of what it was like for these pioneers of software's Pioneering Era.

In my original contact with potential contributors, I asked them to consider the following as they began to write their recollections:

- "I did this and here is what I learned."
- "The field at this time was doing X; I {agreed} {disagreed} with it and here is why."
- "I worked with some other pioneers, such as L, M, and N, and here is what I remember about them."
- "People today say ABC about what it was like in the early days, but my recollection is that it was CDE."

- "I was involved with project GHI, which was interesting because it pioneered PQR."

- "There was a terribly {funny} {tragic} incident that I was involved in, and here is what happened."

- "What we did back then seems strange to us today, but here is what we did and why we did it."

In short, I was looking for a very personal view of that Pioneering Era. You are the judge of how well that attempt has succeeded. The stories that follow may possess style and content as different as the very different pioneers who wrote them, but my hope is that you will find them, at heart, a very human view of what it was like back then. When everyone in the software field was a pioneer!

2

BEFORE THE BEGINNING: THE PRE-SOFTWARE ERA

This book is a collection of very personal stories in which software pioneers share their reminiscences about events in the early days of software development. Whether you lived through those early days or want to understand what it was like back then, these stories provide a glimpse into the fascinating events of that fascinating era.

This first story is different from the others in a couple of ways. The author, David Myers of Australia, pioneered in an era before software existed. His story sets the stage for the stories that follow. Whereas all the other contributors have software-related stories to tell, Myers reminds us of a time when software was only a gleam in the eye of hardware engineers seeking to make their electronic (and mechanical!) boxes more versatile.

The other difference in Myers' story is how he prepared his manuscript. Myers retired from the field in the 1970s, and he is the product of a much earlier era than the other contributors to this book, most of whom are still active in the field.

Let me describe for you how I received his manuscript. The story was typed—that is, it was not prepared with a word processor but was typed on a typewriter. The ribbon on the typewriter was obviously near the end of its usability, and the characters on the pages were faint and uneven. The mistakes were repaired with strike-overs. Footnotes were indicated by hand-inserted digits at a level above the line of type. The right margin was very ragged. Some of the keys on the typewriter were obviously worn, and those characters were less than clear on the page. A cover note accompanied the story, handwritten by Dr. Myers. In this note he said, "the ancient typewriter just lasted the distance."

It is easy to imagine that after he finished writing these reminiscences he packed the typewriter and its tired ribbon and bent keys away into an attic somewhere, where it will symbolically join the buggy whips and slide rules and other artifacts made obsolete by an onrush of new technologies. In a very real sense, the twentieth century has seen the rise—and the demise—of more technologies than any previous century in history. Somehow it seems fitting that the earliest of our pioneers was the only contributor to submit his story using a mechanism made obsolete by the remarkable new mechanism he helped to develop.

LIFE BEFORE SOFTWARE:
A FEW REMINISCENCES

David Myers

In the midst of the avalanche of effort currently being expended on the development and use of computer software it is interesting to reflect on the "state of the art" before the word *software* came into use. My own activities in the world of computing were confined mainly to that earlier period. I have never written a program for a digital computer!

As a schoolboy in the 1920s I became involved in computing after reading a description of the automatic totalizator devised by G. A. Julius and hearing a talk given by him to an engineering audience.[1] An engineer at heart, I was fascinated by his use of mathematical analogies to calculate and display the individual odds at a race track. Many years later, I argued with him that his machine would be more efficient and less cumbersome if the linkages between components were electrical rather than mechanical. He brushed me off by pointing out that electrical devices were "permissive" and that a failure in power supply, even if only temporary, would lead to riots at the race track, probably followed by wrecking of the tote. He understood mob psychology.

At that time the idea of using electrical devices to solve numerical problems was restricted by the difficulty of maintaining accuracy for long periods and by problems associated with storing and displaying numerical data. (An outstanding exception was the ordinary electricity meter that continuously multiplies voltage and current, integrates the product with respect to time, and displays the result on a visible counter.) Electronic devices became more sophisticated, but their use for computing was still limited by the difficulty of distinguishing between two quantities in a decimal system. Measurements in an electronic circuit had to be accurate and reliable enough to distinguish, for example, between 7 and 8. They could, however, easily distinguish between 0 and 1, off and on, no and yes. It was the development of electronic pulse techniques, stimulated by the wartime emphasis on radar and supported by a reappraisal of George Boole's philosophy of symbolic logic, that led to a new appreciation of what could be done electronically.[2]

During World War II, there was a pressing need to solve mathematical problems arising mainly from the use of radar and from the production of food and equipment. While employed by the Australian Council for Scientific and Industrial Research (CSIR, later CSIRO) I wrote a report on the mechanical aids that could be used to solve such problems. These were all analogue machines. They had the apparent virtue of dealing continuously with variable quantities. At the same time, much progress had been made in the use of "step-by- step" processes and the mechanical aids to their solution. In association with the statistician E. A. Cornish, also of CSIR, I forwarded my report with a recommendation that CSIR establish a unit to deal with mathematical instruments.[3] This was accepted, and a Section of Mathematical Instruments (MIS) was formed. I was asked to serve as its officer-in-charge, and when I changed direction soon thereafter by accepting an appointment as Professor of Electrical Engineering at the University of Sydney, the MIS came with me. I had just returned from a visit to the United States and England to bring myself up-to-date with computer developments. The most significant progress there was the successful design of electronic computers in which data storage was achieved by the use of acoustic delay lines or cathode-ray tubes. Magnetic tape or disks were sometimes used as a backup.

These machines, enormous in cost and size by present standards, nevertheless constituted a turning point in computer development by demonstrating the practicability of electronic digital computers. Babbage, without access to electronics, had limited success in doing so with mechanical computers but he did illustrate the value of stored programs, an essential factor in high-speed operation that, in turn, made accurate, step-by-step problem solving feasible. This, of course, reduced the apparent advantage of the analogue machine, which, for the most part, could only be reprogrammed either by physical adjustments or by acquiring a new machine. Programming an electronic machine became a worldwide activity, and it has been said that the developments of the late 1940s were the foundation of the software industry. There were, of course, other contributions, such as the sophisticated use of desk-type accounting machines and punched card devices, but the versatility and speed of the electronic computer gave promise of a great future.

At the time, the size and cost of the new machines appeared prohibitive. When asked many times how soon they would replace such machines as cash resisters in shops, I often replied "not in our lifetime." But the contemporary expansion of the role of semiconductors in electrical circuitry, followed by the use of printed circuits and silicon chips, all conspired to make nonsense of my assertion

In attempting to find ways of reducing the size and cost of electronic computers, MIS in Sydney concentrated on components, such as the design of vacuum tubes to perform logical functions, various forms of magnetic storage, and methods of display. Being pressed by prospective users and anticipating a long delay in acquiring or building a computer, we designed a differential analyzer[4]—a mechanical device for solving differential equations as described by Bush and Hartree but with electrical interconnection of units.[5] It was used to deal with problems ranging from the production of salt by solar evaporation[6] to the astronomical theory of globular clusters.[7] It soon became obsolete when the size, cost, speed, and versatility of electronic computers brought them into everyday use in the community.

In the meantime the MIS was asked by the Snowy Mountains Authority to design and make a digital computer to assist in the balancing of demands for electricity generation and irrigation. This task was successfully undertaken by Murray Allen and David Wong and was probably the first significant solid-state digital computer built in Australia for industrial use.[8]

From that time onward, the speed of change was even greater than we could have predicted. As most readers of this book are familiar with the breathtaking growth of the computer industry and with it the software industry, I can now put my pen down and relax. In any case, my active participation in the field tapered off at about the time software became the main center of exploration, making most fixed-purpose machines redundant. It has been a privilege for me to work for most of my life during the formative years of computer developments and so to help lay the foundations of the software industry.

ENDNOTES

1. G.A. Julius, *Inst. Eng. Aust.,* Trans. 1, 1920, paper 2, p. 221.

2. G. Boole, *The Mathematical Analysis of Logic,* Blackwell, Oxford, 1947.

3. D.M. Myers and E.A. Cornish, CSIR, Div. of Electrotechnology, Report ETR 13, 1946.

4. D.M. Myers and W.R. Blunden, *Proc. Conf. on Auto. Comp. Machines,* CSIRO, Department of Electrical Engineering, University of Sydney, 1952.

5. See V. Bush, *Franklin Inst. Journal,* Vol. 212, No. 4, 1931, p. 575; and D.R. Hartree, *Nature,* Vol. 135, No. 3423, 1935, p. 940.

6. D.M. Myers and C.W. Bonython, *Jour. App. Chem.,* Vol. 8, 1958, p. 207.

7. A.W. Rodgers and D.M. Myers, *Monthly Notices of the Royal Astronomical Society,* Vol. 114, No. 6, 1954, p. 620.

8. M.W. Allen, *Proc. Conf. on Computing and Data Processing,* Vol. 2, Weapons Research Establishment, 1957.

3

SETTING THE STAGE: THREE ERAS OF SOFTWARE HISTORY

In this section of the book, I share my story with you. I immodestly put it early in the book because I believe it structures the computing age and provides a framework into which the other stories can fit. I hope you will agree.

The idea for this book, and for my own story that follows, began when I was asked to prepare some remarks to be presented on the occasion of my receiving an honorary doctorate from Linköping University in Sweden. I was (and am) deeply proud of this honor, and I was especially pleased that it would be presented by my friends and colleagues in Sweden, where I had spent several delightful summers as a visiting professor. I decided that the presentation of such an honor was an appropriate time to talk about my own reminiscences in the software field.

But trouble intervened. The ravages of old age struck—ravages I had optimistically thought were off in some distant and unimaginable future (don't we all think that?). I developed a bulging disk and degenerative arthritis in my lower back. Travel, as well as many other activities of a normal life, became impossible. I had to tell the people in Linköping that I could not attend the award ceremony.

The most amazing thing then happened. My colleagues at Linköping decided that, if I could not come to their ceremony, they would bring their ceremony to me. And so they did. Let me present you with a brief picture of my honorary doctorate award ceremony.

The scene is a restaurant at a lake resort in Indiana. Six of us are sitting in a private dining room: two gentlemen from Sweden, who have flown to the United States to make the presentation; two of my best friends from Seattle, Ed and Carole Presson, whom my Swedish hosts have flown in to witness and be part of the ceremony; and my wife and me. A video camera has been set up on a tripod in the corner, and still cameras lie on the dining table. Outside, mostly out of sight and sound, are the other patrons of the restaurant. The dean, who has come from Sweden to make the presentation, is saying the official ceremonial words, placing the doctorate ring on my hand, and the doctorate hat on my head. I am as proud as I have ever been in my life. I glance in the mirror; the hat on my head looks strange and unstylish and out of place, and I do not care. As we leave the restaurant, I proudly wear this marvelously symbolic hat on my head. Restaurants patrons titter and point, but the aura of the award and my pride in it buffers me from their attention.

That once-in-a-lifetime evening remains as clear in my mind as if it happened yesterday. I hope you don't mind my sharing it with you. And now, on to my own story.

SOFTWARE REFLECTIONS—A PIONEER'S VIEW OF THE HISTORY OF THE FIELD

Robert L. Glass

I cannot imagine a more satisfying career than the one I have had. I began my computing/software professional work in 1954. There were very few computing professionals in the field back then. Computing had only recently emerged from the university laboratories to industrial applications, and I was present from the very beginning of that transition.

I have chosen to base this presentation on my recollections of the history of the field because present-day computer scientists seem to have many mistaken impressions of what those early days were like. As editor of the *Journal of Systems and Software,* I frequently receive papers that try to characterize those early days and miss the mark badly. The most frequent mistake is the assumption that progress in those early days was slow and plodding and that not much was really happening in the field. Nothing could be further from the truth.

What is the best way to characterize the over 40 years that I have been a professional in my field? That is a long time—indigestible if I attempt to present it as one long string of recollections. Fortunately, I can easily divide that long history into three eras, three very different periods of time in which the field was progressing in very different ways. For the purposes of this talk— and to match my personal recollections—I will divide this period of time into three eras: the Pioneering Era (1955–1965), the

---

This material is based on a talk prepared for the occasion of my receiving an honorary Ph.D. from Linköping University, Sweden, 3 June 1995.

Stabilizing Era (1965–1980), and the Micro Era (1980–the present).

In the remainder of this presentation, what I would like to do is describe each of those eras in turn using two different devices. First, I will paint a picture using my personal recollections of the era, attempting to re-create what those days were like. I will then supplement that picture with some factual recollections of that same era.

THE PIONEERING ERA—A PERSONAL VIEW

Come with me to my workplace at Aerojet-General in Sacramento, California. The year is 1961. The Pioneering Era has been underway now for over five years. I sit at a desk in a cubicle with five other people, in two rows of three, each of us facing the wall of an adjacent cubicle, our backs to each other. Two women and four men are in my cubicle; in fact, a goodly percentage of those working in my organization are women. (One of the odder changes that has happened in the field over the years is that there are *fewer* women than in its early days.)

My desk—and those of my co-workers—is full of paper but nothing electronic. There is no computer, no terminal, not even the mechanical calculator that graced my desk until a few years ago. The computer—the only one—is nearby, in something we call "the machine room." When we want to run a job on the computer, we do one of two things: we sign up for machine time and then run the job ourselves when our turn comes up, or we turn the job in to the operational staff and they place it in a queue and run it when it comes to the head of the queue.

Running a job means putting the punched cards—the program, its data, and its control information—into the machine's card reader and waiting for the results to come back on the printer. For some jobs, when we are running the jobs ourselves, outputs appear on the computer's console that tell us how it is running. In addition to watching the flickering lights and the spinning tapes on the machine for recognizable patterns of behavior, our programs can actually cause "sense lights" on the computer's console to light when some event of note has occurred.

A schism is growing among programmers about what our job really is. Some say that our primary job is to run our programs, be present at the console, monitor the printouts, and change the program's behavior if things are not going well (just as the console has sense lights, it also has sense switches via which we can send information to the running program). Others, like me, say that our job occurs primarily at our desks, writing those programs and preparing them to run in such a way that the operational staff can make any dynamic decisions that must be made (and trying to get the program itself to make most of those decisions instead). It is a battle that will be resolved in favor of my position in another few years, only to arise again when the desktop computer offers a whole new way of doing business!

Looking around at my colleagues, people I like very much, I suppose I must reluctantly characterize them as socially weird. They—and I—have chosen to be in a profession that few have entered. We make a product that cannot be seen, requires no resources to manufacture, has no volume, and has no weight. It is impossible to explain to noncomputing professionals what we do. We are proud of what we do—crafting problem solutions that cause the computer to do our bidding with our minds, not our hands—but society sees us as different from its norm, and society is right. That does not, however, diminish our pride in our profession. We love what we do, and we cannot imagine doing anything else.

On our more perverse days, we characterize ourselves in another way. Because we programmers are clustered in cubicles all around the outside of the machine room, we imagine ourselves to be zookeepers, tending the needy computer, feeding it our cards, and cleaning up its paper excrement.

We are a fun-loving group. The field is so new that the notion of management by schedule is still foreign. Making predictions about when a project might be complete is next to impossible. We work hard, of course, and management pretty well believes in us and our ability to do the job as it should be done. But we also play hard. Computing is a fun activity, and laughter often emerges from our cubicle and the ones nearby.

The Pioneering Era—Factual Recollections

Let us step outside my cubicle now. I want to share with you some facts about what was happening during the Pioneering Era, 1955 to 1965. The most important development was that new computers were coming out every year or two, each obsoleting what had gone before. These new computers were invariably different from, faster than, and cheaper than the computers that preceded them. And because the case for each new computer was compelling, we software people rewrote our programs to run on the new computers each time a new one came along! The pace of change was horrendous, far faster than at any time since.

During the Pioneering Era, computer hardware was application-specific. Scientific and business tasks required very different machines, and the programmers for each area never met organizationally. Business computers functioned with variable word length—"set word mark" and "clear word mark" instructions were in the instruction set—and they did decimal arithmetic. Scientific machines used fixed word length (different machines used different word lengths, but the field was temporarily standardizing on the 36-bit word—it could hold six 6-bit characters), and they did binary arithmetic.

Because of the frequent translation of old software to meet the needs of new machines, the "high-order language" (HOL) is brought into use very early in the field. Early FORTRANs appeared in the mid-1950s, the first COBOL emerged from a couple of previous business data-processing languages in the late 1950s, and ALGOL appeared on the scene in the early 1960s. Just as programmers debated about the nature of their job, they also debated about whether real programmers should do assembly language or whether using these new-fangled HOLs was also legitimate.

The frequent rewriting of old software triggered another phenomenon. Lots of software researchers (largely in industry) worked on the notion of the automatic translation of one assembly language into another. This problem resisted solution. A computer could easily translate part of the code, often 60 to 80 percent; but the remaining 20 to 40 percent required human translation, and it was the difficult, complex part of the code. Every few years someone new to the problem claimed to have a solution; we old-timers would perk up our ears, ask the key questions, and realize that the new solution had not yet encountered the scuttling problems we already knew about.

Software was, incredibly, free! Hardware vendors gave away systems software (because they could not sell their hardware without it). A few companies sold the service of building customized software, but there were no software companies selling packaged software. You could sell your time, but not the product.

The notion of reuse flourished. Because software was free, user organizations commonly gave it away. Groups like IBM's scientific user group SHARE offered catalogs of available reusable components, mostly mathematical routines like trigonometric functions but also sorts and merges and more. To have some of your products in the SHARE catalog was the highest honor the field offered. I recall being deeply proud when a debugging routine I had written was listed with SHARE.

Computing organizations were experimenting with two approaches to computing. One, called "open shop," was characterized by the programming taking place in the user organization. The other, the "closed shop," had the programmers clustered around the central computer in a centralized organization. Most programmers, those of us who loved to program, preferred the closed shop, where we could be comfortable with our peers (who understood our weirdness) and where we could share information about this fast-paced new profession

Academia did not yet teach the disciplines of computing, computer science, or information systems. The beginnings of what would later be called "software engineering" were emerging in practice, however. We learned the value of modular programming and what Parnas later called "information hiding" as early as the 1950s. I well remember a software product my team obtained from another company (free!) that was easy to work with because it clustered a collection of subroutines around its primary data structure, allowing access to the structure only through those subroutines. We now call the concept data abstraction, and we have broadened it into object-orientation, but we were aware of those ideas and their value in the early 1960s.

THE STABILIZING ERA (1965–1980)— A PERSONAL VIEW

In the late 1960s the Pioneering Era was passing, but those of us in the field did not know it yet. In 1967 I changed aerospace companies and moved, like an itinerant (space)worker, to Boeing in Seattle. I still had a desk in a cubicle, but because I had moved from applications development to software staff work, my cubicle was bigger, and only three other people sat near me in a space larger than those old six-person cubicles.

I still did not have a computer on my desk, and the machine room was further away (we no longer felt like zookeepers!). I was lucky, however, because as a member of the software staff my cubicle was in the Boeing Computer Center building, and so the computer was only about 100 yards from me. For most others in the company, the computer center was blocks or, perhaps, even miles from where they worked.

Except for peculiar applications like on-board computers, programmers no longer ran their jobs, because the whole job-queue system had been institutionalized. There were people who were assigned to transport jobs between pickup locations scattered throughout the company and the computer center. Others scheduled the central computer's time, deciding what ran when. Some operated the computers and controlled the computing output, so that key printouts did not fall into the wrong hands (salary information and payroll checks, for example). In short, an enormous bureaucracy had grown up around the central computer center.

As in any bureaucracy, problems abounded. Probably the worst was turnaround time, the time between the submission of a job to the computer and the time it was returned. At best, turnaround time was measured in hours. At worst, it was measured in days. Typically, turnaround was "overnight"—jobs submitted at any time during a day were run overnight and returned the next morning. The notion of timesharing, using terminals at which jobs could be directly submitted to queues of various kinds, was beginning to emerge and meeting with some resistance from traditionalists. After all, with the old system, programmers had learned to "multiprogram"—to work on several projects simultaneously—so that they would have something to do between turnarounds. Furthermore, programmers did a great deal of desk checking, since wasting a computer run could be the waste of several days. Would timesharing lead to carelessness, to "shooting from the hip"? The jury was still out in 1967.

At about this time I attended the announcement of the new IBM 360, the machine that—although we did not know it at the time—was to change the Pioneering Era into the stabilizing one. IBM made a big splash with the 360. They rented a movie theater, and invited all of their key customers to sit in on their glitzy presentation. At the theater I attended, I was terribly impressed to see IBM customers in state police uniforms and nun's habits. Computing was beginning to broaden its appeal, I could see dramatically. Soon, we would no longer be weird.

But the "weird" image was still apparent in 1967. The number of jobs for programmers exceeded the number of programmers to fill them. Programmers tended toward independence and they sometimes took advantage of their value in the field. Some have said, looking back on this era, that "programmers were out of control." Certainly we resisted management's attempts to place controls on us. (After all, those early attempts at management control were fumbling and often wrong—especially if the manager was one who did not understand the technology!) Although I am willing to concede that management is still, today, the major problem of the software field, I am still unwilling to say that more control is the solution to poor management.

THE STABILIZING ERA (1965–1980)— FACTUAL RECOLLECTIONS

The IBM 360 signaled the beginning of the Stabilizing Era. Why? Because from the moment the first customers took delivery of their new 360s, the era of a new faster and cheaper computer emerging every year or two was over. We no longer changed computers every few years, we no longer needed to rewrite our software every few years. We software people could finally get down to the business of writing new software and diminish the time spent on rewriting the old.

The 360 swept several other key developments into the field: Scientific and business applications were merged onto one machine. The 360 was deliberately designed to solve both classes of problems. It offered both decimal and binary arithmetic. It did not offer the variable word length, but business applications people had learned to do without it. Within a few years of the advent of the 360, the organizational separation of scientific and business applications people would diminish, if not end. The impact on the sociology of the field was massive. (As with many social phenomena, local loyalties made the transition stormy at some companies.

Although scientific programmers usually had bachelor's degrees, business programmers sometimes had only associate degrees. There was a superiority complex problem that brewed trouble. At one such company, a scientific programmer only half jested: "I don't mind working with business programmers, but I wouldn't want my daughter to marry one!" (This was the time, in our broader society, of the civil rights movement. The same thing was sometimes said by racist whites about minority coworkers and the phrase had become a symbol of racism.)

The massive operating system, still coming largely free with the computer, controlled most of the standard services that a program needed as it ran. The creation of OS360 was the largest software project to date, and a few years later that troubled creation spawned the milestone software engineering lessons-learned book *The Mythical Man-Month* by Fred Brooks. Early 360s and OS360s were trouble prone and offered far less capability than promised by the vendor (capability that would come, but much later).

A cumbersome job control language (JCL) raised a whole new class of problems. The programmer who formerly simply stuffed cards into the card reader and pressed start, now had to write a program in a whole new language to tell the computer and its operating system what to do. JCL was soundly disliked. Probably its complexity was due to the breadth of possible services it needed to provide—for example, all the services needed by both scientific and business programmers—but whatever the reason, JCL was the least popular feature of the 360.

Just as the 360 merged scientific and business applications onto one hardware system, IBM expected to merge all programmers onto one language. PL/1 was a massive language for its day, offering all the capabilities of the scientific FORTRAN and the business COBOL, and some of the capabilities of the still-new ALGOL language as well. Whereas the 360 succeeded, PL/1 failed. Early compilers were slow and buggy, and the economic motivation to change hardware did not apply to the drive to change languages.

There was more than the IBM 360 happening during this Stabilizing Era. Software began to have value. A few daring software houses began to offer products. It was a difficult transition, however. Some said that, to prevent the growth of a separate software industry, the hardware companies intentionally kept the price of their software low. Whatever the reason, few software houses succeeded. I even built a product for sale myself during this period; in spite of the advertisements and notices I ran, I never received a single order.

As the software field stabilized and programmers could concentrate on building new products, several things happened. Software became a corporate asset, and its value—as the years went by—became huge. Software maintenance became an issue, perhaps the largest growth profession of the era. Lientz and Swanson of UCLA did some pioneering research on maintenance, discovering that far more of it was about enhancing software (60 percent) than correcting errors (17 percent). Many seemed to say "uh-huh" about their finding and then continued to treat maintenance as a task that should be minimized, even obliterated.

Stability also brought with it the emergence of academic computing disciplines. The first computer science programs opened in the late 1960s. The first management information systems programs opened soon after. (Note how long the profession of computing existed before there was an academic discipline of computing!) Software engineering, however, was not to split off from computer science and become a discipline of its own until well into the Micro Era to come. However, software engineering research continued, even though that academic discipline did not yet exist. A great deal of energy was poured into Problem-Oriented Languages (POLs, programming languages focused on particular application domains). But as computer science strengthened as a discipline, it lost interest in an application focus, and POL research dwindled and died. It was replaced by something called "Extensible languages," generalized languages that could be tailored by programmers into the POL they needed. But programmers had little interest in inventing new languages when there were problems to solve and programs to write, and that idea, also, failed.

A very bad computing trend also began during this Stabilizing Era. Computer scientists began to tout their new ideas as being of major significance to the field. Artificial intelligence was the first of the high-hype disciplines. A machine called the "Perceptron" was claimed to simulate the functioning of the human brain, and the expectation was established that it could do anything the brain could do. As time passed, and other new ideas flowed forth from the brilliant minds of computing researchers, similar claims continued to emanate as well. All too frequently, the researchers claimed "order of magnitude" benefits for their new concept. Amazingly, some practitioners and computing journalists bought into each of these newly hyped concepts, even when they were fully aware that the payoff from the previously hyped concepts had never been achieved. The credibility of the computing field began to diminish. Either the practitioners were inept because they could not convert these new concepts into their predicted benefits, or the researchers were ignorant or unethical because they made claims with no basis. Either way, the computing field was badly tainted—and continues to be badly tainted—by this hype.

One of the highly hyped concepts, "structured programming," burst on the scene during the middle of the Stabilizing Era. Practitioners were trained in its use, and computer science programs made sure they taught its concepts. If your programs were not structured, you were a bad programmer. Religious wars broke out about the value and use of the GO TO statement. The benefits of the structured revolution were never, in fact, measured, but the revolution took effect, and surveys show that most programs of the 1990s are quite well structured. What little data we have tends to show that the use of the structured techniques, like the use of most new concepts advocated by researchers, improves programmer productivity by roughly 5 to 40 percent. That is, the new concepts are worth implementing—but they are not worth what the hypesters have claimed for them.

As the field stabilized, it became possible to talk about "controlling the field." Control battles broke out in unlikely places. The U.S. Justice Department sued IBM for antitrust violations, claiming it had gotten too large and was manipulating the field. (Justice also sued AT&T for controlling the telephony field at the same time. Oddly, IBM beat Justice but Justice beat AT&T and forced it to break off the "Baby Bells.") During the Stabilizing Era, many referred to the hardware industry as consisting of "Snow White and the Seven Dwarfs." Snow White was IBM (the use of the term was sarcastic; most computists of the day believed that IBM was far from pure and welcomed the Justice suit). The Dwarfs were the seven much smaller computing hardware companies of the time. Prominent among the dwarfs were RCA, GE, and Xerox, all of whom shrank and eventually disappeared from the computing field.

Standards organizations also became control battle grounds during the Stabilizing Era. He who defined the standard could make it match his own technology, and probably gain significant competitive advantage thereby. The field deeply needed standards—progress had been so fast that little time had been given to defining standard ways of doing things—but it often got only badly bent versions of what it needed as the vendors went to war to ensure their own voice in what happened.

A battle emerged, as well, over where software would come from. Hardware vendors, keeping their prices low, kept a brake on the emergence of a new software industry. Software vendors emerged a few at a time in spite of the braking action. Most software—especially customized applications—continued to be done in-house. The stage was set for software control battles to come.

THE MICRO ERA (1980 TO THE PRESENT)— A PERSONAL VIEW

Welcome to my office! It is 1982 now, and things are much different in the programmer's environment. I have a private office, for example. I'm in a one-person cubicle without a door, but I finally have the privacy I need for those moments of creative thought that are so often required to build software.

And look here—on my desk there is a computer! One of these new microcomputers. I no longer take my jobs to a terminal or a batch pickup point; my computer power is right here.

Having a computer on my desk opens up some new ways of doing programming. I no longer need to multiprogram, working on more than one problem at once, wasting time when I "context switch." I no longer do much desk checking, because it is easier to get the computer to play computer than to do it myself. If I wonder about the cause of a bug, I concoct a fix and try it out immediately. The profession of programming has quickly become more about trial and error than about planning, more about electronics than about paper and pencil. Mostly, these are wonderful and good changes. But not entirely.

In 1982, not everyone has joined the Micro Era. Lots of mainframe programmers still do things the old ways. I have chosen to join a micro group because I want to find out what this new technology is all about. But the cultural transformation and differences are profound. Mainframe people tend to be institutionalized, stable, maybe even stuffy. Micro people tend to be weird and a bit out of control. Wait a minute—this all sounds familiar. Just an era or two ago these adjectives were used on the mainframe people. In many ways, computing is a field where "everything old is new again."

THE MICRO ERA (1980–THE PRESENT)— FACTUAL RECOLLECTIONS

So many of us have lived in and functioned in this latest era of computing that I am reluctant to dwell very much on it; however, let me share a few thoughts with you. First of all, the Micro Era is most important because it is leading us to ubiquitous computing. It has been a long time since the days of weird programmers who could find no one to talk to about what they do. Now everyone is an expert on computing—or at least thinks they are.

Plenty of our past problems have been solved. The old JCL nightmare has given way to user-friendly and programmer-friendly interfaces, and the Graphical User Interface (GUI) is everywhere, becoming probably the greatest real computing breakthrough of the 1980s. The price of computer power has dropped dramatically, making ubiquitous computing possible. The value of software has been firmly established, software houses have joined the Fortune 500, and Bill Gates became the richest man in the United States about five years ago, and is now the richest man in the world.

Many of the old battles for control have been resolved, with the marketplace providing the resolution. IBM became king of the mainframe mountain, only to find the mountain much smaller than it had imagined. Intel is the king of the computer chip and, some would say, the king of all computing hardware. Microsoft is the king of micro software. (Is there a Snow White and the Seven Dwarfs of software?) The battle for king of mainframe software continues, but again the mountain is shrinking. Companies like Computer Associates and SAP are winning the mainframe package war, the accounting Big Six get much of the customized software consulting business, but in-house developers—in spite of more and more pressure for the idea of end-user development—build and maintain humongous quantities of customized applications. (End-user computing? Remember open shop computing? Could it really be true that everything old in computing is new again?)

The field still has its problems. Evolution, and not revolution, seems the order of the day. The software part of hardware architecture—the part the programmer must know about, like the instruction set and the interrupt structure—has not changed much since the advent of the first IBM mainframe and the first Intel chip. Not much is happening in new programming languages, with the most-used languages in the field now anywhere from 15 years old (C, C++) to 40 years old (FORTRAN, COBOL). The Fourth Generation Language certainly never achieved the "programming without programmers" status some claimed for it, and the whole idea is still pretty much limited to one application domain—the generation of reports from databases. The hypesters still dominate software researchers and vendors, and there is little evaluative research attempting to measure their terribly exaggerated claims.

But there are signs of hope. Object-orientation continues to have promise as a new technology—although not as much as the hypesters claim—because it is a very different way of building software. Client/server and the Internet/intranet offer significant economic and sociological advantages as a hardware approach, although those who also claim software productivity benefits for the approach are simply proclaiming how little they know about building software (how could an approach that requires all the application-focused problem-solving techniques of yesteryear, then adds to that task those of managing system distribution and building a better user interface, possibly be easier?) There is an increasing clamor for more and better software research, as people like Fred Brooks (who sees no software silver bullet on the horizon), David Parnas (whose Star Wars papers pretty much say the same thing), Vic Basili (who constantly suggests ways that software researchers can do a more relevant job), and Walt Tichy (who points out how little experimental and evaluative research is really getting done) ask for better approaches.

CONCLUSION

Where have we been? I have presented my notion of three computing eras: the Pioneering Era, from 1955 to 1965, characterized by a high level of excitement, a tendency toward being scary because of the pace of change, and a time of loneliness, as the computing specialist existed in a world that had little understanding of what he or she did; the Stabilizing Era, from 1965 to 1980, characterized by a level of comfort (as the pace of change slowed), a time when the field became entrenched and institutionalized, a time when inertia began to become the norm; and the Micro Era, from 1980 to the present, characterized once again by a high level of excitement and a tendency to being scary, but with the notion of ubiquity totally displacing the earlier feelings of loneliness.

What will the next era be? Prognosticators fail much more often than they succeed in our business, and I have done more than my share of laughing at those failed pundits. But somehow I cannot resist putting myself in that same position. I would like to suggest several interesting candidates for the next major era of computing:

- A new era resulting from a major new hardware offering. In the past, new computer hardware has triggered most of the changes in the field. The 360 and the micro each ushered in a major change in how computing did business. Will that happen again? Will a newer, cheaper, better kind of hardware—perhaps the network computer—undercut the computers on the market today? Or are today's computers so cheap through mass marketing that the ability to create a new niche is gone forever?

- A new era resulting from a sea change in software. Many people characterize today's software products as "fatware," offering far more capability than the average user even understands, and gobbling up enormous quantities of computer memory to make all those capabilities possible. Is it possible for a newer, simpler, cheaper software product—perhaps Java-built—to enter the marketplace? Or, once again, has mass marketing brought the price down so low that no one can get in underneath?

- A new era resulting from a transition to application domain focus. Most researchers suggest new ways of building software that are application-independent. Most practitioners know that this "one size fits all" approach simply does not help us progress any more. Will we get new, application-focused tools and techniques to help us improve the quality and productivity of software people working in particular domains? Can there be 4GLs beyond the current ones for report generation from databases? Will the emergence in the research field of the notion of domain analysis pay off?

- A new era emerging from the automation of the software development process. People have predicted this one for more than a decade now, and we seem no closer now than we were when those predictions began. This is my favorite "don't bet on it" category, but if the researchers working in this area ever do make real progress, we'd all better be aware of it. And its influence on the progress of the field would be profound.

But my favorite summary is far afield from all of this hypothesizing. (Is it just coincidence that "hype" and "hypothesize" begin the same way?) I would prefer to tat up this presentation with this thought: This software field of mine has provided me with an unimaginably exciting professional way of life. It has been a wild, stimulating, crazy ride. And my wish for myself—and all the other computists who are reading this—is that the future will be just as wild, just as stimulating, and just as crazy.

Stay aboard—our ride has just begun!

4

MAKING THE MARKET:
VENDOR PIONEERS

The role of vendors in the early history of computing was fascinating. This dramatically new product, the computer, was available from only a very few companies because it required enormous technical skill and a pioneering attitude to conceive of and dare to build such a product. Even the companies that did become computing vendors were not at all sure that the future of the computing industry was very bright. Early predictions suggested that only a handful of companies would eventually want to buy or lease computers; thus the market was assumed to be small and the profits commensurately elusive.

In spite of that outlook, a few companies moved forward at full speed. IBM, of course, was one of those. Other companies moved more hesitantly. UNIVAC, as we will soon see, was in that category. The stories in this section present an insider's view of the computing vendor world. Watts Humphrey was a software pioneer at IBM, and Norm Schneidewind pioneered at UNIVAC.

Their stories are fascinating. Humphrey speaks from his view near the top of the company and recounts story after story about the evolution of IBM thinking as well as IBM products. I especially like his story about IBM's major blunder in de-emphasizing software as a corporate product at almost the same time that the rest of the world was realizing that software had value and could be marketed without being attached to hardware. "About a year later," Humphrey recalls, "IBM San Jose introduced a new file product." When it was introduced it did not sell well. "The product developers found that IBM's old sort program had not been upgraded for the new file product," and for the first time, Humphrey recalls, "hardware managers found that, without programming support, hardware would not sell."

In spite of those blunders (and almost everyone in the computing business was engaged in trial and error in those days), IBM succeeded dramatically. UNIVAC, alas, did not. In Schneidewind's story, we see him choosing between working for IBM or for UNIVAC—and making what, in retrospect, was the wrong choice. I especially like his story about one of the reasons UNIVAC's marketing efforts were inferior to those of IBM. "Both [IBM and UNIVAC, then known as Remington Rand] had a commission plan for the sale of punched card equipment, but only IBM had a commission plan for the sale of computers. Thus Remington Rand's sales people had little incentive to sell computers." It is easy to see through Schneidewind's retrospective that UNIVAC's loss to IBM in the computing marketplace was determined very early and at a very human level.

It was not just vendors, of course, who pioneered the computing and software field. There were also application developers and research and development specialists. In this chapter, the stories of representatives of all three areas are presented. The chapter begins with vendors' stories because, in those early days, vendors tended to steer the field. The appearance of a vendors' product in the marketplace caused enterprises to begin to consider what these powerful but strange new devices could do.

REFLECTIONS ON A SOFTWARE LIFE

Watts S. Humphrey

My first exposure to software permanently changed my life in a way I had never expected. I joined Sylvania Electric Products in Boston in the spring of 1953 and was put in charge of a small engineering group developing a cryptographic communication system. Since this system used advanced digital logic, Sylvania management suggested that I attend an MIT (Massachusetts Institute of Technology) course on computer programming. This was a two-week summer course for engineers from local industry.

When I walked into class the first day, a pretty young woman sat at the reception desk. Although the first day was probably interesting, I did not notice very much. I was much more interested in meeting this young woman. My brother and I shared an apartment in Boston, and that evening we mapped out a strategy for me to meet this woman. The first step was to start a conversation, then I would ask her to have lunch. Assuming all went well, I would invite her for a late afternoon sail on the Charles River in an MIT sailing dinghy.

On the second day, I struck up a conversation. Barbara had just joined the MIT technical staff, and she came from Chicago where I had gone to the university. We even had mutual friends. Overall, the strategy worked out very well and by the following Christmas, Barbara and I were engaged. We were married the following May. Judging from the first 42 years, seven children, and seven grandchildren, the marriage will probably last.

While nothing else in the class could compare with Barbara, the course was technically interesting. It was taught by Maurice Wilkes and some associates who came from England to teach the

My work after joining the Software Engineering Institute in 1986 has been supported by the U.S. Department of Defense.

class. The computer was Whirlwind, which just about filled MIT's Barta building. Wilkes' team had developed a symbolic assembler that provided relative addressing and something called B Boxes for indexing addresses and counting loops.

The programming environment was pretty crude. I remember punching the first program on Flexowriter tape and hand feeding it to the tape reader. The output was on a cathode-ray tube. To store data, we used magnetic wire, and the computer memory was ferrite cores. These had just been upgraded from the old Williams tubes that stored bits as charged spots on cathode-ray screens. These charged spots decayed quickly, so every memory bit was read and rewritten every few milliseconds. The Williams tubes were about 8 inches in diameter and 16 inches long. I remember this because MIT gave away the old tubes, and we used one as a cookie jar. Whirlwind was a nice machine to use, and it was pretty fast. It had a clock speed of slightly over a megahertz.

THE CONTROL PROGRAM WARS

My principal work for the next few years was at Sylvania on various special computer systems for the U.S. military. I was not involved in much of interest from a software perspective until shortly after I joined IBM in 1959. The Advanced Systems Development Division (ASDD) was headed by Jerrier Haddad, and our mission was to develop and initially introduce advanced computer systems. Haddad viewed communications as a natural companion to computing, and I remember attending a meeting where he invented the word *teleprocessing*. Among the ASDD projects was the Sabre system for American Airlines and several projects for the brokerage, insurance, and railroad industries.

One big technical issue at the time was how to program these large complex systems. The hot debate was about the feasibility of developing general-purpose control programs for large communications systems. Up until then, all of these systems had been developed for unique customers. I had a small programming group headed by Alex Reid, who had concluded that general-purpose control programs could be built. The special systems community, however, argued that general-purpose control programs were not technically feasible. These large products were indeed difficult to develop, and it was not at all clear how to settle this debate without actually building such a system.

The special systems argument was based on the contention that customers' needs were too varied to permit standardized functions. At the time, the idea of producing systems with a large number of selectable features had not been tried. There simply was not enough memory or file space for the extravagant amounts of code that would be needed. These early systems generally stored their programs in core memory or on magnetic drums. Large disk files were not yet available. The Sabre system, in fact, used specially developed disk drives to store the flight and passenger information.

The special purpose/general purpose argument raged until the System 360 proposal in 1962. When Fred Brooks described the planned operating system for the 360 computer family, it was obviously a general-purpose control program. When the 360 proposal was accepted, the special purpose/general purpose argument was won by the generalists. The company had to make a functioning general-purpose control program, whether it was feasible or not. Of course, after considerable pain they did.

THE 9020 EN-ROUTE AIR TRAFFIC CONTROL SYSTEM

Shortly after the System 360 was launched, the IBM Federal Systems Marketing Region decided to bid on the new FAA En-route Air Traffic Control System. This was to be a nationwide network of interconnected computer and display systems to provide aircraft position and flight data to traffic controllers. The systems would be installed in multiple centers throughout the United States. The proposal was hotly contested, and every major computer company was expected to bid.

IBM launched a major effort to win the contract. There were, however, substantial disagreements between the marketing and development people. The FAA had specified a polymorphic system of up to four interconnected computers and eight memory units. These systems were to be capable of graceful degradation in the event of the failure of any single element and even some multiple units. The development group contended that such multiprocessing systems could not be programmed. The marketing people argued that IBM must bid the system as requested or we would lose the business. It was then Thanksgiving week 1963, and the bid was due by Christmas.

At this point, I was asked to take charge of the FAA proposal effort, reporting to Vin Learson and John Gibson, two IBM senior vice presidents. Both the marketing and development divisions were told that for the purposes of this proposal they were to report to me. Although this was a marvelous way to settle an argument, it did not address the technical issues. Based on a technical review, however, I was convinced that the systems could be programmed. Fortunately, at least for IBM, the original FAA contract was for the hardware system and a Jovial compiler. The FAA planned to separately contract for the software. Later, in fact, the IBM Federal Systems Division (FSD) won and successfully completed the FAA programming contract. Ironically, the president of the IBM FSD division at the time was Bob Evans, who had previously managed the 360 development group that argued that the proposed polymorphic system could not be programmed. This system was later called the FAA 9020.

Once the development and marketing disagreements were settled, we were faced with producing a superior proposal. The hardware development team selected the IBM 360 Model 50 as the base for the special system design. Although IBM had yet to announce the System 360, much of the Model 50 hardware development was already done. The engineers produced a polymorphic design that involved stripping all the I/O and memory from standard Model 50 computers. They also designed a family of separate memory units, connected to the Model 50s via a memory bus. Separate I/O controllers were also designed, using the Model 50 frame and connecting to the system through an I/O bus. Several special architectural features were added to the 360 architecture to permit these CPUs to pass data, sense status, and synchronize operations.

Once we had a system design, the next question was performance. The FAA had used Lincoln Laboratories to write the system specifications. Lincoln had devised four benchmark programs to evaluate system capability. All the bidders were to write these four programs for their systems and to provide both the run time and the memory space required by each. Based on these eight numbers, Lincoln Laboratories would evaluate the capability of the various systems.

Since we expected this proposal to price out at about $100,000,000, it was important that the four kernel programs be written as tightly as possible. The marketing division had assigned a team of their best system engineers to write the programs and assured me they were as good as could be produced. I decided to check, however, so I went to the manager of the IBM architecture group, Gene Amdahl, who had designed the System 360 instruction set. Amdahl agreed to take a team of his best architects and personally review the kernel programs over the weekend. By the next Monday, they had improved the programs by an average of 40 percent. In one weekend, Amdahl and his people earned $100,000,000 for IBM.

In any event, IBM submitted its proposal and won. The result was the FAA 9020 system, which has been controlling U.S. airspace ever since. Until the last few years, its performance has been superb. The equipment has now become so old, however, that many of the parts are well beyond their design lives. Thus, after 33 years, hardware system failures are now common. It is also interesting to note that the IBM-developed software worked well but took a great deal more memory and CPU power than Lincoln Laboratories had projected from the four program kernels.

THE RCA SPECTRA 70

In 1965, I was an IBM director on corporate staff. At the time, we were very concerned about RCA's impending announcement of their Spectra 70 series of computers. Since this system architecture had been modeled on the 360, the big concern was that these machines would be able to run IBM's software. The worry was that this software was not a separate product and was freely available to IBM users. No one knew how to prevent RCA customers from taking full advantage of IBM's software work without paying for it. Fortunately for IBM, the RCA engineers made a number or architectural improvements over the 360. Thus, the Spectra 70s would not run the IBM software without a significant conversion effort. Although the Spectra line did sell a modest number of machines, it was never a serious threat to IBM's System 360.

TSS AND VIRTUAL MEMORY

Shortly after the System 360 announcement, IBM faced a marketing disaster. MIT had, with IBM's help, developed MAC, an early
time-sharing system. This system started as a simple interactive
communication system run by MIT on an IBM 7090 computer.
The original design had a simple open architecture that permitted users to add features. MIT shared this system with several New
England universities, and its functions grew quickly. In only a couple of years, it had very impressive capability and a large number
of enthusiastic users. At about the time of IBM's System 360
announcement in April 1964, MIT decided to replace the early
MAC system with a newer hardware and software system.

A problem that troubled the MIT scientists was memory management. With an unpredictably large number of time-sharing
users, memory management would be a serious problem. It was
impractical to assign each user specific memory space since there
were too many potential users and their usage times were not
predicable. The amounts of memory demanded by each user
would also depend on the jobs they were running. Jack Dennis
and others at MIT devised the concept of a virtual memory to
solve this problem. The user would be given a large amount of virtual memory, and the computer would assign multiple memory
pages of several thousand bytes as the user needed them. Since
the users were time shared, these pages could be kept on disk or
drum storage and automatically paged into memory when that
user's time slice came up. The pages were then automatically
saved when the user's slice was over and again automatically
retrieved for the user's next turn. MIT had tried to convince IBM
to include this feature in the System 360 architecture, but the IBM
engineers had decided against it. In spite of IBM's decision, MIT
decided to make virtual memory a key requirements for the new
time-sharing system.

Virtual memory became a big issue when MIT chose the GE
system over IBM's proposal for a standard System 360 machine. A
large number of customers liked the idea of time-sharing systems,
and virtual memory was very appealing. These customers
included Lincoln Laboratories, Bell Telephone Laboratories,
General Motors, and several important universities. The IBM marketing position was that if IBM lost the Lincoln Laboratories, Bell
Laboratories, and GM bids to the virtual-memory GE 635/645 sys-

tems, we could expect to quickly lose a lot more business. The IBM arguments about the use of virtual memory were contentious. On one side, the marketing people argued that without a virtual-memory system, IBM would lose a great deal of business. On the other side, the leading critic was none other than Gene Amdahl. He and the 360 architects argued that virtual memory was not needed because memory was rapidly getting larger and cheaper, and the need would soon be met with gigantic physical memories.

At this point, I was asked to take over the time-sharing business, again reporting to an IBM senior vice president. I was given my own marketing team, a software development group, and authority over the hardware engineering team I would need to design and build the systems. We designed the IBM System 360 Model 67 virtual-memory system for the Lincoln Laboratories, Bell Laboratories, and GM bids. We also proposed a new TSS (time-sharing systems) programming system to support the Model 67. With this system, we won the Lincoln Laboratories, Bell Laboratories, GM proposals, and many others.

At about the same time, GE teamed with a group at MIT to develop their GECOS time-sharing system. This work was managed by "Corby" Corbato and was planned to provide sophisticated support for a broad range of commercial and academic time-sharing customers. GECOS was a key feature of GE's aggressive effort to become a major factor in the general-purpose computer business.

In launching the IBM development of TSS, I was fortunate to recruit Andy Kinslow as the architect. He had previously worked on IBM's original time-sharing system at ASDD. We also recruited Joe Rodgers, an experienced program manger from IBM's Federal Systems Division. Because IBM's commercial software development group was then struggling to develop the OS/360 support for the newly announced System 360 machines, we were unable to obtain any experienced IBM software developers. We thus had to staff the entire TSS development with a small team from ASDD, new hires, and subcontract personnel from CSC (Computer Sciences Corporation) and CUC (Computer Usage Corporation), two newly formed software companies. Later when the OS/360 work was under better control, we were able to put Scott Locken in charge of the final TSS development work. He brought much needed large-system development experience to the team.

Although the original TSS design for the Lincoln Laboratories bid had been quite simple, Bernie Galler and others of the University of Michigan, with General Motors' support, argued for a much more sophisticated system. These were very influential customers, and it was likely that if we did not include their desired features, they would cancel their original orders and go to GE. Since there was no obvious way to later add the desired new features, we changed the original simple design to include the more sophisticated virtual-memory design that Michigan advocated.

The requirements expansion forced by the University of Michigan, with GM's strong support, caused the TSS development work to slip by about six months. Unfortunately, in final system test, initial TSS system performance was also found unacceptable. At the same time, the GE/MIT GECOS virtual-memory development was in similar difficulties. Because of the delays in both these systems, customers had grown more concerned about standard data processing. By this time, the initial 360 programming releases had been delivered, and customers were rapidly converting to them. Instead of fixing the TSS performance problem, IBM thus decided to discontinue work on TSS and concentrate on OS/360 and the vanilla System 360 machines. While IBM delivered the committed TSS systems to those customers who insisted, it moved the rest to the standard 360 systems.

Although the time-sharing folks lost the TSS battle, they actually won the war. The entire System 360 was ultimately enhanced to the System 370, which included virtual memory as a standard feature. The IBM TSS was not a great business success, but it was a technical and marketing triumph. It led the way for IBM's later use of virtual memory and multiprogramming systems and it built skills the company needed for the real time, multiprocessing, and communications programming work to come. It was the kind of accidental prototype that Fred Brooks describes so well in his book, the *Mythical Man Month*.[1] TSS also taught several of us indelible lessons about requirements growth, real-time performance, and the unreliability of early programming estimates.

OS/360

When the IBM 360 hardware and software systems were announced in April 1964, full OS/360 support was promised for

18 months later. Interim basic programming support (BPS) was provided by the end of 1964. The hardware designs were already well advanced and, fortunately, the system architects had designed a system feature called an emulator. This was a microprogrammed feature that allowed 360 systems to emulate the instruction sets of earlier systems. Thus, users of IBM's earlier 7000 and 1400 systems could continue to run their old applications on the 360 machines without the new 360 programming support. Thus the 360 Model 65, for example, could be made to run just like a 7090, 7080, or 7070. In fact, some customers even ran Model 65s in the 7080 emulator mode using the 7080 compatibility feature to run the earlier 705 computer programs. The Model 40 and 50 machines could also be made to emulate the 1400 series machines.

After the OS/360 system design was established, Fred Brooks retired from IBM and went to the University of North Carolina. While he had done a marvelous job of leading the 360 programming system concepts and design team, he did not stay to see his concept delivered.[2] Some time after Brooks left, the OS/360 programming development work got into serious trouble. The work was late and there were growing concerns about the delivery schedules. These concerns grew when the first delivery dates were delayed. IBM then announced another date and this too was missed. Marketing was soon in a panic.

This was in late 1965 when we were in the middle of TSS development. Gardner Tucker, IBM's director of research, asked me to submit a brief paper on my thoughts about how IBM should manage programming. By then I had managed several hardware and software projects and had probably committed as many management blunders as anyone around. I was also convinced that the biggest software problem was the lack of effective project management. This was what we would later call CMM Level 1 behavior.[3] My paper was thus a tirade on the need for disciplined planning, scheduling, and tracking. I did not learn until later that this paper exercise was part of Vin Learson's search for a new IBM programming manager. Since I was asked to take the job, I assume my paper won the competition.

The OS/360 was indeed a troubled project. My first need was to find out where the work stood. An experience in my first week on the job was an omen of what I was to find. I received a marketing "Blue Letter" announcing programming support for the new IBM Model 91 computer, IBM's largest machine. I went to the

Poughkeepsie Laboratory in New York that day to ask about the work on the Model 91 project. Not only was there no plan for the completion of the project, but the project was neither staffed nor funded. In fact, no one in Poughkeepsie had even heard of the "Blue Letter" announcement. I then called Jack Rodgers, the marketing vice president, and told him to withdraw the Model 91 programming support. I told him we had no staffing or plan to develop the software, and if marketing sold any of these systems, they would have to develop the software themselves.

While this position caused a flap, it turned out to be very fortunate for IBM. Not only did marketing stop making any programming announcements without our approval, but a hardware problem was discovered in the Model 91. Within a week, the labs found that many of the Model 91 circuit chips had a cracked stripe. This was a problem in the semiconductor devices that caused circuits to fail much faster than anticipated. The Model 91 computers were then delayed nearly a year to fix this problem. During this delay, the Model 91 software project was funded and staffed, and the software was ready before the hardware. Later, in fact, Joe Brown, who was the hardware manager for these large systems, used the new software to test the hardware.

After the Model 91 flap, I personally visited IBM's larger software development laboratories and found they were operating in a state of near panic. At the time, I was responsible for a programming group with 15 laboratories spread through nine locations in the United States and six countries in Europe. Most of these labs had parts of the 360 development work.

In each laboratory I visited, I asked management for their plans and schedules. No one had anything other than informal notes or memos. When I asked for the managers' views on the best way to manage software, they all said they would make a plan before they started development. When I asked why they did not do this, their answer was that they did not have time. This was clearly nonsense! The right way to do the job was undoubtedly the fastest and cheapest way. It was obvious that these managers were not managing but reacting. They were under enormous pressure and had so much to do they could only do those things that were clearly required for shipping code. Everything but the immediate crisis was deferred. I concluded that the situation was really my fault, not theirs. As long as I permitted them to announce and ship products without plans, they would continue to do so. Thus, to fix the problem, I had to make planning an absolute requirement and convince IBM of this necessity.

My next step was to go so see Frank Cary, then IBM's senior vice president for development and manufacturing. I told him that since all the delivery schedules were not worth anything anyway, I intended to cancel them. Next, I would instruct all the software managers to produce plans for every project. From then on, we would not announce, deliver, or fund programming projects until I first had a documented and signed-off development plan on my desk. Not only did the manager have to sign off but so did every manager who had a group involved in that project.

Cary agreed, and we made an immediate announcement. As part of his agreement, Cary also asked me to review these plans with marketing. They asked me to present the programming story to the several thousand IBM sales representatives at four annual 100 Percent Club meetings. In these talks, I told the sales force that the planned software functions would be spread over many releases and that we would give them dates in a few weeks when we had plans to back them up. When we gave them dates, however, they could count on them. Later I learned that this was the first time many in the IBM sales force had heard a software story they believed. Even though it was bad news, software status was no longer a mystery. The schedule problem was something they knew how to handle.

It took the laboratories about 60 days to produce their first plans. This group, who had never before made a delivery schedule, did not miss a date for the next two-and-a-half years. Even then, the only reason they started to miss schedules was that we had not understood the compounding effect of multiple releases. When release 1 slips, it impacts releases 2, 3, and all subsequent releases. Even though I had added a contingency on all the dates, the few inevitable small delays soon compounded. As a result, I later decided not to announce future programs with more than a 12-month delivery schedule. Somewhat later, we even refused to announce any programs until we had running code.

Following these policies, IBM started delivering programs on schedule. In fact, the software was often ready ahead of the hardware. These initial practices were the foundation for the later development of Capability Maturity Model[4] (CMM) Level 2.[5]

OS/360 Performance

One of our serious problems was OS/360 performance. The first release was so slow that the fastest IBM machine at the time, the Model 75, could not keep up with a card reader. The card-reading problem, it turned out, was fairly easy to fix. An experienced programmer in one weekend reworked the reader interpreter and got a 1,000 times improvement. The initial programmer had read and processed each card in sequence. The new design read an entire card batch before processing.

The more general performance problem was much harder to solve. It was obvious from various customer test sessions that the system was much slower than the older 7000 series systems. Nobody, however, knew how much slower or for what kinds of work. Since we had to solve this problem quickly, we had to get performance numbers and develop a performance improvement plan.

Since no one knew how to estimate or calculate the performance of such a complex system, we decided to use some kind of standard benchmark. The solution was to select a family of about two dozen customer FORTRAN and COBOL programs. We then ran these programs on the 7000 and 1400 series machines and also measured them on the 360 systems.

The initial tests confirmed that running OS/360 on the Model 65 was even slower than running the same COBOL or FORTRAN programs on the 7080 or 7090 emulators on the same Model 65. This was clearly a software and not a hardware performance problem. Although this performance was terrible, the numbers helped the engineers understand and address the problem. By the second OS/360 release, performance passed the emulators, and within a year, performance was up by about ten times. Although still not great, it was at least acceptable.

Software Pricing

During 1966 and 1967, a U.S. government antitrust lawsuit against IBM had a strong influence on IBM's thinking. One key issue in the lawsuit concerned what was called "bundling." This involved selling together various elements of a system for a single price. The government's position was that, because of its great size and market power, IBM could bundle many elements of a system and offer them at one big price, and smaller companies could not compete. Unless the smaller companies offered similar complete systems, they had no way to compete with any of the pieces. The fear of IBM's legal department was that this bundling practice would be an early casualty of any government consent decree.

As part of my job as director of programming, I was put on the first IBM task force on software pricing. Howard Figuroa from the corporate policy department ran the group and he assembled a talented team of legal, financial, marketing, and technical people. The task force assumed that the programming would be separately priced from the hardware. We had to figure out how to handle the pricing and policy issues. The group originated the idea of a copyright for the programs and a license for program use. The only difference from today's offerings was that the company would only offer programs for a monthly charge.

The logic was that this would best maintain IBM's ownership of the programs. The concern was that if IBM offered programs for a single charge, this was tantamount to a sale. If it were truly a sale, IBM might not be able to control the customers' later actions. For example, if customers could merely copy and resell the programs, IBM might not be able to stop them or recover its costs.

The protection problem was a serious one that we were unable to completely solve. It is still a serious problem today. We debated various types of protection schemes, including cryptographic systems, hardware interlocks, and other policing mechanisms. We concluded that these were all either too expensive, ineffective, or very inconvenient for users. We thus concluded that the best protection was contractual, coupled with the inherent honesty of most computer users. Judging from the volume of pirated software today, this was not a good assumption. Unfortunately, even today, no one has devised a better solution.

A PRICING FLAP

By early 1968, the issue of software pricing was being widely discussed in the press and by leading customers. I was asked to participate in a panel discussion at the annual ACM (Association for Computing Machinery) meeting in Edinburgh that year and to answer questions from the press. Since I knew pricing would be a hot issue, I cleared my remarks with Hillary Faw, who was then the IBM director of policy development.

At the ACM meeting, I commented on the public perception that as a result of pricing the software, the hardware price would be reduced by 25 to 40 percent. I pointed out that product costs were largely determined by the number of people working on the various product elements. While I could not tell them what the price impact would be, I said that only about 3 percent of IBM's employees then worked on software. A much larger price change would thus seem unlikely.

These remarks created a bit of a stir, and the press called IBM headquarters to get confirmation. Since neither Hillary Faw nor I had cleared my remarks with legal or line executives, management was quite upset. When the pricing announcement was made a couple of months later, however, the hardware prices were reduced by exactly 3 percent.

One incident shows the impact of pricing on the programming community. The IBM group in the Time Life building in New York was developing a new COBOL compiler version, and we decided it would be the first independently priced product. For the first time, the development group had to get market forecasts for their product and work with finance and marketing to set the price.

A little later, I heard that Time Life was going to kill the COBOL project. It seems that the first price they had gotten from finance was too high to yield a forecast that would make a profit. Dick Bevier was one of the key programming managers at the time, and he explained the facts of pricing life to the developers: initial forecasts are almost always too low and the first prices are almost always too high. The development manager's job is to work with marketing, forecasting, finance, and development to bring the forecast and price into line. Within a month, they announced the product, and it was a success.

THE 370 SYSTEMS

In 1969, I was System Development Division vice president of technical development. This included responsibility for all of IBM's programming and the 360 and 370 systems architecture. The systems architecture group essentially had responsibility for the hardware principles of operation. Don Gavis had OS/360 development and Dick Case managed the architects. The 370 systems were being designed as evolutionary improvements over the 360, and Gavis proposed that we change the plan to include virtual memory. This change was highly desirable from a programming perspective, and the software managers were uniformly in favor. The hardware managers, however, were strongly opposed. They had already designed many of the 370 machines, and this change would cause a full year's delay.

At this point, Bob Evans was made president of the Systems Development Division. After an extensive review of all the arguments and a thorough marketing study, Evans sided with the programmers. The IBM virtual System 370 resulted.

THE IBM SYSTEM Q

In 1969 we began to think about what should come after OS/360. I was asked to run a task force of the leading software managers and technologists to examine this question. We formed a group of about 12 people that met over a period of several weeks. While I do not remember everyone who was there, the group included Tom Apple, Marty Belsky, Dick Bevier, Jim Frame, Don Gavis, and Horst Remus. We heard testimony from marketing, technology, and systems people from all over the company. We then produced an IBM strategy for how programming system support should evolve in the future. We called this strategy System Q.

During the meeting, we heard a great deal about the anticipated rapid growth of memory size and the advances in semiconductor technology. As a result, I proposed that we set the minimum memory for the System Q at one megabyte. This proposal was hooted down as wildly unrealistic. Even as informed and perceptive a group as this could not visualize the enormous growth in computer memories and the degree to which future programming systems would consume memory. In retrospect, my proposal of a one-megabyte minimum memory was far too timid.

To put this memory-size issue into perspective, the most widely used computer at the time was the IBM 1400. Its entry-level memory size was 1,400 characters. Even OS/360, our largest operating system, was originally designed with a starter version for a 16K 360 Model 30. Within a year, however, this was expanded to 32K.

One of the principal tenets of the new System Q was that compatibility was essential. That is, every system must be able to interchange data and application programs with every other system. The systems had to provide a smooth transition from the current IBM product line and to stress usability and ease of installation. We were all concerned with the enormous time and effort required to install the current IBM systems and wanted the new systems to be essentially self-installing.

One interesting anecdote from the System Q saga concerns the engineer we initially assigned to work out its introduction strategy. At that time, the San Jose Laboratory was developing a number of advanced disk file products. One manager whose pet project had not been funded was Al Shugart. Al was assigned to my staff to develop the System Q introduction strategy. It turned out that, while Shugart was traveling back and forth from California to arrange for his move to New York, he was also starting a disk file company called, of all things, Shugart. After Shugart left IBM, the company disbanded its software organization and System Q died. Shugart, by the way, is currently CEO of Seagate, the largest manufacturer of personal computer disk drives.

WALKING ON WATER

During the four years from January 1966 to December 1969, I ran all of IBM's commercial programming development work. In this time, we established a phase review system to ensure that the projects followed an orderly development process. This included a planning and commitment system, a quality staff to ensure that the work followed established practices, and a review policy that provided a hearing for disagreements. We had every laboratory install and use the Clear library control system to manage software changes. We also established an education program to ensure that all programming managers knew how to plan and manage their projects. Al Pietrasanta designed and launched this project management training program. In the next few years, this training was given to over 1,000 software managers. All in all, in today's CMM terms, these activities essentially built a Level 2 process.

Because of the growing interest in communications and interactive support and the increasing availability of communications hardware, we decided to develop an interactive programming support environment. This environment would allow every engineer access to the computer systems from a terminal in the work space rather than punching a deck of cards and submitting them for batch runs in the computer center. Bob Rutheroff had been a key OS/360 designer, and he agreed to take on this assignment. His plans were so impressive that, at the annual IBM programming conference that year, I announced that there would be a demonstration of this system at the swimming pool; Rutheroff would walk across.

BREAKING UP THE EMPIRE

From 1966 to 1969 IBM also established technology missions for all of its software laboratories. Time Life had languages and compilers; Poughkeepsie, New York, had sorts; Lidigo, Sweden, had utilities; Raleigh, North Carolina, had communications; and San Jose, California, had data management. Each of these laboratories was charged with developing a strategy to be the leader in its area of specialty. Over a brief span of time, these laboratories developed remarkable skills and abilities. They were soon at the forefront of their technologies and were becoming international experts.

In 1969, IBM management decided to reorganize again. I was asked to run the IBM Glendale Laboratory in Endicott, New York. Programming was split up, with every laboratory housing its own programming resources. A skeleton central programming group was retained in Harrison, New York, as staff advisors. Product planning, staffing, and funding were all given to the laboratories. Ted Climas was assigned to run the central staff, and he did as good a job as anyone could with the job. Even Climas, however, could not defend the mission assignments against the resource needs of the hardware system and product managers. The missions were thus dissipated. However, because the phase review and commitment processes had been imbedded in IBM's administrative bureaucracy, these practices were generally maintained.

The IBM programming missions were dissipated just after programs had become priced products. A host of competitors were entering the software business, and the IBM hardware managers only thought of programming in terms of hardware support. They could not see why IBM should develop or support any software products that did not directly support the hardware.

The sort mission is one example of the damage this attitude caused. Whereas the Poughkeepsie Laboratory had the sort mission, their principal job was to develop IBM's large system computers. The San Jose Laboratory was responsible for file products. Since competitors already provided sort programs, neither laboratory saw any reason why IBM should develop sort programs of its own. They thus disbanded the sort mission and reassigned the sort specialists to other work. When the sort mission disappeared, so did IBM's premier position in sort technology.

About a year later, the San Jose Laboratory introduced a new file product that offered moderate price performance advantages. It was expected to generate substantial IBM revenue. When it was introduced, however, this new file product did not sell very well. On examination, the product developers found that IBM's old sort program had not been upgraded or optimized for the new file. The customers needed sort support, and the competitive sort program suppliers were not interested in supporting the new file. For the first time, the hardware system and product managers found that, without programming support, the hardware would not sell. They then had to start designing many hardware products to run existing software rather than the software being designed for the hardware products.

IBM's failure to foresee the importance of software could not have come at a worse time. IBM's June 1968 introduction of priced software had launched a new software industry. Customers were increasingly sophisticated, and a growing number of competitors had the resources to enter the new market. The hardware people, however, controlled IBM's development strategy and funds. They had no interest or appreciation of the potential of the software business, either as a source of revenue or as a threat to the hardware business. They did not realize that, if IBM did not have a strong software capability, the software suppliers would define how the users saw and used the hardware.

LET 1,000 FLOWERS BLOOM

One immediate and almost tragic consequence of IBM's disbanding its software organization was the loss of a strong advocate for product-line compatibility. In 1970, at the same time that programming was disbanded, Spike Beitzel was named senior vice president over IBM development and U.S. manufacturing. Soon after, he approved the development of a new line of small computers. This work would be done in the Rochester, Minnesota, laboratory and would be freed of any compatibility constraints with the old 360 or newer 370 products.

The new System 3 was followed by the Systems 32, 33, and 38. These machines had a relatively large following at the entry level. Unfortunately, no provisions had been made for data interchange or other communication with the 360 and 370 systems. I was so irate about this plan that I sent a letter to Beitzel warning him of the risks and strongly recommending that IBM establish a compatibility strategy. My letter was picked up in discovery for the U.S. government anti-trust suit and was later published as part of that material.[6] This letter stressed that the most important future need of computer users would be the dynamic interchange of work among computing systems, both local and remote. At the time, IBM was the only supplier that could provide such systems. The letter went on to say, "interconnected systems, as well as interconnected networks of systems, will be of growing importance in the 1970s and a major factor in the 1980s."

This letter was ignored, and IBM proceeded with an incompatible family of systems just as the Digital Equipment Corporation (DEC) introduced a highly successful family of fully compatible computers. Their principal selling feature was compatibility across the entire DEC line from the smallest to the largest systems. DEC quickly grew to become the second largest company in the computer industry.

THE FS SYSTEM

In 1970 IBM launched the new FS system development effort. The FS concept was to build a high-level language system that would be tailored for communications and real-time applications. The machines would be a complete break with the 360 and 370 families, offering only emulator and translation support. The FS strategy was based on a sophisticated machine architecture that would provide a high-level language instruction set. Many of the operating system and memory management facilities of traditional control programs would be built into the hardware systems and implemented in microcode.

During the next three years, FS development took nearly half of IBM's system development resources. Every major laboratory had an FS project, and the only significant other work was to complete the 370 and Model 3X small systems that had already been announced. Unfortunately, the FS software work lagged behind the hardware. When the software people started to look at the FS architecture, they were concerned about the performance of standard commercial applications. On review, it turned out that leading customers' bread-and-butter COBOL applications would not have acceptable performance on FS. When marketing learned this, they rebelled. After spending what must have been $50 million or more on hardware and system development, the FS system was killed.

EXCLUSIVITY

By the early 1970s IBM was under serious attack from plug-compatible manufacturers. Their motivation was to get a free ride on IBM's software development. By making plug-compatible hardware, they could get the benefits of IBM's software support without paying for it. This attack started with graphic displays and terminals and quickly spread to file and tape systems. Soon after, Gene Amdahl left IBM to form the Amdahl Corporation, which made plug-compatible CPUs.

This was the same problem IBM had worried about with RCA some years earlier. Now, however, the IBM software was gradually being priced so that it could be protected. The operating systems and device support, however, were still largely free. This caused a double problem for IBM. First, they lost business to the plug-compatible competitors, and, second, the competitors could capitalize on IBM's full range of system support. They not only got free software support, they also got a free ride on IBM's systems marketing and installation work. The IBM response to this was called exclusivity. That meant that when IBM developed new hardware, the programming support would work only on the new hardware and not on the old. This was viable as long as the new hardware was sufficiently attractive to motivate customers to upgrade to it. Unfortunately, this meant the new hardware had to be much better. It also meant the customers for the older IBM hardware would no longer continue to get free enhancements to their programming support.

When the new hardware was not attractive enough, the customers bought the plug-compatible competitors and used IBM's old software. Although IBM tried various ways to withdraw the old software, that was not generally possible. Many of IBM's product managers were able to accelerate their rate of new product introduction but some could not. The biggest impact was that IBM could no longer afford to rent machines to customers. IBM thus moved to a purchase strategy.

THE TRANSITION TO A PURCHASE BUSINESS

IBM had long rented its machines to customers on a 30-day agreement. These machines could be returned to IBM at any time with no charge. This was very attractive to most customers, and it provided IBM with a steady stream of revenue. It also provided a ready market for new machines. A new system could be sold quite easily by merely focusing on the added monthly cost of a new rental and not rejustifying the rentals the customers were currently paying for the equipment to be replaced. Thus, every sale meant an increase in IBM's monthly revenue.

Moving to a purchase strategy severely affected IBM's ability to maintain a smooth revenue stream through economic downturns. Also, as IBM sold off its large inventory of installed rental equipment, they generated a huge and temporary revenue bulge. However, once the early purchases of installed rental equipment were largely completed, not only did IBM no longer generate rental revenue, but the purchase revenue bulge passed as well. This produced an extended period of slow and sometimes negative revenue growth.

All this came about because of the value of IBM's programming support to its customers. This was the raison d'être for the plug-compatible competitors, and they in turn were the threat to the installed rental equipment. After all, if competitors could sell a cheaper machine to do the same job, customers could actually eliminate their monthly rental bill by buying a plug-compatible machine to replace it. Often, in fact, these suppliers could demonstrate paybacks of less than 12 months. As long as the price was low enough, it was an easy sell. Again, the emerging software business had a long-term impact on IBM's hardware businesses.

The IBM PC

In the early 1970s, various competitive start-ups launched small personal computer (PC) products that began to get market attention. Frank Cary, who was IBM chairman at the time, rightly saw this as a critical future product area and insisted that a PC program be launched. After several abortive efforts, Cary finally established a special group that was cut off from all of IBM's business controls. He told them to act like a start-up company and to build their own PC. They did exactly what they were told and had a PC ready within a year.

To do this they had to rely on commercially available semiconductor chips from Intel. Also, because of the dissolution of programming, no IBM programming development resources were available to the PC group. They thus contracted out the software to a little start-up software company called Microsoft, run by Bill Gates. Although many among the corporate staff had serious concerns about this strategy, this program was being directed personally from the chairman's office and nobody's opinion was wanted. The PC was an initial great success. In the long run, Microsoft and Intel were the real winners.

Programming Quality and Process

In 1982, a few years before my retirement from IBM, I was asked by Jack Kuehler to take over the programming quality and process staff. Kuehler was about to be named IBM president, and he was concerned about the quality of IBM's programming work. The company had established a corporate instruction, CI105, that required each new product to have better quality than its IBM predecessor product as well as better quality than the leading competitor. The hardware community aggressively implemented this policy, with impressive results. The software community argued that CI105 did not apply to them. The president of one of IBM's divisions even made a presentation to the then IBM CEO, John Opel, arguing that CI105 could not work for software. Opel disagreed and told him that CI105 applied to all IBM products. A short time later this division president was replaced. The common assumption was that his CI105 presentation had something to do with it.

In any event, my group was told to get software in compliance with CI105. We established a task force of experts from the major laboratories and spent several months studying the issue. In the end, they could not agree. Bill Florac, the quality manager in my group, had his team produce a proposal. We took this to senior management for agreement and then tried to sell it to the laboratories.

Several laboratories agreed, but Poughkeepsie did not. Although they would not make a counter proposal, they insisted that our proposal would not work. I called Jack Kuehler and asked if he would help. We scheduled a meeting with the Poughkeepsie programming director for the next week. When I told him that Kuehler wanted to hear what Poughkeepsie recommended, he decided to accept Florac's proposal.

Whereas the quality measurement approach we selected was not particularly good, it was the best we could devise. We argued that IBM would never learn to measure software quality until it started doing so. Interestingly enough, this system has now been in place for more than 12 years and it has produced remarkable results. In the first 2 years, for example, customer-reported software defects for new MVS software products were reduced by an average of 50 percent per year. At the time, IBM spent about $250,000,000 a year on U.S. software maintenance. Thereafter, even though we continued to ship increasing volumes of new software, annual software maintenance costs actually declined.

One example of the impact of this was an event that happened shortly before my IBM retirement. At a meeting in my organization in California I ran into Naomi Trapnell, the wife of Fritz Trapnell, who had managed the OS/360 in 1966. Fritz Trapnell was then programming director for Amdahl Corp. At dinner that night, Fritz asked me what IBM had done to improve its programming quality. It seems that several Amdahl customers had noticed the sharply improved quality of IBM software and had told Amdahl.

LIVING HAPPILY EVER AFTER

As I neared retirement from IBM, I considered what to do next. I was 59 years old and had the energy to tackle a new challenge. I had recently visited many of IBM's customers and found their software work poorly managed and consistently late. Nobody was happy with their software development groups and nobody had any viable programs for improving things. It was obvious that the management methods we had used in IBM had been effective, but very few people were using them. It was also obvious that software was a critical technology whose importance would continue to increase for the foreseeable future.

I decided to make an outrageous personal commitment: I would devote myself to changing the way the world developed software. Although I had no expectation that I could actually change the world, making an outrageous commitment was highly motivating. I was not sure how to address this commitment, so I want to see an old friend, Erich Block, who headed the National Science Foundation. I told Block about my outrageous commitment and he suggested I work for the Software Engineering Institute at Carnegie Mellon University (SEI). He even give me a letter of introduction.

Thus, on retiring from IBM, I joined SEI. I am now an SEI Fellow and have worked on many aspects of software process improvement, including the Capability Maturity Model (CMM)[7], the Personal Software Process (PSP),[8, 9] and my current work on the Team Software Process (TSP).[10] Although it is too early to tell, it looks as if we are starting to change the way the world develops software.

CONCLUSION

As I look back on my software life and all the exciting tasks I have been given, several conclusions stand out:

- Hindsight is marvelously clear when writing a retrospective. Although I was deeply involved in all that I have described, the future was not obvious at the time.

- I have indeed been fortunate, not just because of my wonderful wife and family but because of all the exciting assignments I have been given.

- While I am proud of what I have personally done, it is clear that I could have done very little of this on my own. I have worked with some marvelously capable and creative people, some of whom I have mentioned and many I have not.

- Surprisingly, after all these years, big projects, and prestigious titles, the most rewarding work has been the most recent. The challenges in this field are incredible, and it appears that they will continue to be more incredible and more rewarding in the future.

It ain't over yet folks!

ENDNOTES

1. Frederick P. Brooks, *The Mythical Man-Month, Essays on Software Engineering, Anniversary Edition*, Addison-Wesley, Reading, Mass., 1995.

2. Brooks, *The Mythical Man-Month*.

3. Humphrey, *Managing the Software Process*, Addison-Wesley, Reading, Mass., 1989.

4. Capability Maturity Model and CMM are service marks of Carnegie Mellon University.

5. Humphrey, Managing the Software Process. Mark C. Paulk et al., *The Capability Maturity Model: Guidelines for Improving the Software Process*, Addison-Wesley, Reading, Mass., 1995.

6. Richard Thomas DeLamarter, *Big Blue, IBM's Use and Abuse of Power*. Dodd, Mead and Co., New York, 1986, pp. 361–362.

7. See Humphrey, *Managing the Software Process*. Reading; and Paulk et al., *The Capability Maturity Mode*.

8. See W.S. Humphrey, *A Discipline for Software Engineering*. Addison-Wesley, Reading, Mass., 1995; W.S. Humphrey, "Using a Defined and Measured Personal Software Process," *IEEE Software*, May 1996, pp. 77–88; and W.S. Humphrey, "The PSP and Personal Project Estimating," *American Programmer*, Vol. 9, No. 6, June 1996, pp. 2–15.

9. Personal Software Process and PSP are service marks of Carnegie Mellon University.

10. Team Software Process and TSP are service marks of Carnegie Mellon University.

How I Watched in Pain as IBM Outsmarted UNIVAC

Norman F. Schneidewind

My Introduction to the Commercial Computer Field

Beginning in 1956, as a newly hired engineer at the UNIVAC St. Paul, Minnesota, plant, and later in the Los Angeles regional office, I witnessed the early battles between IBM and UNIVAC for supremacy in the computer marketplace. Ironically, in 1955, UNIVAC had the lead in the scientific market—in those days a distinction was made between scientific and business computers—but UNIVAC saw its lead evaporate in 1956 due to a combination of IBM's foresight and the incompetence of UNIVAC's Remington Rand management. As you will see later, various segments of the UNIVAC product line were owned by various companies at various times during the time span covered by my account. Where it is appropriate to refer to the entire corporate entity, I use the name "UNIVAC." Where it is more appropriate to refer to a particular company's influence on the fate of the UNIVAC product line, I use that company's name (for example, Remington Rand).

In 1956 I had job offers from both IBM and UNIVAC; I chose UNIVAC because the evidence suggested that UNIVAC was in the lead in the scientific computer field, which was my primary interest at the time. One piece of evidence convinced me that UNIVAC had the lead at that time. I was invited to UNIVAC's St. Paul plant for interviews. There I saw impressive research developments in the laboratory and production in the factory of scientific computers. Although I would eventually be assigned to UNIVAC's Los

Angeles regional office, which was responsible for sales and technical support of UNIVAC products in the area, I was interviewed in St. Paul because this was the headquarters for UNIVAC Scientific engineering, production, application, and sales. So this meant that I was exposed to much more of UNIVAC's computer capabilities than would have been the case had I been interviewed in Los Angeles.

In contrast, because of IBM's emphasis on sales activity—a policy that would prove crucial in its victory over UNIVAC—I was interviewed in IBM's Los Angeles regional and branch offices, where I observed punched card equipment, typewriters, and time clocks—the core of IBM's office business at the time. Thus, I was not exposed to IBM's computer prowess, as was the case with UNIVAC. As it turned out, what I was witnessing was illusory; in reality UNIVAC's early advantage was beginning to evaporate as IBM's management, led by the younger Thomas Watson, Jr., realized the potential of the computer and began to aggressively develop and market competitive products. When I informed IBM of my decision to join UNIVAC, the Los Angeles branch manager remarked: "Young man, you are making a mistake." Based on my experience with UNIVAC, he may have been right.

CORPORATE COMPUTER CULTURE

Remington Rand, a long-time competitor of IBM in the punched card business, had acquired Engineering Research Associates in 1952, an early computer firm in St. Paul. Engineering Research Associates, founded in 1946, became the nucleus of Remington-Rand's scientific computer business, headquartered in St. Paul. Engineering Research Associates' product line was dubbed "UNIVAC Scientific"; some of its models were the 1101, 1103, and 1103A. Remington Rand was acquired by the Sperry Corporation in 1955 and renamed Sperry Rand. Because the Sperry Corporation had many interests in addition to computers, such as gyroscopes, the Remington Rand management was pretty much left in charge of the new corporation's computer business. Among the founders of Engineering Research Associates was William Norris, and among the chief designers was Seymour Cray (chief designer of the 1103 series). (Because of Sperry Rand's lack of interest in scientific and military computers, Norris would break away from Sperry Rand in 1957 to found the Control Data Corporation; he took Seymour Cray with him.) In addition, in 1955 Remington Rand acquired the Eckert-Mauchly Computer Corporation, which had been founded in 1946 by J. Presper Eckert and John William Mauchly, principal designers of the ENIAC. This acquisition became the nucleus of Sperry Rand's business computer applications, headquartered in Philadelphia. This product line was simply called UNIVAC (for Universal Automatic Computer); example models were the UNIVAC I and II.

As had been the case in IBM under Thomas Watson, Sr., Remington Rand's management philosophy was built around punched cards and the tabulating equipment that processed them. Although Remington Rand recognized that it must get into the computer business and, hence acquired Engineering Research Associates and the Eckert-Mauchly Computer Corporation, it did not make the right business decisions at either the corporate or field levels. For example, a significant factor in Remington-Rand's loss to IBM was that both companies had a commission plan for the sale of punched card equipment, but only IBM had a commission plan for the sale of computers. Thus Remington Rand's sales people had little incentive to sell computers. I had direct exposure to this policy after I had completed my training in St. Paul and was assigned to the Los Angeles regional office. I recall being assigned as the only UNIVAC Scientific technical support person in the region and discovering that the sales people, who had come from Remington Rand, had no interest in selling UNIVAC Scientific computers because they received no commission for selling these computers but received a lucrative commission for selling punched card equipment!

IBM GAINS SUPREMACY

Like Remington Rand, IBM was slow to recognize both the technical and market potential of computers. However, once IBM did understand that its future lay with the computer, it was much more aggressive than Remington Rand in making technical innovations and in providing superior marketing and customer support for these innovations. A typical IBM sales approach was to assemble a large number of both product and application specialists at the prospective customer's site to convey the message that IBM had the resources to ensure the success of the installation if the customer decided in its favor. This strategy could indeed be intimidating as I recall when I was the lone UNIVAC Scientific representative facing this kind of opposition when battling for the Marquardt Corporation sale in Los Angeles. I lost!

Although Remington Rand could have slowed the IBM juggernaut if it had had more effective management, IBM's victory was probably inevitable because of its extremely large base of punched card customers, which provided the foundation for IBM's push into the computer market place, plus its "cradle to the grave" service that distinguished IBM from its competitors. IBM continued this approach with great success. This "full service" approach not only increased customer satisfaction, which led to increased sales, but also succeeded in locking in customers so that they were highly dependent on IBM for continued support. These captives contributed to IBM's market share when it came time to upgrade their computer systems. Being dependent on IBM for support, they were very reluctant to consider UNIVAC or other vendors.

THE TECHNICAL BATTLEGROUND

Remington Rand's problem was not lack of good products. Rather it was unable to exploit good technical ideas in the market place. For example, Remington Rand failed to bring to market scientific computers it had developed in its St. Paul laboratories—mainly designed by Seymour Cray, who would later found Cray Research—that were superior to anything available from IBM. This was an irony for me because I would be assigned to conduct plant tours for visitors—customers and prospective customers—to show them our new developments that would never reach the market place.

However, in early 1956 UNIVAC appeared to be in good shape, having delivered a number of scientific computers to key government agencies and companies (such as Lockheed and Ramo-Wooldridge). The UNIVAC Scientific 1103A was considered to be a good machine. Its Repeat instruction for automatically incrementing operand addresses in an instruction loop was considered a significant advance. The 1103A was considered superior to IBM's closest scientific model—the 701. However UNIVAC's lead did not last long. The following were the major reasons for the reversal of market positions and the factors that made it increasingly difficult for all of us in UNIVAC to compete with IBM:

1. IBM developed and started to deliver the Model 704, which had not only index registers for incrementing operand addresses but built-in floating point commands, as well. The 1103A had neither of these features. With the 1103A the programmer had to use address arithmetic in combination with the Repeat instruction to control the execution of a loop, whereas with the 704 the programmer could load index registers with address increments. The contents of the index registers would be automatically added by the hardware to the base operand addresses during instruction execution. Also IBM's hardware-implemented floating point instructions were faster than UNIVAC's software implementation.

2. Possibly the most significant advance was the development of FORTRAN. UNIVAC had only an assembler. With FORTRAN, IBM users could write programs easier and with fewer errors than could UNIVAC users. Interestingly for me, in the fall of 1956 I accompanied Ramo-Wooldridge computer executives (a 1103A was installed at Ramo-Wooldridge in Los Angeles) to the UNIVAC St. Paul and Philadelphia plants. The purpose of the trip was for the Ramo-Wooldridge personnel to see the latest UNIVAC developments in computer technology. At the Philadelphia plant we met with Grace Hopper, who was working on the development of COBOL. Although this was of general interest to the Ramo-Wooldridge personnel, it was not relevant to their scientific computing applications. Subsequently Ramo-Wooldridge ordered a 704 for general-purpose scientific computing but retained the 1103A because its I/O operations were considered superior to the 704 and, hence was better for Ramo-Wooldridge's real-time applications.

3. Ironically, a UNIVAC technical advance resulted in an advantage for IBM. UNIVAC used a magnetic tape system rather than punched cards for data input. Magnetic tape could be read faster than cards, but the marketplace was

not ready for it. Decades of experience with punched card processing had created a culture. This reverence for punched cards was somewhat justified because of their convenience: data could be keyed, verified, interpreted, sorted, computed, and printed. The only problem with this concept was that the functions performed on punched card equipment were unnecessary for computer processing. Once data were input to a computer, it could process data electronically with no need for external punched card manipulation. Thus, eventually, after computers overcame the punched card mindset, punched cards would be relegated to the role of an input medium and, later, eliminated altogether. But in part, because jobs were tied to the use of punched card equipment, the data-processing field was not ready or willing to assign the punched card such a minor role. Thus in 1956 the data-processing field was not receptive to the idea that data could be keyed to magnetic tape and used as computer input.

One of the issues that seems trivial today but was a major concern at the time was the matter of verifying computer input. A key-punch verifier was used to rekey the original data while reading the card that had been originally key punched. When a mismatch was discovered, the verifier would not punch a notch on the card; this notch signified that the card had been verified for use in subsequent processing steps. UNIVAC's solution to verification was to type two tapes and compare them on the computer for consistency, or to type three tapes and to use a "voter logic" to choose the "correct" character. If there was no agreement among the three tapes, an error condition was signaled. Although it is obvious today that the computer can be used to advantage to make a great variety of input data validity checks, which are superior to external checks like key verification, the punched card culture, promoted by IBM, did not have this perspective in 1956.

Another charge levied against magnetic tape input was that it was not possible to erase and correct a character in the middle of the tape. Technically this was true because the tape-recording mechanism did not allow selective changes. However, a correction tape could be created and input to the computer with the main tape and corrections made in the computer's memory. The punched card culture's solution was to rekey the character at the key punch (for key punches that were capable of storing the data before the card was punched), if the error was caught before the card was punched. If the error was discovered after the card was punched, either the data would have to be rekeyed and a new card punched, or a correction card would be punched and the process described for using a correction tape would be used. Thus neither method for correcting errors had a clear advantage. Rather, the opposition to magnetic tape input was more a reflection of culture and resistance to change than a substantive technical argument against tape input.

MISSED OPPORTUNITY

A typical example of a missed opportunity occurred after I was assigned to the Los Angeles regional office of UNIVAC. I learned through colleagues that IBM had reached an agreement with the UCLA Graduate School of Business to establish a Western Data Processing Center in the school to be well stocked with IBM computer equipment and support staff. It was obvious to everyone except my regional manager that although ostensibly the data-processing center would be used to support instruction and research, it would also provide IBM with the significant marketing benefit of indoctrinating hundreds of future managers in IBM computer technology. My regional manager had not heard of this development. This was bad enough, but when I informed him, his response was: "Let them [IBM] do it." He did not express the slightest concern. He was financially well off because of his commissions as a Remington Rand punched card equipment sales representative for many years and as regional manager (he received "off the top" commissions on all sales made in his region).

CONCLUSION

Although it would seem that the lesson learned from both UNIVAC's corporate experience and my personal experience is that "technology is not everything"—you also need superior marketing and customer support—the lesson was forgotten by IBM, of all organizations, in the era of the personal computer! It was for

Microsoft to use chapters from the IBM play book to make most of the world's personal computer users *and* developers dependent (that is, captives) on its products and services.

5

SOLVING PROBLEMS: APPLICATION PIONEERS

The application developer's role in the early history of computing was pivotal. They performed what was, in a sense, the *real* beginning of the Computing Age. These fancy new computers and this strange new software were finally being used to solve some real and significant problems.

The problems that applications developers attempted to solve cut a wide swath from the very beginning of the field. There were scientific problems that were numerical in nature and small, but still quite complex in their scope. For example, in 1957 I took over responsibility for a program that computed the potential thrust power of various rocket fuel chemicals, and it was used to determine what chemical components might be worth mixing to build rocket engines. The program was tremendous in size—it filled the entire 4,096-word memory of an early IBM scientific computer! I spent as much time shrinking it (in order to fit in some new functions) as I did adding the functions. It was also extremely complex—its algorithm was iterative, and there were failure-to-converge problems aplenty to deal with. As you might imagine, its outputs were key to decisions being made by my employer, the space propulsion company Aerojet-General. For example, at a time when *Time* and *Newsweek* were trumpeting the value of boron as a propulsion additive, we at Aerojet had already run the chemical composition data and found that it was worthless for that purpose. The outputs of my program were more up-to-date than the latest news magazine!

There were also business data-processing problems. For example, in 1961 I inherited a shop-scheduling program that produced daily schedules for the workers on a laboratory assembly line and for the parts flowing along that line. Its algorithm, coded by a brilliant mathematician, was so complex that there were parts of the program I never dared modify. It had to run daily, before the first shift arrived at work, so that the shop workers would know what to do. Its algorithms took account of calendar information, and it would simply not run on holidays, printing out a message, "I'm on vacation, tra-la." That was all well and good until, on the first work day of the new year in 1962, someone forgot to reset the year in the computer's memory to the new one, and the program refused to run—because that day in the previous year had been a holiday.

There was computing in academia, of course. Vendors gave tremendous price breaks on their new machines in order to expose these new tools to as many emerging students as possible, and it was easy for an academic computer center to have the latest equipment for both its administrative and academic sides. For example, at the University of Washington's computer center in the late 1960s I worked on some system software for Control Data's latest and greatest computer, the 6400. Traditional business accounting applications, class scheduling, special-purpose programs to support specific faculty research, and much more were the order of the day.

Finally, there were a few consultants. Not as many as today, but still there were those who sold their services to the rest of the applications developers and their management—to advise them on new computers or work alongside the in-house application programmers, or to look ahead to where the future of computing might be headed.

In short, even though the early applications were a diverse lot, by today's standards they were relatively few in number. Although hundreds of applications were developed in the 1950s and 1960s, thousands or perhaps even millions exist today. We were only beginning, back then, to anticipate the problem-solving power of the computer.

No packaged applications were available in the early days. Word processors were not available because we still thought of computers largely as numeric or business data processors, not as information processors, and because printing devices did not print lowercase characters. Generalized spreadsheets were not available because no one had yet conceived of that brilliant idea, and would not for another 20 to 25 years. (Many business applications had spreadsheet-like special-purpose output, but no one had thought of generalizing the concept yet.) Graphics products were unheard of because little or no graphics printing capability existed, and when such capability first arrived in the 1960s it was clumsy and astonishingly slow. And, of course, no packaged applications were available because software was free and no market existed for them!

The stories that follow are divided into those of aerospace pioneers, information systems pioneers, academic computer center pioneers, and consulting pioneers.

AEROSPACE

For those in the aerospace business during the Pioneering Era of software, it was difficult to tell which kind of pioneer you were. Were you a software pioneer, finding new ways to solve problems using brainpower and without physical raw materials? Or were you a space pioneer, expanding the world's reach into the infinite area beyond our own? The technologies for both endeavors began and evolved together, and for the aerospace software application pioneer, life offered a profusion of opportunities.

The stories of three aerospace application pioneers are included in this section of the book—Barry Boehm, Robert Britcher, and Donald Reifer. Boehm's role began at the beginning, in the 1950s, and he remains a key figure in the aerospace software world today. Britcher and Reifer began their work a decade after Boehm entered the field, but their stories devetail nicely with Boehm's. Britcher was involved in air traffic control, a more down-to-earth (literally!) branch of the aerospace business, and his reminiscences are as alive and relevant as today's air traffic control headlines. Reifer focuses on the importance and difficulty of change in the evolution of software in the aerospace business.

All three stories vividly portray the era. We see the artifacts of early computing in Boehm's space problem/solution anecdotes. He recalls the escape tower on top of the Atlas missile; the flow charts of early programs; the primitive, numeric data input forms; and his own attempt in the 1960s to "get out of the software business," an effort we are all glad failed.

Britcher provides a view of the early development of air traffic control applications. He recalls his early training: so narrow and specific that he had to acquire the more important facets later, "like burrs on a hike through the woods." (Early training in computers and software development was like that—you learned by doing.) He remembers an early computer that "would fill a small gymnasium," and early computer specialists, who worked in strange and uncomfortable quarters: "the men wore shirts and ties and the women wore skirts and dresses." He relates the story of the computer that melted down because someone turned the wrong switch, and he tells us about the people who suffered various personal meltdowns because of the stress of their jobs. Finally, he proffers that "the act of meeting ordinary, daily demands can transform itself into an extraordinary achievement."

Reifer's recollections are of himself as a change agent. During his early excursions to computing conferences, he encountered the famous of the field—"they never look like you expect." He recalls the evolution of "airplane seatmate" talks, from the early days when he tried to explain to the computer-naive what a computer was ("he was amazed by the concept") to more recent times when he does not bother to try ("I would be bombarded with questions about what software package he should use"). Reifer's story includes his attempt to enlighten a general who is genuinely curious to understand the mathematical derivation of the theory underlying structured programming.

Boehm's story is fact-filled; he clearly remembers the intimate details of his early days in the field. Britcher's story is a work of art, a tapestry of fine writing woven around an important and yet very human set of reminiscences. Reifer's story is a chronology; you see his own evolution running parallel to that of the field. One can recall the past in many ways— nowhere is that more evident than in this section.

AN EARLY APPLICATION GENERATOR AND OTHER RECOLLECTIONS

Barry Boehm

This paper is sponsored by the affiliates of the USC Center for Software Engineering. The current affiliates are Aerospace Corporation, Air Force Cost Analysis Agency, AT&T, Bellcore, DISA, E-Systems, Electronic Data Systems Corporation, GDE Systems, Hughes Aircraft Company, Institute for Defense Analysis, Interactive Development Environments, Jet Propulsion Lab, Litton Data Systems, Lockheed Martin Corporation, Loral Federal Systems, MCC Inc., Motorola Inc., Northrop Grumman Corporation, Rational Software Corporation, Rockwell International, Science Applications International Corporation, Software Engineering Institute (CMU), Software Productivity Consortium, Sun Microsystems, Inc., Texas Instruments, TRW, U.S. Army Research Laboratory, and Xerox Corporation.

In this recollection I focus primarily on the experiences I had while developing an early application generator in the area of rocket flight mechanics. I begin by describing some of the events that led up to this work, and I end by describing some of the experiences I have had since.

EARLY EXPERIENCES

My First Day in the Software Business

In early June 1955 I showed up at the personnel office of General Dynamics–Convair in San Diego for a summer trainee job after my sophomore year at Harvard. I was a math major and was very concerned about what math majors did once they grew up. Being an actuary, statistician, or math teacher all seemed pretty dry.

67

The personnel manager looked at his blackboard and said, "Hmm, math major. Well, we have summer openings in Structures, Thermodynamics, and the Digital Computer Lab. Why don't you try the Digital Computer Lab?" Luckily for me, the computer field came along just in time to give math majors a fascinating and rewarding lifetime of mathematics-related challenges and applications.

On that first day my supervisor spent some time explaining what computer programmers did, and then took me on a walking tour through the computer. It was UNIVAC's ERA 1103, with a 12-microsecond cycle time and a whole 1,024 words of main memory, and it occupied most of a large room. What I remember most indelibly was my supervisor's next remark: "Now listen. We're paying this computer $600 an hour, and we're paying you $2 an hour, and I want you to act accordingly."

This was my first exposure to software engineering economics. As behavioral conditioning, it was valuable to me in impressing good habits of desk checking, test planning, and analyzing before coding. But it also created some bad habits—a preoccupation with saving microseconds, patching object code, and so on—that took me years to unlearn after the balance of hardware and software costs began to tip the other way.

Some Early Software Experiences at Harvard

After a summer at General Dynamics building mathematical routines and paper-tape input-output utilities, I returned to Harvard with an urge to learn more about computers and programming. I also returned with altogether too much confidence in what I had learned already. Harvard's computer laboratory had the original Mark IV computer that Howard Aiken had developed at Harvard, and a recently acquired UNIVAC I. One programmed the Mark IV in absolute octal using instructions that opened gates and sent strings of bits down wires to registers.

My big assignment in my first Harvard computer course, Numerical Analysis, was a classic in optimistic effort estimation. It involved programming a number of numerical algorithms and entering various data sets to test and compare the algorithms. I rapidly sketched out the program for the algorithms, and assumed I was pretty near complete. However, I had not considered that the input-output for the Mark IV required a good deal of complex programming that was significantly different from the I/O of the ERA 1103. After a couple of all-nighters, I got most of the cases to run, but my grade in the course went south. It taught me (at the gut level rather than at the intellectual level) that the housekeeping details on a software job generally consume most of the code, and that being a whiz on computer A did not mean that one was a whiz on computer B.

Eventually, I ended up doing some useful software things at Harvard, such as eliminating my job as a Friden calculating-machine operator. I was reducing data on meteor trails for the Harvard College Observatory and developed a computer program to automate all the calculations. Fortunately, the observatory found other things for me to do to earn my keep.

Further Experiences at General Dynamics

During the summer of 1956 and after graduating (still as a math major) in 1957, I went back to programming jobs at General Dynamics. I did not realize it at the time, but several of the regular-guy programmers and engineers I worked with day-to-day would become heavyweights in the profession. For example, my carpool to work included Bob Price, who became the CEO of Control Data, and Donn Parker, who did a lot of the pioneering work on computer crime and computer ethics. In 1957–58, Parker was the leader of the FORTRAN movement within General Dynamics. Its adherents came in wearing FORTRAN T-shirts and joked about the Neanderthal assembly language programmers. I was one of the Neanderthals, still believing that FORTRAN wasted microseconds and restricted my essential access to the machine's registers and exotic instructions.

It was an exciting time to be in both the computer business and the rocket business. One of my assignments involved the Atlas-Mercury astronaut program. The General Dynamics Atlas rocket engineers wanted to put an escape tower on top of the Atlas that would blast free if the rocket started getting into trouble. The engineers were not sure that the escape tower would work in all the situations in which it was needed, and I got the job of analyzing it. This involved modifying a large assembly language simulation of the Atlas rocket, running a lot of cases that might cause problems, and working with the rocket engineers to fix the problem situations. I really identified with the astronauts, who were

putting their lives on the line by trusting that things like this would work. The escape tower did become part of the Atlas-Mercury flight vehicle but fortunately never had to be used.

I did not realize at the time that the Atlas rocket-simulation program was an early example of domain engineering, software product line architecting, and software reuse. The Atlas rocket product line included a number of options for rocket engines, aerodynamic configurations, and flight guidance algorithms. Their performance could be represented by either mathematical functions, tables, or polynomial approximations to the table values. Led by an unsung hero named Herb Hilton, the team developing the Atlas rocket simulation had encoded the most likely options as numerical sequence numbers. Thus, for example, the rocket engine simulation options were encoded roughly as:

/ul//00—no thrust and fuel flow

01—constant thrust and fuel flow

02—constant thrust and fuel flow modified by atmospheric pressure

03—Atlas V.1 booster thrust and fuel flow tables versus time

04—Atlas V.2 booster thrust and fuel flow tables versus time

05—and so on

Other sequences covered aerodynamic, guidance, and special output options. Thus, a simple unpowered coasting trajectory with a simple aerodynamic model and no guidance could be represented by the sequence 00-01-00, whereas an Atlas V.1 booster with simple aerodynamics and a simple guidance scheme would be represented as 03-01-01.

Using this approach, most of the Atlas trajectory analyses desired by the rocket engineers could be accommodated by preparing input cards with these option sequences, plus some general parameters describing the rocket's launch location, initial weight, initial fuel weight, and so on. It was also fairly easy to add new standard options. Exotic options, such as the Atlas-Mercury escape tower, involved special programming efforts. Overall, however, the approach provided great labor savings and rapid service through reuse of the standard Atlas rocket model components.

Rand and Its Environment

In 1959 I left General Dynamics and joined the Rand Corporation in Santa Monica, where I worked primarily as an engineering programmer-analyst. My primary motivation for this move was that Rand was willing to let me work full-time while taking graduate courses toward a Ph.D. in math at UCLA (University of California–San Diego did not exist at the time, nor did any computer science departments).

Another major motivation for my move to Rand involved its world-class staff and research programs. I learned linear programming, dynamic programming, and network flow theory from their inventors, George Dantzig, Richard Bellman, and Ray Fulkerson (with the latter two, I also frequently played weekend tennis matches). Allen Newell, Cliff Shaw, and Herb Simon were developing the Logic Theorist, IPL-V, and other pioneering artificial intelligence (AI) contributions. Another future Nobel Prize winner, Harry Markowitz, was developing the Simscript programming language. Paul Armer, the Computer Sciences Department head, also sponsored "AI summers" in which people like Marvin

Minsky, Ed Feigenbaum, and Dan Bobrow experimented with new AI concepts and floated mind-stretching visions of robotic futures. Occasionally controversies erupted, such as during the summer of 1964 when Hubert Dreyfus came to Rand with his "alchemy and artificial intelligence" challenge: to provide evidence that AI techniques could scale up to handle large, complex problems and commonsense reasoning.

A team led by Willis Ware had developed the Johnniac computer, named after Rand consultant John von Neumann. Cliff Shaw was using it to develop JOSS (Johnniac Open Shop System), one of the world's first on-line interactive time-sharing systems. Tom Ellis invented the first freehand graphic input device, the Rand Tablet; and Gabe Groner developed a robust freehand character recognizer for it. Paul Baran developed his classic 14-report study "On Distributed Communications," which provided the conceptual foundation for packet switching, ARPANET, and Internet. Experts in large-scale software development, such as Pat Haverty, were available from the time that Rand spun off System Development Corporation to develop the software for the SAGE system.

My interest in mathematical economics was also stimulated at this time by Rand's pioneering efforts in cost-benefit analysis, systems analysis, game theory, decision theory, and conflict analysis.

My job at this time involved developing computer models for Rand's engineers and physicists. Unlike the Atlas rocket engineers, the Rand rocket engineers did characteristically exotic analyses. For example, engineers explored firing rockets out of the sides of tall mountains, carrying rockets above most of the atmosphere on huge airplanes, and devising aerospace-planes that could cruise around converting atmospheric oxygen into rocket fuel before taking off into orbit.

After programming some of these special cases, I had a pretty good idea of how to develop a general-purpose rocket simulation to handle Rand's wide range of analyses. Fortunately, Rand's Engineering Department was interested in having such a program, and this became my main job in 1961.

In the following sections I describe the rocket domain model and rocket trajectory application generator, since they formed the experience base for my more recent work with the DARPA Megaprogramming, STARS, and Domain Specific Software Architecture initiatives.

ROCKET TRAJECTORY DOMAIN ARCHITECTING

Desired Technical Capabilities

The first step in domain architecting was to interview the Rand rocket engineers to determine the range of their desired capabilities. These desired capabilities are summarized in the following list and contrasted with the capabilities of the General Dynamics Atlas rocket model.

1. *Wider range of aerodynamic, propulsion, and guidance models.* Atlas was a liquid-fueled, basically cylindrical rocket with booster, sustainer, and vernier engines, with basically preprogrammed guidance options. The Rand engineers needed to investigate solid rockets, various rocket shapes, various engine combinations, and various advanced guidance, navigation, and control options.

2. *Wider range of environment models.* The Atlas simulation included a fairly extensive set of Earth gravity and atmosphere models. The Rand engineers also needed to simulate rockets in the vicinity of the Moon and other planets, and to include such effects as solar radiation pressure on large, lightweight satellites.

3. *Wider range of initiation and termination conditions.* The Atlas simulation basically assumed a ground launch. It typically changed stages as a function of time or weight, or of altitude when the rocket finally came back to Earth. The Rand engineers needed to be able to start in mid-flight or from aboard an aircraft. They had needs to change stages as functions of such quantities as velocity, flight path angle, relative time from the beginning of the stage, or the point at which the rocket's extrapolated trajectory would reach a certain distance or altitude. A related need was for an alternate termination condition in case the primary termination condition could not be met.

4. *Abilities to iterate on a control variable* (for example, a guidance parameter) to determine the value at which a resulting dependent variable (for example, the extrapolated flight distance or range) would reach a desired value or reach its optimum value.

5. *Abilities to investigate several options during a single pass on the computer.* In the batch-sequential computer operations of the early 1960s engineers wanted to get as much mileage as possible from each computer pass.

6. *Ability to provide special outputs,* such as orbital parameters or the rocket's range, azimuth, and elevation with respect to one or more tracking stations.

7. *Ability to specify higher or lower levels of simulation accuracy.*

8. *Ability to simulate backward in time.*

9. *Ability to simulate rocket vibration effects.*

10. *Ability to simulate airplanes and helicopters as well as rockets.*

It turned out that it was feasible to accommodate all of these desired capabilities except the last two, which would have added significant complexity to the system.

Desired Operational Capabilities: User View

Besides the technical capabilities, operational capabilities were also necessary to make the program as easy to use and easy to modify as possible. This was also one of my main concerns, since I would have to do all of the software usage consulting and maintenance myself.

Rand had an IBM 704 computer that ran the Share Operating System. It still ran in batch-sequential mode, in which engineers submitted card-deck inputs and received printouts either a few hours later or the following morning. It had a number of amenities, such as the ability to compile programs and link them to system or programmer libraries of relocatable object modules. It did not have a job control language, but applications could be programmed to provide multiple simulation runs within a single pass on the computer. The primary programming languages supported were FORTRAN and COBOL. By this time I was no longer preoccupied with saving microseconds, and I did most of my programming in FORTRAN. I chose FORTRAN both for ease of maintenance and for portability, just in case Rand's next computer might not be assembly language compatible with the IBM 704.

The users were primarily aerospace engineers. They were not programmers but were largely willing and able to learn some simple programming constructs if it helped expedite getting their analysis jobs done. They wanted simple, problem-oriented input forms. They wanted the inputs to be concise but not so concise as to be hard to read (for example, not 030101). They wanted a good users' manual to explain the inputs, outputs, and control options. They would eventually like graphic outputs but were satisfied with numerical printouts. They wanted an easily extensible system for their unpredictable new analyses. And they wanted to be able to reuse inputs as files or macros.

Domain Model and Interface Specifications

Accommodating all of the desired capabilities for the Rand rocket may appear complicated. Fortunately, the rocket trajectory simulation domain can build on a relatively simple and elegant central domain model:

1. The propulsion, aerodynamic, gravitational, and other forces on a rocket are basically a function of its position vector P and velocity vector V; of the orientation of its body axis A; and of time. So is the rocket's fuel flow or rate of change of mass dm/dt. The individual forces can be added together into an overall force vector F.

2. The rocket obeys Newton's second law, $F=ma$, where m is the rocket's mass and a is the rocket's acceleration vector, or rate of change of velocity.

3. Given that the rocket's position P, velocity V, and mass m are known at time t_o, their values at time $t_o + \Delta t$ can be determined by integrating their rates of change from t_o to $t_o + \Delta t$:

    //eq// $P(t_o+\Delta t)$ by integrating $V(t)$

    $V(t_o+\Delta t)$ by integrating $a(t) = F(t)/m(t)$

    $m(t_o+\Delta t)$ by integrating dm/dt.

There are elaborations on this domain model, such as the need to determine the rocket's orientation vector $A(t)$ and the fact that multistage rockets have discontinuities in the nature of their propulsion and aerodynamic forces. But, overall, these elaborations can be added to the central domain model fairly cleanly.

Core Domain Architecture

Based on this domain model, the core domain architecture involved a trajectory initialization step, the central trajectory simulation loop, and a loop-termination step. The initialization step involved the assimilation of input parameters provided by the engineer. This was followed by a loop involving the three steps of the central domain model shown earlier; the calculation of rocket forces and attitude angles; the resolution of these forces along the rocket's body axes; and the integration of rates of change to determine the rocket's future position, velocity, attitude, and weight. Finally, the loop was terminated with the use of termination conditions supplied by the engineer. Figure 1 summarizes this core domain architecture.

Published Interface Specifications

The key to the practical success of the core domain architecture was the set of published interface specifications for the inputs to and outputs from the Flight Program of propulsion, aerodynamic, guidance, and other routines specified or supplied by the engineer.

Table 1 shows the set of inputs that any flight program subroutine could count on being available. The first quantity shown in the table is the current time. The next three quantities are one

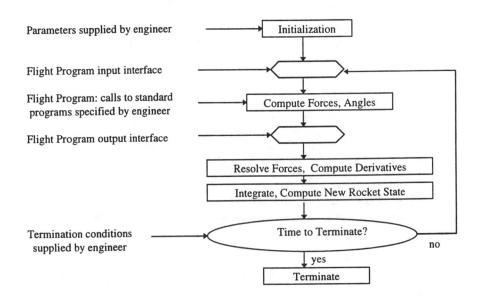

Figure 1. Rocket program core domain architecture

Program Symbol	Quantity
TIME	time t (sec)
ALT,HEFT	altitude h_E above sea level (ft)
ELϕNR	Longitude λ (rad)
PHIR	latitude ϕ (rad)
VELE,VE	velocity v_E with respect to the earth (ft/sec)
GAMMAR	flight path angle γ (rad)
GAMMAD	flight path angle γ (deg)
SGAM,CGAM	sin γ, cos γ
PSIVR	velocity azimuth angle ψ_v (rad)
PSIVD	velocity azimuth angle ψ_v (deg)
SPSIV,CPSIV	sin ψ_v, cos ψ_v
RFT	distance r of vehicle from center of earth (ft)
HD	rate of change $\dot{r}$ of radial distance r (ft/sec)
ELD	rate of change $\dot{\lambda}$ of longitude (rad/sec)
PHD	rate of change $\dot{\phi}$ of latitude (rad/sec)
WGT	weight w of vehicle (lbs)

Table 1. Quantities automatically furnished to flight program subroutines

representation of the rocket's position. The three quantities v_E, γ, ψ_v are one representation of the rocket's velocity, with respect to the rocket's local horizontal plane. The three quantities $\dot{r}$, $\dot{\lambda}$, $\dot{\phi}$ are another representation of the velocity in terms of rates of change of altitude, longitude, and latitude. The final quantity is the rocket's current weight (its mass times the gravitational constant).

Table 2 shows the set of outputs that every flight program (combination of computational subroutines specified by the engineer) was expected to produce. The first three quantities shown in the table are the components of the rocket's thrust vector along the body axes. The second three quantities are the corresponding components of the rocket's aerodynamic force vector. The third three quantities collect any other nongravitational forces, such as solar radiation pressure. The next two quantities, α and β, are the angles relating the rocket's body axis to its velocity vector. The final quantity is the rocket's rate of change of weight.

Note that the output interface specifications indirectly indicate force quantities that the engineer does not have to specify, such as the gravitational force. Such forces are calculated in the same way across the entire trajectory and thus are taken care of by

Program Symbol	Quantity
TAX	thrust T_A along A-axis (lb)
TBT	thrust T_B along B-axis (lb)
TAL	thrust T_{A1} along A1-axis (lb)
AAX	aerodynamic force A_B along B-axis (lb)
AAL	aerodynamic force A_{A1} along A1-axis (lb)
XAX	other nongravitational forces along A-axis (lb)
XBT	other nongravitiaonal forces along B-axix (lb)
XAL	other nongravitaional forces along A1-axix (lb)
ALPHAR	angle of attack α (rad)
BETAR	sideslip angle β (rad)
WD	weight derivative or negative fuel flow $\dot{w}$ (lb/sec)

Table 2. Quantities supplied by the user's flight program

the main program (subject to some parameters that the engineer can specify for the entire run). Also, the input interface specifications indirectly indicate input quantities that the engineer will have to calculate if he or she needs them for subsequent calculations. Examples are the local atmospheric pressure and density, often used for propulsion or aerodynamic calculations but not automatically furnished because their calculation takes considerable time and is unnecessary for major portions of rocket trajectories above the atmosphere.

The "published interface specifications" were eventually published in a book constituting the users' manual for the program, which was used at its peak by over 50 organizations besides Rand. The book, *ROCKET: Rand's Omnibus Calculator of the Kinematics of Earth Trajectories,*[1] is the source of several further tables and figures in this account.

Examples of Flight Program Subroutines

Table 3 shows three examples of propulsion flight program subroutine descriptions. The first subroutine, CONTFL(TH,FL), assumes that the rocket's thrust and fuel flow are constants specified by the values TH and FL. The subroutines are invoked by a standard FORTRAN CALL statement. Thus, CALL CONTFL(300000., 1000.) specifies a rocket engine that will deliver a

	Inputs	**Outputs**	**Action**
CONTFL (*TH,FL*)	None	THRUST, total thrust T (lb); TAX, axial thrust T_A (lb); WD, weight derivative $\dot{w}$ (lb/sec).	*TH*, after being modified by the multiplicative factor C_T, is assumed to be the thrust T in lb; *FL*, after being modified by the multiplicative factor C_{FF}, is assumed to be the fuel flow rate in lb/sec, a positive quantity. It becomes $\dot{w}$ by a change of sign. T_A is set equal to T; thus, all thrust will be axial unless modified by a thrust angle subroutine.
CONTAU (*TA,TB*)	THRUST, total thrust T (lb)	TAX, thrust along A-axis T_A (lb); TBT, thrust along B-axis T_B (lb); TAL, thrust along $A1$-axis T_{A1} (lb).	*TA* and *TB* are assumed to be the angles T_α and T_β, in degrees. They are converted to radians and used in Eq. (B–30) to produce the final T_A, T_B, and T_{A1}.
TBTFTM (*N*)	None	THRUST, total thrust T (lb); TAX, axial thrust T_A (lb); WD, weight derivative $\dot{w}$ (lb/sec).	Tables of T in lb and *FF*, the positive fuel flow in lb/sec, as functions of the time t in seconds, are assumed to be in Table 2. The subroutine TABTFL (TIME, N) is then used to produce T and $\dot{w}$ from t. T_A is set equal to T.

Table 3. Propulsion flight program subroutine descriptions

constant thrust of 300,000 pounds, and a constant fuel flow of 1,000 pounds per second. Each standard ROCKET subroutine is described by a common schema specifying the inputs needed that are not automatically furnished (see Table 1), the outputs produced, and the action performed by the subroutine.

The second subroutine is TBTFTM(N), which assumes that thrust and fuel flow will be determined from a table as a function of the current time, using Nth order interpolation. The third subroutine, CONTAU(TA,TB), assumes that the rocket engine is offset from the body axis by two angles, τ_α and τ_β. It takes the total THRUST determined by subroutines like CONTFL and TBTFTM and distributes it across the three body-axis components TAX,

TBT, and TAL expected by the output interface specification in Table 2.

INTEGRATED ARCHITECTING: CONTROL STRUCTURES, DATA STRUCTURES, AND USER INTERFACE

The overall architecting process involved elaborating the core domain architecture into a set of control structures, data structures, and user interface capabilities. These were determined by trying to accommodate as many as possible of the desired technical and operational capabilities described earlier without overly compromising performance or ease of use and extension. The process thus involved a simultaneous determination of requirements and system architecture, including iteration of prototypes of the input forms and output formats with the prospective users.

Control Structures

Some of the main control structures involved the support of simulating multiple options or branches of a trajectory during a single run. Figure 2 shows the desired capability. For example, an engineer might want to experiment with range-versus-payload-weight tradeoffs using more or less lofted trajectories.

In Figure 2, two branches are created in section 3, using two values of a rocket guidance parameter that will create more or less lofted trajectories. For each of these branches, two further branches are created for section 4 by varying the rocket's burn time during section 3. The longer burn times produce trajectories with greater range but result in less remaining weight for the rocket's payload. The resulting trajectory outputs would enable the engineer to get a feel for the type of trajectory settings best providing the range and payload desired for the rocket's mission.

The overall ROCKET program control structure accommodating the section and branching capabilities is shown in Figure 3. The bottom of Figure 3 shows that the central trajectory simulation loop from Figure 1 is extended to accommodate the printing of trajectory outputs. Proceeding upward in Figure 3, there are

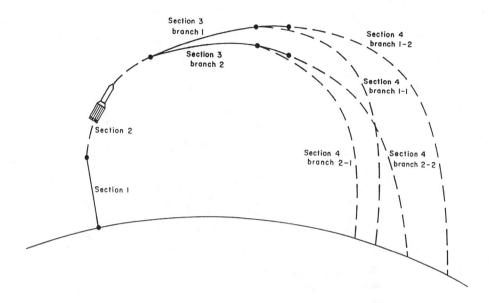

Figure 2. Trajectory sections and branches

loops to cover multiple branches, multiple trajectory sections, and multiple runs per computer pass. The "Compile Flight Programs" and other initialization activities will be covered under the User Interface discussion that follows.

Data Structures

The ROCKET data structures relied heavily on the FORTRAN Global COMMON and EQUIVALENCE capabilities. These have been accurately analyzed as being highly risky and easy-to-misuse data structures.[2] Global COMMON enables any routine to modify a shared variable (for example, the force of gravity) without anyone else's knowledge. The EQUIVALENCE capability enables the same storage location to have multiple names. This also can create dangerous side effects if one of the names is used to modify a variable that is assumed to be stable under its other name. However, these capabilities provided powerful support for the services ROCKET needed to provide, and ROCKET used them in ways that reduced the risks of misuse.

Figure 3. ROCKET program basic flowchart

User Interfaces

Input Form

The user interface for the ROCKET input block is shown in Figure 4. Columns 1 to 4 indicate the position of the data in the input block; thus, we can see that the Descriptive Remarks for the run

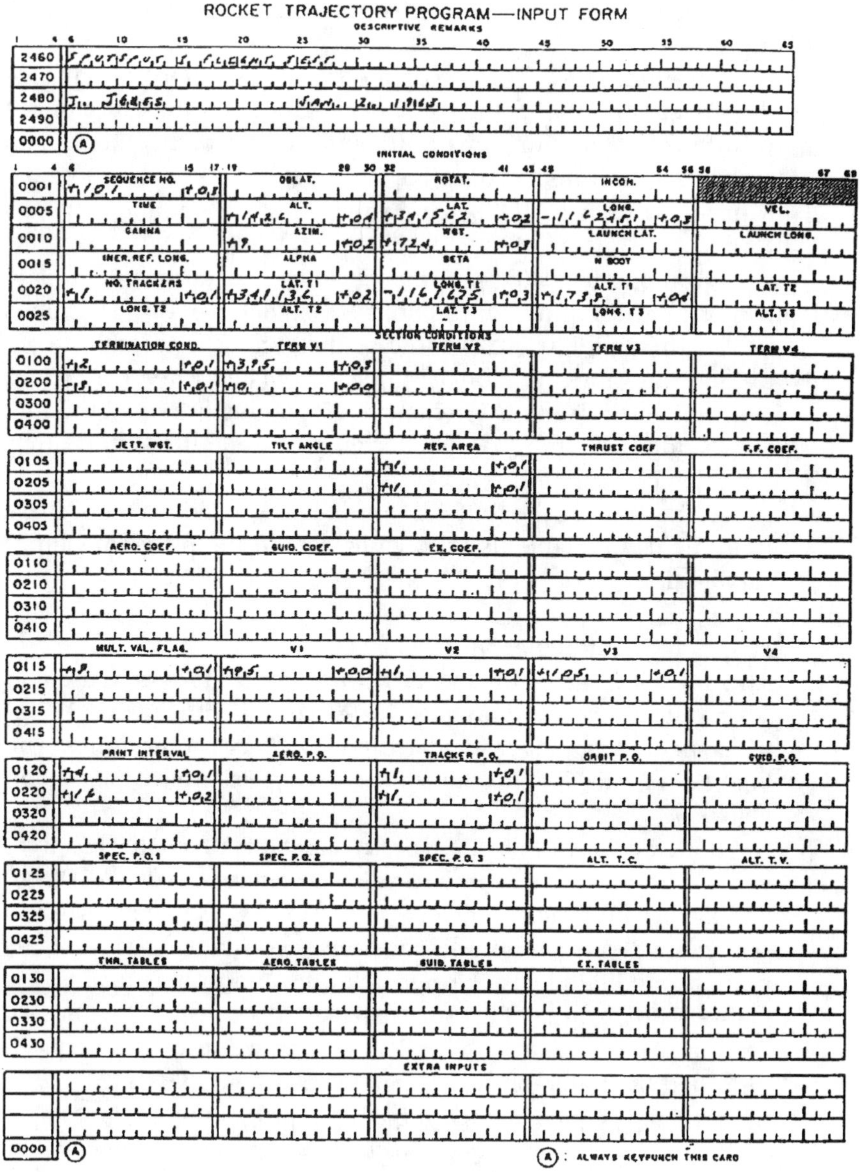

Figure 4. Flight control form: Sputsput I

were stored in locations B(2460-2499). The always-keypunched "0000" cards were used to end FORTRAN READ statements. The first one indicated the end of the character-string Descriptive

Remarks and the beginning of the floating-point numerical inputs.

Locations 0001–0029 accommodate the standard initial conditions and options for the run. Figure 4 indicates that the run will print a sequence number of 101 and operate with a nonoblate (spherical) and nonrotating Earth model. It will start at time 0.0 with an altitude of 1,426 feet, a weight of 724 pounds, and so forth.

Locations 0100–0134, 0200–0234, and so on accommodate the standard inputs for sections 1, 2, and so on. Locations 0100–0101 and 0200–0201 indicate the section termination conditions and values: section 1 will be terminated when the weight (termination condition 2) reaches 395 pounds (when all the fuel is expended). Section 2 will be terminated when the altitude (termination condition 3) reaches 0.

At the bottom, the ROCKET input form provides a set of spare input fields to enable users to easily extend the program's input capabilities.

Flight Programming Form
The user interface for specifying the Flight Program used to "Compute Forces and Angles," as discussed with Figure 1, was implemented as a set of standardized FORTRAN subroutines. The Flight Program for the Sputsput I rocket example is shown in Figure 5.

Both Sections 1 and 2 specify a set of atmospheric forces defined by tables of atmospheric density and pressure (TABDPQ), and a constant drag coefficient of 0.4 (CONCAX). Section 1 also specifies a propulsion model involving a constant thrust of 2,800 pounds, modified by back pressure of the atmosphere against the engine's nozzle area of 0.1 square feet, and a constant fuel flow of 8 pounds per second (CTHAIR). The direction of the thrust is indicated by a table of thrust angles versus time (TBTATM).

Having learned something about programming languages and compilers by this time, I was tempted to invent a special-purpose Flight Programming Language and compiler for it, rather than using FORTRAN capabilities. I decided against this, for the following reasons:

- By using FORTRAN, it would be easy to interface existing FORTRAN programs (for example, detailed engine models or heating calculations) to the ROCKET structure.

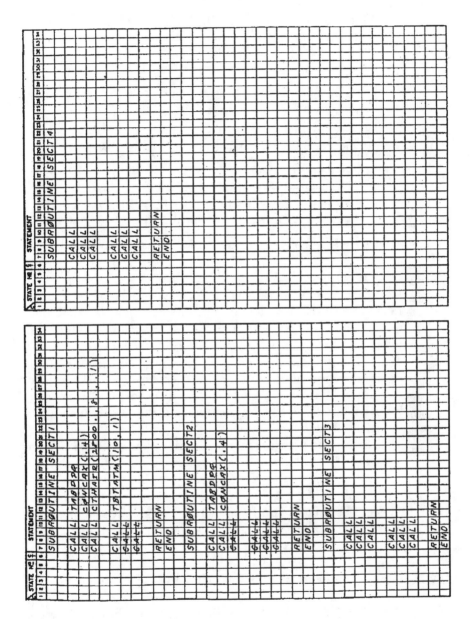

Figure 5. Flight programming form: Sputsput I

- The simple FORTRAN CALL's on the Flight Programming Form covered most uses. Any extensions could be naturally specified via additional FORTRAN statements.

- FORTRAN was widely known by engineers; a special language would be one more thing to learn.

- Despite predictions as early as 1958 of its demise, FORTRAN appeared to have a lot of staying power.

- The FORTRAN compiler and related utilities (for example, diagnostics, debugging aids) provided a lot of capabilities that would be time consuming to develop, and maintain, by myself with a special-purpose language.

I have never regretted my decision to use FORTRAN.

Output Formats

Figure 6 shows the initial set of trajectory outputs for the Sputsput I example (it was preceded by a printout of the user's descriptive remarks and inputs). The standard outputs (time, altitude, latitude, longitude, and so on) are preceded by the sequence number, 101. In this example, the user also specified a printout of the range, elevation, and azimuth of the rocket from a tracking station (on the Input Form the tracking station coordinates are specified in locations 0021–0023 and the tracker printout specified in locations 0122 and 0222).

The outputs were the most awkward part of the ROCKET user interface. The engineers were accustomed to reading them, and engineering assistants were generally available to turn the results into graphs, but a graphical output capability was much needed. In the following section I summarize a follow-on user-interactive program, Graphic ROCKET.

ROCKET Development and Usage

The overall ROCKET development took six months of roughly full-time effort. About four months involved architecting, which included prototypes of key capabilities. Coding and integrating took about a month, as did testing. Testing of complex numerical programs is quite difficult; one large trajectory program operated

```
SEQ  TIME (SEC)      ALT (FT)         LAT (DEG)        LONG (DEG)       VEL (FT/SEC)     GAMMA (DEG)      PSI Y (DEG)      RANGE  (NMI)
SEQ  WGT (LB)         AX ACCEL (G)     THRUST (LB)      FLOW (LB/SEC)    AX AERO (LB)     AL AERO (LB)     ALPHA (DEG)      DT (SEC)

T     RANGE 1 (NM)         ELEV 1 (DEG)          AZIM 1 (DEG)          RANGE 2 (NM)          ELEV 2 (DEG)             AZIM 2 (DEG)
T     RANGE 3 (NM)        ELEV 3 (DEG)              AZIM 3 (DEG)

101  0.               0.14260000E 04  0.34156199E 02 -0.11624809E 03  0.                0.89999998E 02  0.89999998E 02  0.
101  0.72400000E 03  0.33964846E 01  0.24590550E 04  0.80000000E 01  0.                0.               0.               0.

T      0.47532069E 01      -0.66014365E 00      -0.57416642E 02

101  0.25000000E-00  0.14284113E 04  0.34156199E 02 -0.11624809E 03  0.19303332E 02  0.89948092E 02  0.89999997E 02  0.
101  0.72200000E 03  0.34056824E 01  0.24590726E 04  0.80000000E 01  0.16985039E-00  0.               0.               0.25000000E-00

T      0.47531945E 01      -0.65617739E 00      -0.57416575E 02

101  0.40000000E 01  0.20532620E 04  0.34156199E 02 -0.11624809E 03  0.31576619E 03  0.89762916E 02  0.90000001E 02  0.42496520E-03
101  0.69199999E 03  0.34956604E 01  0.24636137E 04  0.80000000E 01  0.44616695E 02  0.               0.               0.50000000E 00

T      0.47529109E 01       0.58330090E 00      -0.57414012E 02

101  0.80000000E 01  0.39598972E 04  0.34156199E 02 -0.11624802E 03  0.63745308E 03  0.88643006E 02  0.90000039E 02  0.37328859E-02
101  0.65999999E 03  0.34875564E 01  0.24769574E 04  0.80000000E 01  0.17176650E 03  0.               0.               0.09999999E 01

T      0.47640932E 01       0.43607044E 01      -0.57392259E 02

101  0.12000000E 02  0.71387610E 04  0.34156199E 02 -0.11624746E 03  0.95280907E 03  0.85508741E 02  0.90000349E 02  0.31305349E-01
101  0.62799999E 03  0.34120332E 01  0.24975453E 04  0.80000000E 01  0.34839664E 03  0.               0.               0.50000000E 00

T      0.48100212E 01       0.10607587E 02      -0.57212479E 02

101  0.16000000E 02  0.11542792E 05  0.34156199E 02 -0.11624600E 03  0.12589630E 04  0.83301985E 02  0.90001173E 02  0.10401177E-00
101  0.59599999E 03  0.33403347E 01  0.25229389E 04  0.80000000E 01  0.53006693E 03  0.               0.               0.09999999E 01

T      0.49377645E 01       0.19033702E 02      -0.56729384E 02

101  0.20000000E 02  0.17132414E 05  0.34156199E 02 -0.11624359E 03  0.15590458E 04  0.82060971E 02  0.90002524E 02  0.22371864E-00
101  0.56399999E 03  0.33195157E 01  0.25504167E 04  0.80000000E 01  0.67811262E 03  0.               0.               0.09999999E 01

T      0.52231273E 01       0.28976689E 02      -0.55906550E 02

101  0.23999999E 02  0.23900005E 05  0.34156199E 02 -0.11624031E 03  0.18627982E 04  0.81269211E 02  0.90004370E 02  0.38703240E-00
101  0.53199999E 03  0.33991912E 01  0.25775287E 04  0.80000000E 01  0.76907033E 03  0.               0.               0.09999999E 01

T      0.57412052E 01       0.39403109E 02      -0.54724091E 02

101  0.27999999E 02  0.31885611E 05  0.34156198E 02 -0.11623607E 03  0.21857246E 04  0.80548162E 02  0.90006747E 02  0.59743144E 00
101  0.49999999E 03  0.36171047E 01  0.26072376E 04  0.80000000E 01  0.79360494E 03  0.               0.               0.09999999E 01
```

Figure 6. Sample output: Sputsput I

for two years before it was discovered that one minor gravitational parameter had been entered with a positive rather than a negative sign.

For ROCKET, there were several trajectory programs I could use for test oracles, such as the General Dynamics Atlas simulation, an Aerospace Corp. rocket simulator, and some special-purpose models I had developed at Rand. Fortunately these initial tests picked up the serious defects in the program. The residual defects found during ROCKET usage were special cases that gave quite obviously erroneous outputs.

After about a year's use of ROCKET at Rand, I prepared an export version for the IBM SHARE users' group library. Before exporting it, I did the equivalent of a post-deployment review. This picked up a number of shortfalls. For example, I had written a "common pitfalls" section of the users' manual, including such advice as "Don't leave the rocket's initial weight input blank; it will make the weight equal to zero and cause an abort when the program tries to compute $a = F/m$." On review, it made a lot more sense to just test for such inputs before starting the simulation.

Eventually, the program was used regularly at over 50 installations. It turned out to be quite portable, running on IBM (7000 and 360 series), Control Data, DEC, GE, Honeywell, and UNIVAC machines. It was not a big burden to maintain, although there were occasional peaks of activity to add new capabilities, such as aerodynamic heating and nonstationary trackers.

Some Lessons Learned

The following are remarks contained in a 1965 paper that I wrote about my experience with the ROCKET program.[3] They were suggestions for developers of similar large general-purpose computer programs.

1. Use a general programming language which is not tied to a particular machine;
2. Slight gains in efficiency, purchased at the cost of logical simplicity of the program, are a poor bet in the long run;
3. Develop the sections of the program in modular form;
4. Thorough documentation with numerous examples saves everybody's time in the long run;

5. An extensive field-test period for both program and documentation eliminates a lot of embarrassing situations;

6. Anticipate the direction of extensions to the program and provide a clean, well-defined interface for tying them into the program.

On reviewing these now, they seem like good remarks, but well short of what they could have been. It was only years later, when I read papers like David Parnas' "Designing Software for Ease of Extension and Contraction" that I could see and appreciate how much more could be done using more thorough definitions of "in modular form" and "clean, well-defined interface" to anticipated extensions.[4]

Some Follow-ons: Graphic ROCKET and POGO

Graphic ROCKET

In the mid-1960s, Rand developed a set of powerful interactive graphics capabilities and was looking for useful application areas for them. ROCKET's lack of a graphic output capability made it a good candidate application.

John Rieber, Vivian Lamb, and I developed Graphic ROCKET in 1966–67. It ran on a dedicated IBM 360-40 that Rand was using for interactive graphics research for ARPA. Graphic input-output was done using an IBM 2250 display with both light-pen and free-hand Rand Tablet inputs, plus a Stromberg-Carlson SC-4060 graphic output device.

Figure 7 shows the general nature of the user interaction, and Figure 8 shows an example input screen with the counterpart of the Sputsput I propulsion inputs. The program turned out to be quite popular with Rand engineers but not very popular elsewhere. The main reason was economics. At Rand, the engineers were research subjects operating on a paid-for computer. Elsewhere, IBM 360-40 prime-shift time cost $50 per hour, a difficult figure to justify when engineering assistants were paid around $5 per hour.

For comparison, I've provided the conclusions from an early paper on Graphic ROCKET:[5]

Figure 7. User viewing graphic ROCKET display

1. The major benefit of interactive operation is the reduction of calendar time required to analyze a mission or the increased number of alternatives that can be investigated in a given time.

2. Even with its higher overhead rate, interactive operation can provide more efficient machine usage, since human judgment can reduce the number of runs required to establish a result.

3. Even a good batch-mode program needs considerable redesign to reorient it toward interactive processing.

4. User enthusiasm for interactive operation depends mainly on two factors: the degree of user-orientation of the language, and the degree of the user's involvement with his problem.

5. Man-machine interfacing for problems involving design creativity is still a little-understood subject. In designing

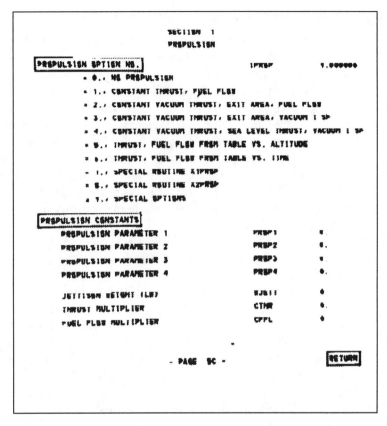

Figure 8. Graphic ROCKET display, showing section 1 propulsion system

such systems, one shouldn't try to build a closely optimized system around anticipated usage patterns. Instead,
one should build a flexible system, wait and see how the
analyst uses it, then modify it to serve him better.

Conclusions 1 and 2 provide some rationale for benefits and
savings due to interactive operation, but this rationale was not sufficiently persuasive for most organizations. Conclusions 3 and 5
are the strongest in retrospect. I was particularly surprised by the
amount of breakage in converting ROCKET to Graphic ROCKET.
Some capabilities, such as branching, just were not needed.
Others needed total reorganization, such as batch versus interactive input validation.

Programmer-Oriented Graphic Operation (POGO)

Another unpleasant surprise with Graphic ROCKET was the amount of effort required for maintenance. Just adding a single option or parameter to an input screen, such as Figure 8, involved reorganizing the screen "real estate" and reworking a number of graphic system calls whose parameters involved the numerical raster coordinates of the boxes, character strings, or input fields.

After a few months of doing this, we decided to use the Rand Tablet's dragging and dropping features to develop a screen-building and modifying capability for Graphic ROCKET. At the time, we were limited to using integers to indicate where to place parameters when a user entered them into an input slot and where to transfer control when a box was clicked on. But with the ability to move the slots and boxes around, even this level of capability improved our maintenance productivity by more than a factor of 2.

It turned out that developers of other Rand models and simulations were also looking for easy ways to develop interactive graphic interfaces. So we packaged the screen-builder and screen-linker capability with Graphic ROCKET's curve-display capabilities to provide a support tool for such applications. The result was POGO, the Programmer-Oriented Graphic Operation.[6] It was used to provide graphic user interface (GUI) capabilities for several Rand models, particularly in the medical area. But for the same economic reasons, it was little-used outside Rand. It was only about ten years later, in the late 1970s, that similar GUI-builders began to be economically feasible at TRW and elsewhere on machines like the DEC VAX. Only about ten years after that did the term "GUI builder" became widespread through emerging PC capabilities.

Broader Lessons Learned: Domain Engineering, DARPA, and Megaprogramming

A broader set of lessons I learned from the ROCKET, Graphic ROCKET, and POGO experiences involved the power of domain engineering and domain architecting in achieving savings through software reuse. The domains could be oriented around applications, such as rocket trajectory simulation, or around support elements, such as GUIs.

These lessons had a negative side as well. My experiences with the IBM SHARE library involved successful sharing of FORTRAN mathematical subroutines as well as ROCKET, and I was convinced that many more software programs could be successfully shared. This led to my developing a catalog of potentially reusable software programs at Rand.[7]

Unfortunately, the programs in the Rand Computer Program Catalog were not reused very much at all. In trying to analyze why, I discovered how many incompatible assumptions could be built into software programs. Some of the reasons for failure became clear to me somewhat later when I read Larry Constantine's excellent analysis of module cohesion and coupling as critical success factors for software reuse.[8]

Beyond these general criteria, however, it appeared that there were further keys to domain-specific reuse involved with shared assumptions and domain-specific interface specifications. These were worked out for the ROCKET components but were absent for the programs in the Rand catalog.

From time to time afterward, I came upon people and organizations who had developed domain architectures and successful associated software component libraries, such as Toshiba in industrial process control,[9] Raytheon in business data processing,[10] and a signal-processing group at TRW in the 1980s led by Lyndon Hardy and Roger Vossler.

These experiences came to the fore again when I went to DARPA in 1989 and was looking for themes for the DARPA software research and technology program. They provided an experience base and example set of success stories for the DARPA Megaprogramming initiative,[11] the Domain Specific Software Architectures program,[12] and the domain-oriented reuse component of the STARS program.[13] These in turn led to the successful establishment of larger Department of Defense initiatives, such as the Army Software Reuse Initiative[14] and the Software Reuse Initiative.[15]

EPILOGUE: MY EFFORTS TO GET OUT OF THE SOFTWARE BUSINESS

While I was developing Graphic ROCKET and POGO, I was also trying hard to get out of the software business. As interesting as these general solutions were, they were basically providing services to engineers and system analysts. These systems people were working the real-world decision issues and formulating the technical problems rather than just reacting to them through programming solutions. At the time, it seemed to me that they were doing much more useful and satisfying things than programmers were.

Eventually, I got into doing command-and-control system studies. Some were for exotic satellite command and control systems whose titles were even security classified. Others were for urban systems such as the New York City Fire Department. Another involved applying Paul Baran's packet-switching ideas to make a survivable command-and-control system for the Minuteman ICBM system (coincidentally, my wife, Sharla, had developed the original packet-switched network simulation with Paul Baran).[16] Through this packet-switching analysis activity I became involved in the initial ARPANET Working Group and with many of the ARPANET pioneers, such as Larry Roberts, Frank Heart, Bob Kahn, Len Kleinrock, Vint Cerf, and Steve Crocker.

CCIP-85: Back into the Software Business

It was a command-and-control study that got me back into the software business. In 1971–72, Rand lent me to the U.S. Air Force to run a mission analysis called Information Processing/Data Automation Implications of Air Force Command and Control Requirements in the 1980s (CCIP-85).[17] The study involved about a dozen analysts and nine subcontract studies analyzing the U.S. Air Force's existing command-and-control operations; determining the biggest gaps between their future information processing needs and projected information processing capabilities; and formulating an information-processing R&D roadmap to reduce the gap between needs and capabilities.

The original expectation was that the biggest gaps were in such areas as supercomputing and large-screen displays. But, as the study went on, it was increasingly clear that the U.S. Air Force's biggest command-and-control information-processing problems were in the software area. The Strategic Air Command's 465L system software had to be 95 percent redone to make it operationally useful. The Ballistic Missile Early Warning System software identified the rising Moon as a Soviet missile attack. Software caused numerous long delays in cutover of new command-and-control systems. Software errors dumped $50 million satellites into the ocean.

A good many of the software rework and delay problems needed management solutions more than technical solutions. On the other hand, CCIP-85 had briefings on some new and exciting software engineering technologies that addressed many of the critical software needs. Dan Teichroew's emerging PSL/PSA system had great potential for addressing the U.S. Air Force's software requirements problems. Harlan Mills briefed us on the exciting software productivity and reliability results IBM was getting with structured programming technology on *The New York Times* project. Eldred Nelson and John Brown briefed us on TRW's suite of automated test tools, and Win Royce's waterfall model. Jules Schwartz presented SDC's (System Development Corporation) early efforts in building and using an integrated software development environment. IBM, TRW, and SDC also had some early quantitative data on how those techniques affected software cost and quality.

As the study went on, I found that the problem of producing software for large mission-critical systems was very important for both national defense and industrial competitiveness. At the same time, a number of exciting new software technology and management approaches were coming along that looked as if they could be orchestrated into good solutions.[18]

It was enough to draw me back into the software business. In 1973, I left Rand and joined TRW as their director of software research and technology. My charter was to come up with an integrated set of procedures, methods, and tools that would bring the software problem under control.

At the time, I remember estimating that it would take a good five years to do this. It was not the first or the last software underestimate I have made. We have made a lot of progress since then, but the magnitude of the software problem seems to grow as fast as our ability to develop solutions. The challenge, though, is still as important, exciting, and fun as ever. I feel incredibly lucky to have happened onto the software engineering field so near its inception, and to have shared its challenges with so many of its outstanding pioneers.

ENDNOTES

1. B.W. Boehm, *ROCKET: Rand's Omnibus Calculator of the Kinematics of Earth Trajectories*, Prentice-Hall, Englewood Cliffs, N.J., 1964.

2. W.A. Wulf and M. Shaw, "Global Variables Considered Harmful," *ACM SIGPLAN Notices*, Feb. 1973, pp. 28–34.

3. B.W. Boehm, "Development and Usage of the ROCKET Trajectory Program," *Proc. Design Automation Working Group Conf.*, June 1965.

4. D.L. Parnas, "Designing Software for Ease of Extension and Contraction," *IEEE Trans. SW Engr.*, Mar. 1979, pp. 128–137.

5. B.W. Boehm and J.E. Rieber, "Graphical Aids to Aerospace Vehicle Mission Analysis," *Proc. AIAA Annual Meeting*, October 1967.

6. B.W. Boehm, V.R. Lamb, R.L. Mobley, and J.E. Rieber, "POGO: Programmer-Oriented Graphics Operation," *Proc. SJCC, AFIPS*, May 1969, pp. 321–330.

7. B.W. Boehm, "Rand Computer Program Catalog," The Rand Corporation, D-14653, April 1966.

8. L.L. Constantine, *Concepts in Program Design*, Information and Systems Press, Cambridge, Mass., 1967.

9. Y. Matsumoto, "Some Experience in Promoting Reusable Software: Presentation in Higher Abstract Levels," *IEEE Trans. SW Engr.*, SE-10(5), Sept. 1984, pp. 502–512.

10. R.G. Lanergan and C.A. Grasso, "Software Engineering with Reusable Design and Code," *IEEE Trans. SW Engr.*, SE-10(5), Sept. 1984, pp. 498–501,

11. B.W. Boehm and W.L. Scherlis, "Megaprogramming," *Proc. DARPA Software Conf.*, April 1992, pp. 63–82.

12. E. Mettala and M.H. Graham, "The Domain-Specific Software Architecture Program," *Proc. DARPA Software Conf.*, April 1992, pp. 204–210.

13. J. Kramer and J. Foreman, *STARS Newsletter*, DARPA, 1992–96.

14. J. Hess, "Army Software Reuse Plan," U.S. Army, 1992.

15. D.J. Reifer, "DoD Software Reuse Plan," DISA, 1994.

16. P. Baran and S.P. Boehm, "On Distributed Communications, II: Digital Simulation of Hot-Potato Message Routing in a Broadband Distributed Communications Network," The Rand Corporation, RM-3103-PR, August 1964.

17. Air Force Systems Command, "Information Processing/Data Automation Implications of Air Force Command and Control Requirements in the 1980's (CCIP-85)," AFSC, April 1972.

18. B.W. Boehm, "Software and Its Impact: A Quantitative Assessment," *Datamation*, May 1973.

A VIEW FROM BELOW

Robert N. Britcher

I started programming in 1969, just as the output of programming was becoming known as software. My first job was working on the Federal Aviation Agency's 9020 en route air traffic control system, part of NAS, the National Airspace System. NAS encompasses much more than the en route computer system. It is a system of systems that includes navigation, weather, logistics, facilities, procedures, people, the entire air traffic milieu in fact. We called our project NAS, because NAS is easy to say.

I was one of thousands of youngsters getting into computers—programming was then as it is now a young person's field. In the late 1960s, industrial programming was surging. In the main, industrial programming meant programming large systems for the U.S. government: the air traffic control system, space systems, defense systems, communications systems. Computers were not yet widespread, but we were beginning to rely on them in important and subtle ways the public did not, and perhaps still does not, appreciate.

I worked with large systems throughout my career. I have never worked in the world of Microsoft or America Online, where, I understand from my golfing buddy Henri, programmers are not paid for their carefulness, but for their panache. Henri used to work on large systems. He puts it this way: "What we did then was engineering; it happened to involve programming. What I do now is programming; there is no engineering involved and none required."

In the winter of 1969, I joined a hundred or so other prospective programmers in IBM's basic programmer training. Most were college graduates who had majored in such subjects as chemistry, English, political science, music, you name it. For 16 weeks we learned IBM's System/360 assembler language, with a week of FORTRAN tossed in. We were given no introduction to computer science, nor the principles upon which computing and computer programming were built. The stored program, the assignment of values to variables (which were somehow resolved as computer storage locations), and manipulating those locations through indirect addressing were notions one picked up along the way, like burrs on a hike through the woods. The early education of programmers was similar to Thoreau's description of his education at Harvard: it introduced him to some of the branches of learning, but to none of the roots. After learning about flow charts and loading registers I was given a choice of assignments. I chose NAS because my college roommate worked there, and "there" was near Ocean City, New Jersey, where I had vacationed for years as a kid.

The 9020 System was not the first application of automation to air traffic control. Automated radar surveillance had been developed to support traffic around the airports and approach-control areas in the mid-1960s. But the 9020 System was the first national automation system, because it supported all twenty domestic en route centers with a single set of computers and programs.

The en route centers had experimented with automation as early as the 1950s. By 1959, the center at Indianapolis had a computerized flight system. Fix arrival times for each flight were calculated on an IBM 650, a quinary computer drum that worked like an abacus. It had 2,000 words of storage, and programmers had to know the speed of the drum to program it. The 650 would get so hot that a floor fan had to be installed to keep it from overheating. But it was less powerful—had less storage and fewer relays—than the 403 accounting machine on which the flight data was printed. The printed sheets coming off the 403 were cut into strips by a device invented on the spot called "the stuffer and cutter." The strips were put into pneumatic tubes and circulated to the various air traffic control sectors. From the first, engineering prevailed.

The 9020 System took almost ten years and $100,000,000 to build. It was built three times, although today we would call the first two prototypes. The 9020 computers—an IBM System/360 multiprocessor specially built for the FAA—were ordered and installed before anyone had written specifications for what they would do. In fact, it was not until Model 3 that the system's requirements were specified. Models 1 and 2 were simply coded.

The 9020 System is not fancy. (I say "is" because Model 3 is still in the field and with few exceptions—the central 9020 was replaced in 1986—it is the same system developed 30 years ago.) It converts analog radar data to digital data and presents it on air traffic controller situation displays. The computer correlates the radar with flights, each of which appears on the display as a small moving triangle connected to a "data block" containing the aircraft's call sign, flight identifier, and altitude. The system calculates and prints flight data pretty much like the 650.

The 9020 is huge. It would fill a small gymnasium. (The 9020s are still used in the display subsystem. But, even the IBM System/370 3083s that replaced the central computer in 1986 are monsters by today's standards.) The NAS computers are not only huge, they are noisy. I worked in the computer room for a year and I became hardened to sound. Programmers and operators screamed at each other all day long without realizing it. Outside, the quiet was stunning.

The software suite is also large. NAS takes about a million-and-a-half programming statements to run, build, and maintain. About half of these were written in assembler language and half in JOVIAL, a high-order language originally developed for the U.S. Air Force.

The 9020 System was built at NAFEC (National Aviation Facility Experimental Center), which lies about ten miles west of Atlantic City, New Jersey. It had been a naval air station during World War II, and it still looked that way in the 1960s. The white weatherboard buildings stood among the tall Jersey pines like a picture on a postcard. I worked in one of the larger barracks, the officers' club. But that was after I had worked in the tape library behind the computer room and in a trailer.

In my building, as in the others, the windows were painted shut. Cigarette smoke soiled the air. Listings and punched card decks and their carrying boxes were everywhere. The room next to mine had been a shower, and the chairs, when unoccupied, would run down to the drain in the center of the room. Rodents kept us company. A large cinderblock building, Building 149, frequently contained the 9020 computer complex and the air traffic control labs. It was located near the air strip, a good distance from the barracks; so we often drove. Sometimes, instead of driving to the lab, we would leave and go to the Atlantic City race track.

The man in charge of NAFEC was Commander Buck Commander. He and his wife lived on the base in a graceful white house near the front gate. Occasionally, his voice could be heard over the loud speakers warning of some official visit. Otherwise, things at NAFEC were very unofficial. It was a long way from Washington and a short way to the beach. But everyone worked hard. The development of the 9020 System was a seven-day-a-week, 24-hour-a-day proposition. Almost in opposition to the laid-back climate, the men wore shirts and ties and the women skirts and dresses. There was an air of formality among the programmers, which suggested earnestness.

Some of the programmers on the early systems had college degrees, some did not. Those who did not were called technicians. Amanda Blizzard was one of the technicians on NAS. She had grown up in the area, not far from NAFEC. She owned a farm. Both her rooster and her husband were named George. Neither worked terribly hard, she said. Amanda was good at her job, in spite of her eccentricities—from time to time she spoke in tongues and would beat her head against the wall to relieve back pains. Because she was not a college graduate, her job was limited to maintaining the JOVIAL COMPOOL, the data declarations. She was not allowed to touch "code," which meant the logic. Coding instructions was for college graduates and those with advanced degrees.

Wacky things happened on those large computer systems, as they do everywhere. But there was one project I worked on in the 1970s that was unusually rich. It was a very successful project, one of the great feats of diligence in the early years. As systems go, it was not much. It was easy to define. Photographs of the earth taken from a satellite (Landsat) had to be corrected before they could be developed. There were what engineers call intrinsic errors, errors in the image, caused by the earth's not looking like a photographic plate, and errors in the camera. Geometric and radiometric errors to be technical. A special computer, an array processor, was used on this special project. To programmers working on the project this meant something. Perhaps to you it means nothing. It also meant nothing to the managers of the project. This special computer was built with two power supplies: one for the fan and one for the processor. Every night someone would turn off the processor. Then one night someone turned off the fan and the computer melted. Months before this, the project overran its entire budget in one unlucky afternoon when it was learned that the specially built disk-control unit, estimated to cost $200,000, would run over $2 million. Not long after, a programming manager broke both his feet jumping off a garage and had to be replaced. He said he tripped, but no one believed him. He crossed several state borders to get away and fell into the Gulf of Mexico. Shortly thereafter, a programmer crossed over the yellow line on a back road and hit a car head on. The woman driving the other car was killed instantly. The programmer kept coming to work, but he sat at his desk, staring at the wall in front of him. He spoke to no one after the accident. I would pass by his office from time to time. He sat like a board in his chair with his arms folded across his chest looking straight ahead. He was looping, someone said. Soon after, a young programmer drove her Corvette into the side of a stone barn beside a field of corn. From the looks of the tracks, the police said she must have rehearsed. Afterward, programmers would not touch her code. Maybe they felt it was sacred, or they were afraid of it—that somehow her terror and despair were contagious. Sometimes though, the terror is being separated from the code. A lead programmer on the project bought a trailer and lived in the parking lot at work so he could be near the code, to feel its cool rush around him. Not just his code, but all the code, and the libraries and macros and job control statements, and all the gear. He would awaken at 2:30 in the morning thinking he had forgotten to clear a buffer and would pad across the parking lot in his thongs to the computer room, fire up the machines, and look at dumps. There he would find his buffer cleared and breathe easier. But he would find another bug. Soon it would be 7 a.m. and the operators would show up in the computer room asking if he had been there all night. He said he did not know, but wondered if the coffee was on.

Then there was Ved's listing. Listings were important in the 1970s and 1980s. Ved and I and a few hundred other people worked on the Strategic Air Command's Digital Network System—SACDIN. It was another dreadful project that ended in a great system, another reminder that the act of meeting ordinary, daily demands can transform itself into an extraordinary achievement. Thousands of programs and hundreds of people. In the end our code was buried in missile holes. I wrote a program, called EAM, to send the Emergency Action Message. It could end war.

Afterward, there would be no programming, only code. The code would go on heaving until the machines died. I had not thought about it, but I suppose the code is still there, ready to be executed. It should be better than new. New code is usually not so hot.

One hot July day, a new cleaning crew showed up on the project. Only the supervisor spoke some English, I was told later. The next morning we came to work and our listings were gone. There was no paper anywhere. There must have been some misunderstanding about what exactly was trash. The problem was that Ved had written all his notes from a design inspection on his listing. There was no choice, he said. We had to retrieve that listing. However, by this time, it was in the truck by the loading dock, along with hundreds of other listings and waste paper. It took a couple of hours to track this down. It took another hour for us to figure out that we had to go into that truck and look for it. The truck was an 18-wheeler, big enough to live in. Four of us went to the dock. There was a hill of paper in the trailer. You had to have tactics. One guy clambered up the right side, where it looked like firm footing. John, Ved's manager, went straight up the front to the top to see if he could get at the back. Two of us just started in. Ved was not among us. He was back in the air-conditioned office trying to see if he could get by without the listing. I recall that distinctly. Around noon we broke for lunch. Someone had brought chicken salad sandwiches and potato chips and sodas. We bolted it down and kept going. About one o'clock the smell in the truck reminded me of an incident that occurred in the summer of 1967.

That was the year a friend of mine, Gary, and I sneaked into my fraternity house in the afternoons before work to play pool. It was closed for the summer, but I had a key. It was hot as hell in there, like in the trailer. The third or fourth time we were there we smelled a rancid odor that seemed to be coming from the walls. The pool table was on the first floor in the middle of the house between the living room and the dining room and next to Mrs. Peters' (the house mother) apartment. "There is something dead in here," Gary said. We finished the game of eight-ball and left. The next week we came back. I had forgotten about the smell, but when we opened the door we were flattened by it. It seemed like you were swallowing it. It occupied your mouth and nose and gut like a live thing. It was tremendous. "There is something dead in there alright," I said as I shut the door, "and it is not a pigeon, either." Gary said it must be a dog. But how did it get in? It was then that I remembered Mrs. Peters. Mom P. we called her. My father had told me she lied about her age to get the job. She was really over 80 he said. She smoked ferociously. I remembered Mom P. telling me she was going to Colorado for the summer. But I was not sure. Maybe she had not gone to Colorado.

After some careful thought, we went around the side of the house. There was a window in the apartment bedroom. Gary hoisted me part way and I managed to get a foothold. The window was not locked. I got it open somehow. Half-way through I was thinking about what I might find and about the stories passed down through the family about Gettysburg after the battle, how the stench of decaying horses and men and mules would not depart the Blue Ridge Valley—that it stuck like lower back pain. I got sick right there on the oriental rug. I kicked open the bedroom door. Nothing. Then the bathroom. Nothing. I got more confident. She is not in here, I yelled. I went out the back door and saw Gary heading up the street. Months later, when school started and Mom P. had returned, someone found the rotted capons in the unplugged freezer behind the pantry. The fire company cleaned it out and buried it somewhere.

It was not long after lunch that one of the guys found Ved's listing. I think it was John. He came out of the truck waving it triumphantly. By that time I could care less. He told me he would take us out for lunch tomorrow. Barbecue, he said. I told him we needed to have a better backup plan.

Speaking of paper and backup plans, the manager of the Landsat project was addicted to eating paper. He would bring a tablet to meetings, and every fifteen minutes or so, you would hear a rip from down the table. At the beginning of the project he would tear a page into small pieces and stuff them into his mouth incrementally. Later on, I noticed he was devouring entire sheets. I suppose the stress got to him. Once, his deputy had given him an important memo from NASA and, before a copy could be made, he ate it. The deputy had to scramble a little but managed to get the agency to send it again. I heard, after the project was over, that the project manager changed his life. He took time off, went to parks, and lived in tents. Someone who had seen him a couple of years later told me he was eating wood now.

Herman Valentine asked me not too long ago if the programming of large systems has improved. Have better methods and tools helped, he asked? My first day at NAFEC, on the 9020

System, my manager took me to Building 149 to see a test of Model 2. He told me it would take a while to bring the system up. The object file had to be read in through the card reader. This amounted to six or seven boxes of cards. If there were a jam, it could take much longer. I was impressed when I saw the data blocks glow on those green tubes and the flight strips chugging out of the flight strip printers. I wondered how anyone could program something as big as an air traffic control system knowing the handful of instructions I was taught in class. I could not make the leap from loading a register to handing off airplanes between sectors. So I went into testing instead of programming.

What I did not know then, but felt, was that there was no intellectual control in programming. The idea of using precise abstractions to model computer programs, to design them, was not commonplace. It still is not. At that time, while we were lugging card decks around in the south Jersey rain, a few men and women were laying the ground work for programming as a branch of algebra. Structured programming, ALGOL, programs as axioms, modules defined by the rules of mathematics: these were underway while, at NAFEC, hundreds of kids were simply coding the nation's first air traffic control system. We have now dignified this race to the machine by calling it "prototyping." The deliberate laying in of logic through verifiable steps is still not in vogue.

But in the early years, what we did not know did not hurt us. Looking back, we were more rigorous than programmers of today because the work was physically arduous. You could not go fast. We were not saddled with automation. Edsger Dijkstra, who mixes his own ink and often wears it on his sleeves, said it best to a friend of mine, Patricia, standing on the escarpment overlooking the Atlantic near Salve Regina: "Tools can overcome complexity so well they invite it." By tools, he meant not just software, but graphics and other aids to comprehension.

"Things are definitely different now," says Patricia. A few months ago she showed me her new workstation. She was about to run Taligent, a product sold by IBM, Apple, and Hewlett Packard. She powered on and the computer produced a farm, a beautiful scene, reminiscent of a Robert Altman movie. In the distance, behind rows of tulips, each of a slightly different color, there stood a near-perfect replica of a barn and silo and an amiable farmhouse, like in Pennsylvania Dutch country, like the farm across from my office. Before I could take it all in we were telemarketing.

There were windows upon windows. One contained icons for folders, stationary, and documents, even trash. There was a window for business cards and one for financial spread sheets. Another invited me to select one of eight natural languages by dragging and dropping the mouse on the appropriate flag. At the bottom of the screen, a ticker rolled off the daily stock quotes. I browsed a catalogue selling gloves, soft garden gloves, goat skin, and suede, the textures rendered as if snipped from "Gardener's Eden." The phone book was the most impressive. I picked a client's number from a list. The phone dialed automatically. Had voice-activation been installed, I could have simply spoken the name. All the while, clips of the movie Dracula were being shown in the upper left part of the screen. Movies, not stills. The protagonist was sucking the blood out of some innocent, while I contemplated my next sales call.

Patricia thinks it is a good thing there is more government supervision of large computer systems now. It is because programming is harder than ever to see, she says. With punched cards, there was a machine or a tool for each job. You could tell who was doing what. You coded on paper for keypunching. Flowcharting templates helped with logic design. Sometimes typewriters were used for high-level design. The physical brought regimentation and authority. Lines were well marked. Only those people called programmers working under the flag of programming wrote code, not everyone. A friend who worked on NASA's Space Shuttle System tells of the lab manager where flight control software was tested. Julius, an older fellow, was always there, it seemed, logging in the card decks, explaining the rules and regulations about entering the lab to novice programmers. Everyone learned and obeyed. I had a similar job my first year at NAFEC— without the authority. I was a go-between for the programmers and the FAA operators. I logged patches to the system before various tests. There was continual controversy. Should I be allowed to insert the cards in the card feeder, and punch "enter" and "end-of-file"? Or was my job limited to logging the patches and handing them over to the operator? This was never resolved satisfactorily. I learned much later that when it comes to job security no job is too small.

In the 1970s we moved away from punched cards. Programmers on most large systems were now using video display terminals. The programming languages had not changed much,

mostly assembler language, with a few compiler languages, like
FORTRAN and JOVIAL, sprinkled in. You could create, compile,
and test programs by typing. The video display terminals replaced
coding sheets and contributed to the death of erasure. Entire data
bases could be summoned with a few keystrokes. I was glad my
father made me take typing in high school, just in case I went to
work for an insurance company, he said. With terminals, coding
was easier. But it had a greater impact on design. By the mid-
1970s, designing programs was catching on. Flow charts were
replaced with design languages. Still, terminals encouraged short
cuts. Programmers went too fast, largely because copying was
faster. Source libraries were on mainframes and public. It was all
too easy to copy someone's text and forget to make a critical
change. Fearing the worst, Harlan Mills, at the time an IBM Fellow
and advisor to the division president, warned against terminals.
"Hurried programs will bristle with errors." Mills was fond of saying that programmers write programs without having read any,
including their own.

Terminals also brought social change. At first, too few terminals were available to put one on each desk. So they were placed in terminal rooms, two terminals to a table. There was space for a listing next to the terminal. If you needed a document as well, you held it on your lap. By midmorning the terminal rooms were full. There were distractions, sometimes welcome, but cooperation among programmers, and their programs, improved markedly. If someone had just finished debugging a macro, he or she would announce the name of the library, and you could fetch it and look at it right then. Programmers discussed their programs and bugs and computer time, the latest standard, some new operating system discovery, a restriction on the size of arrays, or the awful severity of the new configuration control package.

Inspections—the more-or-less formal process of programmers reading and critiquing each other's program or design or test cases—came in with terminals. Inspections moved large-scale programming into the light, making it more communal. More important, with inspections it became easier to measure milestones, such as the completion of design or coding. Subtly and decisively, inspections slowed programmers down. Programmers who did not like to read texts read them. The hidden strength of cards, the scrutiny born of tedium, was displaced. At first I found inspections painful. We all did. Then, as now, schedules were demanding. No one knew the cost of inspecting, so we sucked it in and worked more overtime. Or we cheated and waived inspections.

Today there are workstations and a mountain of programs to go with them. Not quite like Taligent's telemarketing, but almost. We call these supporting programs tools. Sales reps even refer to them as technologies. But they are just computer programs. Like compilers, they are used to write other programs for nuclear power plants and strategic weapons systems and hospitals, the programs we call applications. Sometimes they are advertised under the title of computer-aided software engineering, or CASE.

The tools roll together the typewriter, the plastic template, the keypunch, and sometimes the thinking. Now when I walk down the hall I cannot tell if programmers are working out their ideas incrementally with precise abstractions, or if they are just coding. Recently, I read two or three papers describing projects that used compilable designs. The programmers quickly slid away from the conceptual and wrote code. The idea was to shorten the coding cycle. But the result was no design. When it came time for a design review, special overhead foils were created. Some projects have found benevolent products that encourage uniformity without penalizing initiative. When there are hundreds of programmers, all but a few of whom want to do things their own way, tools, used properly, keep the work lined up and heading in the same general direction. Everyone records design or test cases or schedules the same way. Managers prefer this.

Workstations have moved programmers back into the safety of offices, where we started. The programming cycle is now largely electronic, although we generate more paper than ever and need more printers and couriers. Programmers still get together for inspections, but electronic mail has replaced the rap of terminal rooms, which are gone. (Although some companies have experimented with bullpens, like those at NAFEC.) They have been replaced by meeting rooms with large Formica tables and comfortable chairs, like those in the board room of Wilmer, Cutler, and Pickering. This is a marked change from the digs at NAFEC, where there were no meeting rooms, and consequently, very few meetings. When I think about those early years, I cannot recall attending more than a few meetings. We worked well together, between departments, with the FAA, with other contractors. Did we avoid meetings simply because there were few places to meet? My department got together occasionally, but we met in our manager's office. There was room to bring in a chair or two. Mostly, we stood, which helped move the meeting along. Now, with many nicely appointed meeting rooms, we meet often and for long periods. The rooms are always booked, like motels. And like motels, the rooms are reserved with the help of computer programs.

For seven years, beginning in 1987, I worked on the FAA's Advanced Automation System. It was to be the system to replace the 9020 System, as well as the systems in the terminal areas. There would be no cards and no listings. This is the age of workstations. And the age of publicity. Both were prominent on the Advanced Automation System. It was our yen for automation combined with our yen for aggrandizement that did the project in. Pundits spoke louder than science and engineering. Computers, we now believe, can do more than arithmetic and convert signals and store them; they can replace air traffic controllers—and bankers and physicians and even executives.

Most readers in this field know about the Advanced Automation System. It continues to haunt the newspapers and television. It began in concept in 1981 and ended in 1994. Billions of dollars were spent on it. Unlike the Landsat System, it is hard to describe. You cannot learn anything from the name. You know it is about air traffic control because I told you, or because you read about it in the papers. Maybe part of the problem was the name. It sounds like the system to end all systems.

The idea was to combine the system for controlling airplanes around airports—the terminal areas—with the en route system. This meant combining the 180 or so terminal approach control facilities, or TRACONs, and the 20 en route centers. Individually, they had evolved somewhat comfortably over the years. Consolidation seemed to make sense. First, in 1981 over 11,000 air traffic controllers were fired by the Reagan administration, not one at a time, but all of them at once. At the time, nearly everyone in America was beginning to believe that computers could do work better than people—not just one man inside the FAA or several on the committee to oversee this or that inside the government, not just computer manufacturers and computer programmers around the land, not just a few youngsters in Cherry Hill, New Jersey, or a handful of academics. This belief began with Alan Turing's claim that, by the year 2000, computing machines would be able to perfectly imitate human intelligence. And we were egged on by the media and by Reagan himself, who greatly admired Buck Rogers. Second, shutting down over a hundred facilities would save billions in operating costs. Third, there was pressure from the airlines to invent new algorithms so that planes could fly with fewer restrictions and thus save fuel. The result: fewer people, less fuel, less money, cheaper flights, fewer delays, more computer programs.

At $3.5 billion, the Advanced Automation System was one of the largest civilian computer contracts ever; maybe the largest. The money would pay for a so-called complete modernization.

On the Advanced Automation System, everything was to change: facilities, machines, people. For example, each air traffic controller would operate an entire configuration of computers and communications channels and software and peripheral devices, all hidden away inside his or her own workstation, fronted by a 20-inch by 20-inch Sony color display. The controllers could tune the splendid graphics to suit their own situations and preferences. There would be new algorithms. A new digital voice system was coming along. There would be the latest in fault-tolerant computing, algorithms to protect the air traffic control algorithms, so the system would (almost) never fail. The system would be written in Ada, bearing on its back ferocious government supervision, carried out, in part, by private-sector subcontractors and there were lots of meetings in paneled rooms, because no one was ever quite sure about the whole thing.

The Advanced Automation System took up a quarter of the entire military-industrial epoch before it collapsed under its own weight. One programmer described the project this way: "Working on the AAS was like working on a car inside the garage with the motor running. Eventually, even the crickets hopping around the tires suffocate."

Which brings me back to Herman's question: What about methods? While I was on the Advanced Automation System, I had the chance to study several large computer systems and projects, mostly those related to air traffic control and space, including the NASA Space Shuttle system. I poured over their defect data, their cost data, their schedules, projects spanning four decades, from the 1960s through the 1990s.

What I found was this: the inspection and testing process, defect discovery and repair throughout the development life cycle, seems to drive success—delivering a usable system on time. I could not correlate success with programming methods such as design methods, language, or coding practices. A certain number of defects will be introduced regardless. What appears to matter a great deal is the application of professional engineering. By that I mean technical management: establishing precise plans and procedures; defining computer programs in terms of their correctness, not just their development, and evaluating them quantitatively with respect to budgets and schedules; using models; developing a detailed system integration plan; and measuring results scientifically (projects that rely on status reports, such as "test cases run," do not fare well).

My experience is, of course, anecdotal and narrow. I willingly admit that, in the last 30 years, I have changed my mind so many times about programming and computer systems I will never be able to say "I know." There is one thing, however, that rumbles around in my head, that has the air of truth about it, something another buddy, Al, told me years ago. It makes more and more sense as we push on with newer and bigger things, more computers and thousands more programs, geographically dispersed, yet aspiring to become a single family, decked out in brilliant graphics. Al advised me "to be among the measurers, not among the measured; then, you can safely descend to that lowest of all professions: punditry."

ALMOST THIRTY YEARS AS A CHANGE AGENT

Donald J. Reifer

INTRODUCTION

When Bob Glass asked me to write this story, I shivered. I then asked myself: am I really an old-timer? would anyone actually be interested in my recollections? what changes have really occurred in the field in the last 30 years? The more I thought about answering these questions, the more excited I became. When you contemplate such topics after about 30 years in the field, you come to the realization that computers and software have totally reshaped our society in a short period of time.

Like most old-timers in the field, I started in software purely by chance. I took a job with Hughes Aircraft Company in the late 1960s after receiving a bachelor's degree in electrical engineering. I had decided to get my degree under the GI bill after serving four years in the U.S. Air Force as an electronics technician. Hughes made me a great offer: a masters fellowship and prorated salary of $12,000 a year. As a masters fellow, I was automatically enrolled in their rotator program. I would switch jobs every six months as I worked part-time and went to school full-time to get my masters degree under their sponsorship. At the end of two years, I would be free to select the job I liked best. My goals were to get into the area of digital design and get some experience under my belt.

It is interesting to note that none of the schools I considered enrolling in had a degree program in computer science. Like most, my school, Newark College of Engineering, had a mainframe. But, I was not required to use it as part of my undergraduate course of study. We still used slide rules to do our calculations.

We typed our papers on typewriters and lived without beepers, copy machines and faxes. If we needed multiple copies, we used carbon paper. Transistors were the "in things" and nobody had even thought of the Internet. My senior project was a 22-function electronic calculator that I designed and developed at a cost of about $1,000 (most of the parts luckily were donated— to a poor college student this was a year's wages). My forecast was that such calculators would become available at a much lower price once fabrication techniques of integrated circuits were perfected. I was into the topic of amorphous semiconductors and really keen on integral calculus.

THE EARLY YEARS

Hughes immediately placed me in a software organization. They were developing programs for radars and missile systems and were looking for programmers. There were not many available. Therefore, they decided to develop what they needed from their crop of university new hires. I spent my first summer in Venice, California, learning to program fixed point machines in assembly language. I also learned FORTRAN and IBM/360 BAL (basic assembly language). Input was through punched cards and paper tape and you learned to multiprocess as you waited for your batch jobs to either run or bomb. Programming fascinated me. When my first six months ended, I elected to stay and take another job in the same software shop. I never did rotate elsewhere because I liked what I was doing. Like many my age, I changed my career goals on the fly based upon what life offered.

I opted to work toward a masters degree in operations research. This also was a change, because at first I was going to specialize in digital design. I was more and more interested in management and found quantitative methods and math modeling to my liking. This proved to be a good move because during my second assignment at Hughes I worked with managers of relatively large software projects who were developing ways to get their software development processes and costs and schedules under control. Simple processes like configuration management were challenges during this period because few success models existed on which we could base our management systems. Estimating procedures for software costs and schedules were nonexistent. Metrics were things of the future, and many of the simple controls we use on today's projects to make software progress visible were just gleams in people's eyes. I remember recommending a standard Work Breakdown Structure for planning future projects based on results of one of the more successful projects we had. I also remember the tedium I went through to prepare PERT charts for the same project. This was done by hand on big pieces of paper that were taped around the room so we could determine the shortest path through our task plan. We used this approach then because there were no project management packages available and the personal computer had not yet revolutionized the workplace.

During the early 1970s, I worked on software methodology, process, and tool issues at Hughes. The hot topic during these days was testing. Dijkstra, Mills, and Hoare were making substantial contributions to the theories of testing, and I, like many others, was trying to improve the practice.[1] I acted as a bridge between the theorists and practitioners, trying to match new techniques to engineers who were looking for better ways to do their jobs. I devoured articles and books on advanced topics and then ran pilot projects trying to see if they could be used in the real world.

For my first management assignment, I was given responsibility for a number of internal research and development (IR&D) projects for Hughes. I led several small teams who evaluated software technology and tools to determine their applicability for use on avionics projects. I also developed some software cost estimating procedures that we could use on the job as part of these research efforts. To my surprise (and that of my management), I found that I could write. This skill and the presentation skills I developed while pitching the results of my projects to my bosses again and again (primarily to get funding) would serve me well in the future.

I was particularly intrigued at this time with the constructive approach to programming. In theory, you would not have a testing problem if you designed the program right the first time. Proofs of correctness were advocated by many leading theoreticians to validate that the program was designed properly before it was implemented. However, after careful study, validating the correctness of program designs using proofs seemed practical only for very small programs. Needless to say, I looked for alternatives because the technology could not be matched to the needs of the projects I was working on.

To bridge the gap between theory and practice, I put two new concepts into practice at Hughes during the early 1970s: simulation and modeling techniques and coverage analysis. Simulation and modeling techniques were mainly used to verify the functioning of our algorithms and logical designs before we implemented them. Simulation and modeling were also used to help set realistic timing and sizing budgets for our programs because they had to operate in flight computers that had severe memory and speed limitations. Coverage analysis ensured that the tests we used to verify our programs exercised an acceptable percentage of the program code and logic. Coverage analysis became practical during this period because a number of software tools became available that automated the process of analyzing the code. Based on this experience, I became convinced (and still remain so) that techniques like coverage analysis could become practical if and only if the tools needed to put the technology into widespread use became available to potential consumers at affordable prices.

For my next management assignment, Hughes decided to put me in charge of automating the Hughes El Segundo factory complex. This was my first major project management job. It involved managing large teams that were primarily developing real-time software for manufacturing and production control. Our showpiece project was an automated storeroom built using state-of-the-art Hewlett-Packard minicomputers and robots. Based on my positive IR&D experience, I decided to use simulation techniques to model and prototype factory improvements before we implemented them (at considerable cost). Luckily, Hughes had invested in some applicable work in another division, and I was able to use their experience (and people) to sell my plans. Simulation ultimately proved to be a valuable tool because it allowed my team to assess the impact of different automation approaches before we implemented them. In essence, we took the techniques we had used to verify program logic and extended them for use in verifying the logic that governed the flow of parts and assemblies in a manufacturing plant.

In the early 1970s, the recently published Rand Corp. CCIP-85 study (Command and Control Information Processing in 1985) was shaking up the military/aerospace complex. It projected that software costs on large command and control systems would soon eclipse those of hardware based on trends being experienced on such large air and missile defense systems as Sage and Safeguard. Hughes management was skeptical about these projections, as were most of the military people with whom I talked. Their skepticism may have been somewhat justified by the fact that computers were extremely expensive in those days and networking and communications gear was developed on a custom basis, not supplied off-the-shelf. Therefore, hardware was the cost driver on most projects, and software was not yet viewed as the glue that pulled systems together and made them work to satisfy the needs of the user.

I was asked to independently assess the CCIP-85 study conclusions and report back to management. During my investigations, I became familiar with the pioneering work of Dr. Barry W. Boehm. In 1971, I was thrilled to meet him as we talked over the results of his study[2] and his team's efforts in developing the simulation languages. Meeting him was an important milestone to me because Barry's work has had a profound influence on me over the years and I view him as my mentor. In due course, I told management that I thought the CCIP-85 study was on the mark and they should make strategic investments in software. My advice fell on deaf ears because nobody seemed to believe that a firm's profit and loss in the future would be governed primarily by its software capabilities and capacity.

After receiving my masters in operations research, Hughes selected me for a Certificate in Business Management program (MBA equivalent) at the University of California at Los Angeles. While working full time and fathering two children, I continued my studies for another two years at night. Where I got all the energy evades me. In retrospect, those were great times. I was growing as the industry grew and was able to put many forward ideas into practice in a very forward-thinking firm. I worked on the bigger programs and used the skills, knowledge, and abilities I had gathered in school and on the job to engineer innovative solutions to their development problems first as an analyst and then as a manager. I also enjoyed my family.

I also received several rewards for my work. I went to conferences, listened to industry leaders, and participated in professional societies. The first major conference I went to was the Fall Joint Computer Conference. I remember how excited I was to go to this conference. This event drew tens of thousands of people to the Anaheim Convention Center and Disneyland Hotel. State-of-the-art equipment, like the Xerox Sigma 7 computer we were soon going to use on the Hughes Phoenix missile combat officer's trainer for the Navy's F111 fighter-bomber, were on display. I was also thrilled to meet the author of the book I learned FORTRAN from at this event, Dan McCracken. Dan, as many of you probably know, became the president of the Association for Computing Machinery (ACM). I was also thrilled to hear Jean Sammet talk about the history of programming languages. It is fun to finally meet the people who wrote the books from which you have learned. They never look like you expect.

THE STRUCTURED REVOLUTION

In 1973 my career took a turn for the better. My best friend, Steve Trattner, had recently left Hughes and joined The Aerospace Corporation. The Aerospace Corporation is a think tank in El Segundo, California, established in the early 1960s to provide general systems engineering and integration support primarily to the U.S. Air Force on space and missile projects. Like MITRE and other such firms, Aerospace is considered quasi-government because it cannot compete with commercial firms due to the nature of its work. Steve encouraged me to submit my resume to Aerospace. Of course, I had mixed feelings. I enjoyed my job and was on the fast track at Hughes. The people there were like family to me. However, Aerospace offered me a chance to take on more management responsibility earlier in my career and work directly with the customer. And, like many young men, I was ambitious and lacked patience. I still keep in contact with many of the people I worked with at Hughes in those early years.

When Aerospace offered me a position running a number of software technology projects, I jumped at it. My first assignment was to develop improved software verification and validation techniques for use in assuring flight software used in the Titan family of satellite launch vehicles, support the development of software for a spaceborne fault tolerant computer, and directly support the U.S. Air Force in their advanced planning and acquisition management activities. Because of the nature of the work, software reliability modeling quickly became a topic of interest to me.

These were the days of Apollo. Draper Labs and others were developing the software that would take the astronauts to the moon (and back to Earth, as many of you saw in the movie *Apollo*

13). Programming was still an art form to which most people did not relate. I remember traveling east on a plane to some business meeting. The guy next to me asked what I did. I told him I developed software for a living. He asked what that was. I went on to explain in very simple language that the software I developed told computers, which were dumb, what to do. He was amazed by the concept. Now, if asked the same question, I would tell the same guy that I was either an insurance or a used-car salesman. Else, I would hear either some software horror story or the guy would bombard me with questions about what software package he should use. This is a real sign that we in the industry have made some progress. Everyone seems to be somewhat software literate. However, they would still have problems understanding what I do if I told them that I am a software engineer trying to institute change in large firms to improve production capability and capacity. It is simpler to tell a little white lie. It allows me to read my book without being bothered during the entire flight.

Working in the software research community was fun. I traveled, met interesting people, and did interesting work. I even got to apply my analytical skills in the area of software reliability modeling. Yes, there were frustrating times. And, much of the software technology we were investigating was immature and would not scale or was deemed too risky by conservative project management. But, I had found my niche. I liked working on projects that were willing to try to use software technology to achieve some positive benefit (for example, to reduce costs).

The craze during this time was structured programming. In the early 1970s, IBM published its positive experience on the New York Times system with chief programmer teams, software libraries, peer reviews, and structured programming. "Get rid of GO TO's" became the war chant. "Have your people conduct code reviews" became the cry. As the customer's representative, I got to visit with IBM and help structure a U.S. Air Force effort aimed at transferring their structured programming technology to the public domain. This involved preparing a series of guidebooks on the topic, developing training materials, and making program support library software generally available. This work came in handy. I remember receiving a panicked phone call from a friend asking me to immediately come to the General's conference room. When I arrived, the General asked if I could prove the structured theory mathematically for him. I did and he thanked me as I departed fifteen minutes later. When I got back to my office, I received another call from my friend. After thanking me, he went on to tell me that this General was interested in the topic because he had a Ph.D in mathematics. I never forgot this lesson. Always be prepared for the unexpected when briefing management—they never cease to surprise you. Most of them have hidden technical talents. They show these off when you least expect it.

In 1975, an Aerospace Division vice president asked me if I would like to take all of the good ideas I talked about and put them to work on the Space Transportation System. He offered me a promotion to a management position in the Program Office supporting the Space Shuttle project. This was a large and prestigious project, and I was ready to make the move. This new position would allow me to put many of the new ideas I was working with in the technology shop into practice as I had done at Hughes. This was very appealing to me. On arriving in the office, my first task was to figure out how much software the Department of Defense (DoD) was responsible for developing because nobody knew. While the National Aeronautics and Space Administration (NASA) was in charge of the Shuttle mission, the DoD had a large role in the project as the vehicle's primary user. I soon learned that the U.S. Air Force, as DoD's acquisition agent, had committed to develop over 100 million source lines of code for the launch processing system at Vandenberg Air Force Base, mission control complex in Colorado Springs, and launch vehicles (that is, the Titan 3C launch vehicle, the new Titan expendable booster, and the Inertial Upper Stage). Like most new managers, I was overly impressed by my role.

My second and more challenging task was to set in place a management infrastructure that would enable the U.S. Air Force to manage the acquisition of software being developed across the nation under about a dozen contracts by over 20 different firms. The nine-part strategy that I used then to manage the effort, shown in the following summary, has proven over the years to be just as relevant to today's large-scale software development efforts:

1. Use one gated process that can be tailored to each of the applications being developed (gates are key points in the process where management makes the decision whether or not you are ready to move ahead based on predefined exit criteria);

2. Focus on paradigms that make the product visible as it is being developed;

3. Use a consistent set of methods and tools;

4. Do not become overly enamored with the technology or by the technologists;

5. Pay particular attention to interfaces, both in the product and across contracts;

6. Foster one team and teamwork in everything you pursue;

7. Manage requirements creep because it has a way of sapping resources;

8. Focus on managing other risks because that is where the return is greatest;

9. Never forget that the sum of a lot of small successes is a big success. To be successful, you need to be continuously perceived as being a success.

During the early 1970s, I started to write. I published about 20 papers during the decade, and the first edition of my popular Institute of Electrical and Electronics Engineers (IEEE) tutorial on software management[3] came out in 1979. I also served on program committees and got involved professionally. During this period, various software engineering technical and standards committees formed under ACM and IEEE sponsorship. The topic was becoming recognized as important by the community, and it was fun to be one of the founding fathers of a movement. I also started to teach. I developed a course on software engineering for UCLA Extension. I also taught an evening class using Shuttle as my example at The Aerospace Corporation. If you really want to know a topic well, teach it. The students will keep you on your toes by asking questions that tax your knowledge of a subject to the fullest.

Getting involved professionally resulted in my becoming somewhat frustrated. Most of the committees I joined were staffed by volunteers from the universities. They were motivated by the "publish or perish" reward system. They seemed to have a bias against publishing anything that did not contain new and novel research ideas. Experience reports and survey articles were frowned upon. I fought hard to get things published that would be of interest to the practitioner. But I felt then (as I still do today) that such articles were not given a fair shake.

One of the highlights of my career was being invited to speak at the 1975 International Conference on Reliable Software.[4] I was on the same program with many of the leaders in the software engineering field. At the speaker's banquet, I had the chance to sit next to and converse with Professor Edsger Dijkstra. I asked him: "What techniques would you use to properly engineer a 100,000 source line FORTRAN program used to support a simulation application?" I was shocked when he answered: "I wouldn't have a 100,000 source line program." Twenty years later, I know he was correct. But, at the time, I thought his answer was very cavalier. As a matter of fact, it put me in a state of shock for a while. How could someone of this stature just ignore the real world, I thought.

My interest during this time period was in software tools. I was convinced that I could not transfer software engineering technology from the small to the large without them. Shuttle was in dire need of industrial-strength tools that could be used to establish a consistent management infrastructure across its contractor community. Most tools during this period were first-generation products that ran on minicomputers. They were not user friendly and tended to be error prone. As a result, we took many schedule and budget hits because we were maturing the tools in tandem with developing our operational software. We searched unsuccessfully for a standard configuration management control toolset (remember, the UNIX "MAKE" utility and source code control system were just being put into service on internal projects by AT&T during this time period). We also tried to find a decent tool to support our preferred structured design methodology. Unfortunately, most of the tools we tried were nothing more than glorified drawing packages. We called the tools "flash and burn" because they focused their energy on generating lines and boxes instead of doing any meaningful design analysis. In addition, many of the firms supplying the products were start-ups. Much of what we wanted we had to pay extra for because these firms had limited financial and personnel resources. I learned another lesson at this time. Money talks. Do not be afraid to use it to get what you want when you need it. If you are having a problem getting a response from a vendor, become the vendor's partner. That will put you in the front of the queue when you call and need service.

During the 1970s, my wife and I had the pleasure of being part of IEEE delegations that visited the Soviet Union and People's Republic of China. We visited many centers of software expertise and helped energize many to pursue the profession. I remember giving the first lecture on the topic of software engineering in China during my visit there in 1978. Not many understood what I was talking about at the time. This was soon to change. I also met with many foreign friends and developed several long-term relationships. These and other visits abroad helped me put the software efforts in the United States in perspective. In my estimation, we maintained the world's best software capability at that time.

Software Emerges as a Discipline

In 1979 I made yet another career change. After working at TRW for about a year in several senior management level positions, I was given the opportunity to form my own firm. I made the jump because I believe that there is never security, only opportunity. My first contract was with the Jet Propulsion Laboratory (JPL). JPL is a quasi NASA organization that handles interplanetary missions. In 1979, the Voyager probe had just visited Jupiter for several hours and sent back stunning pictures of the rings and several newly discovered moons. JPL was starting up a new program called Galileo that would send a probe to study Jupiter and an orbiter to survey its moons for a two-year period in the late 1980s. JPL needed help in managing the development of Galileo software. This was to be the first distributed avionics system to fly into space, and it had to be perfect. If it failed en route or upon encounter, there would be no recovery. You could not just send an engineer into space to fix it. As a matter of fact, it had to fix itself, because commands from Earth would take minutes to reach the spacecraft due to the distances involved. (In retrospect, it was a good thing we paid attention to such details. It was the software that saved the mission recently after the antenna on Galileo failed to deploy.)

I worked side-by-side with JPL and Martin Marietta engineers for over three years helping them pull their plans together and put a flexible software management infrastructure in place. For the time, the project proved very innovative. Every engineer was given a workstation. These were then networked together to allow groups to work with one another across the laboratory. Configuration management was centralized, and one set of methods and tools was used. Of course, it should be pointed out that this was before the days of the personal computer (PC). As a consequence, we had to build the workstations ourselves using 8-bit microprocessor boards and a custom chassis. Software ran under the CPM operating system. Networking was handled using our own hardware, which ran software we developed and supported standard protocols like Kermit. Although we could buy some of our software off-the-shelf, much of what we needed had to be custom made. This included database management, project management, networking, and the array of other software tools that are commonly available off-the-shelf in most offices today. The system that evolved, called the Administrative Office Data Center (AODC), was eventually replaced by PCs when they became available in the mid 1980s. This system was augmented with tools that ran on JPL's more powerful mainframe computers for mission planning, modeling, analysis, and software development (cross-compilers, debuggers, and so on). In retrospect, the effort to build and sustain the AODC environment was worth the pain because it allowed the JPL Galileo software engineering workforce, which was spread across the lab, to work productively together under centralized control as a single team.

As a major lesson learned, I do not think we could have been successful without such a solid management infrastructure supported by JPL's best people and a modern, workstation-based, tool-rich environment. Our strategy, which is common today, focused on disciplining our process, standardizing our products, providing a state-of-the-art work environment, and professionalizing our workforce. Again, we used advanced software engineering concepts on Galileo before they became adopted widely. We had to in order to succeed with our mission. We could not wait for the technology to become ripe. Instead, we had to invest prudently and ripen it. Although there were some traumas, our efforts yielded very positive results.

The Galileo project, like many other government-sponsored programs of the time, planted the seeds from which several successful commercial software firms would grow. Many of the packages we developed for our AODC provided the proving grounds for future PC-based database management and office automation software packages. Such ventures are positive examples of dual use programs in which technology developed for the government can and has been successfully spun out commercially under private sponsorship. I was proud to be part of them.

The mid-1980s were a time of growth for the software industry. A revolution was occurring that was affecting the manner in which society operated. As I have already noted, the PC was born and computers were starting to affect just about every aspect of our lives. They were getting cheaper and more user friendly. Computer and software stores were opening and the average Joe and Jane were becoming computer literate. Kids were using them in the classroom and learning not to be afraid of them. Adult schools were running classes in their use as were the computer stores. Offices were getting rid of typewriters and replacing them with word processors. Machines were getting smaller and cheaper and it was not uncommon for prices of home computers to drop monthly. In addition, because of their multifaceted capabilities, computers were being embedded in products that were affecting our everyday lives (automated tellers, automobile ignition systems, cash registers, microwave ovens, and so forth). The world as we knew it was steadily becoming silicon-based, information-intensive, and software-driven. I was excited to be in the business. The magical image of software was being slowly eradicated.

The challenges we in the software industry faced were also changing during this decade, and we had to change to deal with them. The systems we were building were bigger and issues of scale were more important. Foreign competition also got stiffer. Europe, Japan, and many emerging industrial nations (such as India, Ireland, and Israel) targeted the computer and software industries for growth. In addition, major research initiatives were started in Europe and Japan to improve their technology base so they could compete effectively in the 1990s in these growth markets. At the time, U.S. companies dominated the computer and software industry worldwide. Being behind in a high-technology area like software has its advantages. If you are smart, you can avoid the mistakes the leaders in the field have made and quickly catch up with them.

In the early 1980s I spent a lot of time in Japan. I worked primarily with Hitachi to implement a concept that has been called software factories.[5] Like many innovative ideas of the time, the concept was born in the United States. While several forward-thinking firms had explored the concept in the West, few were willing to pursue it all out because it called for large financial outlays to capitalize software.[6] Software at the time was thought by most to be an expense, not an asset (some managers still think this way). A software factory was a physical plant specially designed to make about 1,000 software professionals highly productive. The facility was wired to link people and machines together with the tools they needed to do their jobs efficiently in an office environment designed for teams and teamwork. The Japanese perfected this concept utilizing their skills in manufacturing methods and production technology and put it to work to build software. They also started to export the concept to other Pacific Rim nations concentrating on linking facilities together so that they could manage the remote development of software by geographically separated teams.

During the 1980s and into the early 1990s, I became involved with a lot of corporate self-improvement efforts. Many high-tech firms realized that their software capability separated them from their competition. They were looking to improve their software capabilities and capacity but did not know what to do and how to do it. My team and I were the experts from afar who were called in to tell them what they were often hearing from their own software people. However, such internal advice seemed to have little credibility, and reputable outsiders always seem to command more respect than internal champions. Often, executive management is more motivated to do something when an outside expert comes in and explains what to do and why they should do it. The two tricks I learned in establishing my credibility with executives were first to benchmark their performance against firms with which they competed within their field and, second, to use other firms as models so they could see what could be done to modify their own situation.

The hard numbers never failed me. As a result of these exercises, my firm developed a number of cost-estimating tools that we calibrated to the data we were collecting to make economic forecasts.[7] In the late 1980s we decided to market these tools as commercial software packages to derive additional income. Getting into the commercial marketplace as a software vendor was an eye-opening experience. It is not something for the faint of heart. You need guts, money, and vision to make it in today's market. Because the technology changes so rapidly, you need to continuously invest in keeping your product current on the machines of your choice. You need to understand your competition and try to beat them to market with technology that motivates buyers to select your product. You need to advertise, go to shows, talk with your users, and influence the influence makers. Even if you can do all this, in the cost-modeling field, you have to be patient and recognize that it takes a long time to make a sale. Needless to say, I could write a book on software marketing based on the many adventures my staff and I had as we ventured forth to make money with software we knew was good because we used it daily in our own business ventures.

In 1993, I made yet another career change. After founding and growing several successful software firms, I decided to try my hand at government service. I was offered a two-year position as the technical advisor for the Defense Information Systems Agency's Center for Software under an Intergovernmental Personnel Act assignment. I would also be given the additional responsibilities of chief of the DoD Software Reuse Initiative and chief of the Ada Joint Program Office during my tour. Those recruiting me described the job as being a change agent for the world's largest software organization, the DoD. In taking the job, I would have to make a number of sacrifices. I would have to take a leave of absence from my job, rid myself of assets that were deemed conflicts of interest, move without my family to the Washington, D.C. area, and take a substantial pay cut. Many have asked me: "Why would anyone in their right mind take this position?" Well, the answer and reason I took the position is simple: "To make the difference." Needless to say, my task of trying to improve the DoD's software capabilities proved to be the most difficult and frustrating job of my career. I liken it to the task of trying to move a mountain with a teaspoon. I learned that you can do it if you are persistent and move the mountain a little bit at a time. I will not bore you with a lot of stories about my adventures in government. I tell those stories elsewhere.

PROGRESS MADE

Those of you who have read this far probably now understand why I have focused this recollection on change. My principal role for the past 30 years has been to help decision makers make needed changes in a field that has been in a constant state of turmoil. That is why I call myself a change agent. Based on what you have read so far, you are probably asking: "Has anything really changed, have the changes the industry has made been for the better, can organizations really change?" or "Has change enabled us to become better over the years?" My answer to all of these questions is a qualified "Yes!"

Since its birth in the late 1960s, the software engineering field has gone through a number of significant changes. The structured programming fad of the 1970s was replaced by the Computer-Assisted Software Engineering (CASE) craze in the early 1980s. Expert systems went through a brief period of popularity and then fizzled because they failed to deliver the benefits they promised. Then, process became the rage in the late 1980s and object-oriented methods became the "in thing" in the 1990s. Software architecture and reuse are now quickly becoming our next silver bullets. What is on the horizon next is anybody's guess. My bet is on visualization and animation because of the push to go on-line via the World Wide Web (WWW) and the need for new and inventive forms of user interfaces that foster group interaction.

Each of these fads represents a transition the field has experienced as the technologies we work with and the problems our users face have changed during the past 30 years. In the 1960s, our industry's focus was on building error-free programs that ran on mainframes. During the 1970s, the direction changed as we tried to engineer software to solve well-defined user requirements better. In the 1980s, we tried to alter and scale our software methods to cope with larger and more distributed systems and take full advantage of the PC revolution. However, during this same time period, software became the cost driver in systems as hardware became viewed as a commodity you could buy off-the-shelf. Competition became tougher. Expectations rose. People became more software literate. So we searched for ways to improve our image, reduce cost, improve productivity, reduce time-to-market, and increase quality. Now, in the 1990s, software is viewed as a producer of jobs and a solution to our problems. Software is also starting to be viewed as a reusable asset as firms begin to introduce standards-based product line architectures specially designed to allow our engineers to systematically exploit libraries of software building blocks.[8]

I believe the industry has matured greatly over these 30 years. We have good technology at our finger tips, proven success models, and a more complete understanding of what it is we are trying to do as a profession. Most importantly, organizations seem to recognize that software is vital to their health and well-being and they need to invest to maintain their competitive advantage into the next century. Just a decade ago, most of these same firms did not recognize that they had to become a software powerhouse. Most were unwilling to invest in software. Many hoped it would go away. We have also seen the birth of the software executive. Many organizations have hired a leader with proven abilities as part of their senior executive team to nurture their software workforce and implement their software strategy. Based on these facts, you can see why I believe a lot of change for the better has occurred.

My experiences over the past 30 years have taught me a great deal about change management. There is nothing so humbling as the technical, managerial, and political problems you encounter as you try to help clients put new ideas to work in organizations that are driven to deliver software products under funding short-falls according to overly aggressive schedules. As a consultant, you learn to search out the opportunities that have a high probability of success. That is how you earn your credentials and large fees. You also learn to help clients create a climate ripe for change. Organizations ready for change can be characterized as follows:

- They recognize they have a problem that needs to be solved.

- They are willing to allocate the resources to solve the problem.

- They recognize that the problem cannot be solved overnight.

- A high-level champion can be enlisted to help you win the political battles.

- The software workforce perceives your recommendations to be credible.

- An internal change agent who is respected by the work-force is there to carry on.

- A project where solutions can be proven has agreed to serve as a pilot.

- People are willing to listen and try new and innovative approaches.

When you come up with your recommendations for change, recognize firms change primarily for business reasons. Your rec-ommendations can have the most positive effect when they impact what a business does and how it does it. Pay particular attention to process and products. Look to the future, not the past, under-standing that your job as a change agent is to tell it like it really is, not to be popular. I remember being ostracized by long-time friends because they thought I made the recommendation to a firm to shut down an operation (in this case, I had not made the recommendation, but in others I had made such hard-hitting suggestions). Always try to quantify the economic impact of your recommendations. That is what gets executive attention. I remember briefing the board of directors of a large Fortune 500 firm on a software strategy several years ago. When the numbers appeared on the screen showing the return on investment projections, I had the president and chairman of the board stand to get a better view because they had difficulty seeing from the back of the room. All these executives really were interested in was the impact of my recommentations on their bottom line. Also, do not forget to assess how your recommendations will affect the people involved. For most firms, that is their most important resource.

I hope that my reflections will help you come to the realization that you can motivate an organization to change if you convince those in power that it is in their best interests to do so. During the 1970s and 1980s, I often felt like I was beating my head against the wall when I counseled those who sought my advice on what changes were needed. Not enough people listened, and being a change agent was a frustrating job. Today, however, I feel a lot better about my role because people seem to be listening to my recommendations and, more importantly, seem to be acting on them. I do not think the reason behind this is that I have become smarter and wiser as I have aged. I honestly feel that people are more receptive to change today than anytime in the past that I can remember. I believe that executives recognize the need for change and are searching to do what is right for their organizations. It is, therefore, a great time to be a change agent and work with organizations to help them make necessary improvements. For those of you whom I have motivated to get involved in change, my advice is: Be thorough, honest, factual, quantitative, and, most importantly, have fun. That is what life is all about.

A WORD OF THANKS AND APOLOGY

I would like to thank Bob Glass for asking me to write my reminiscences. It made me think about things that I would not have thought about otherwise. I would also like to thank my wife, Carole, and my kids, Joe and Jessica, for their help during the years. If it were not for them and their support, it would not have been worth it.

Finally, let me apologize to those of you who remember things differently than I do. As a change agent, I have often upset people because I have told them things they did not want to hear or I have recommended or done things that were unpopular. This often colors perceptions of events. I remember what I saw. This does not mean somebody else's view of the situation is wrong. It just means there are many views, and each has a bearing on the truth. I also remember being told by one of my replacements for my government jobs that about half of the people he talked with did not seem to like what I had done. I told him I was extremely disappointed. I had hoped three-quarters of those I was dealing with would have expressed their displeasure. Such displeasure would have demonstrated to me that the change I was implementing was having an impact (hopefully positive, because I was trying to change a community that had grown complacent and was not motivated to change). Again, I have always tried to do what I thought was right, not what was popular.

ENDNOTES

1. See E.W. Dijkstra, "A Constructive Approach to the Problem of Program Correctness," BIT, Vol. 8, 1968, pp. 174–186; H. Mills, "Mathematical Foundations of Structured Programming," IBM Tech. Report FSC 72-6012, Feb. 1972; and C.A.R. Hoare, "The Emperor's Old Clothes," *CACM*, Vol. 24, No. 2, 1981, pp. 75–83.

2. B.W. Boehm, "Software and Its Impact: A Quantitative Assessment," *Datamation*, May 1973, pp. 48–50.

3. D.J. Reifer, *Tutorial: Software Management*, IEEE Computer Society, New York, 1979.

4. D.J. Reifer, "Invited Tutorial: Automated Aids for Reliable Software," *Proc. Int'l. Conf. on Reliable Software*, IEEE Computer Society, April 1975, pp.131–142

5. M.A. Cusomano, "The Software Factory: A Historical Interpretation," *IEEE Software*, Vol. 20, No. 11, March 1989, pp. 23–30.

6. M.E. Evans, *The Software Factory*, John Wiley & Sons, New York, 1989.

7. *SoftCost-R, SoftCost-Ada,* and *ASSET-R User's Manuals,* Reifer Consultants, Inc., Torrance, Calif., 1992.

8. D.J. Reifer, *Practical Software Reuse,* John Wiley & Sons, New York, 1997.

INFORMATION SYSTEMS

The name of the field in the early days was not "information systems," it was "data processing." People who processed data for a living had been doing it for years on punched card equipment. But the tedium and limitations of punched cards slowly began to give way to the power that the computer brought to the data processing (DP) table.

In this section of the book, we are fortunate to be able to trace our roots back to the very beginning. Frank Land tells us the story of the first business computer, at England's J. Lyons Company, which in the early 1950s was just beginning to realize the potential of the computer to assist in running a business. Astonishingly, as J. Lyons—basically in the tea shop business—began to use computers for its own purposes, it also found it could market them. First it marketed computing service, and later it marketed computing products. Imagine an early-day McDonalds in the computing business; the image boggles the mind!

Land paints some wonderful word pictures of those earliest software application days. Programmers clustered around a lunchroom table, excitedly discussing the cycles they had been able to save by hand-optimizing a key instruction in a key program loop that made a difference of a factor of two in program execution speed. Programmers waiting for the changes to the tax code presented at a once-a-year speech by the Chancellor of the Exchequer to the House of Commons, so that they could prepare and run the program that produced the tax tables for the Inland Revenue. Early system managers sitting in an office whose very walls were papered with the details of a master plan for automating a management information system. Pioneering results lasting far beyond what one might have expected—the 1954 tea contracting program that continued to be used for 25 years; the early specification for a tea blending system that Land has kept to this day. (I, too, have some ancient artifacts of my earliest programming days. The urge to keep those dusty products is a measure of the pride we felt in their creation!)

Our second information systems application pioneer began his tenure in the field almost as early as Land, this time in 1956. Ben Matley's career evolved from data processing to DP education, a transition he recalls as being exhilarating and frustrating at the same time, and in the end somewhat disappointing.

Matley's exhilaration stems from the very pioneering nature of his entry into the field. He remembers the eclectic workforce he joined—aeronautical engineers, foreign language specialists, music majors(!)—all of whom moved into the DP field because it could find no academic DP graduates. No such academic programs existed at the time. He remembers achieving a level of professional stability—four employers in ten years!—virtually unknown in the itinerant, demand-far-exceeds-supply-driven world of programmer hiring.

Matley's frustration stemmed from his transition into software quality control, where he found it difficult to get programmers to accept the notion of an external definition of quality achievement. "We experienced more than 100 percent turnover in programming personnel in a six-month period," he recalls. "Some working conditions were simply not tolerable among crucial workers who could find a new job during their coffee break."

And, finally, Matley's disappointment emerged from his transition into DP education. He participated in the establishment of one of the earliest academic DP programs at a California community college and then found that the largely vocational programs defined at that level were transitioned more or less intact to the four-year schools.

Something huge, of course, has grown from these early days of the information systems (IS) field. Most data I see indicates that fully two-thirds of today's software applications are information systems. The IS language COBOL remains the most-used programming language in the world today, in spite of decades of criticism, condemnation, and predictions to the contrary. Separate from computer science in most academic institutions is an information systems program, which prepares students for this astonishingly large and thriving profession. What Frank Land and Ben Matley pioneered has become a major force in today's society.

And now, on to their stories.

LEO, THE FIRST BUSINESS COMPUTER: A PERSONAL EXPERIENCE

Frank Land

In the 1940s and 1950s J. Lyons was one of the most successful businesses in the country; its products and establishments—Lyons Tea, Lyons Cakes, Lyons Ice Cream, and the Tea Shops and Corner Houses—were household names. It had built its success on quality products and services sold to a mass market and a constant striving for value-adding innovation. Selling to a competitive mass market required tight control over costs and margins and a sensitive response to customer preferences and market movements.

John Kay, in his study of what makes businesses successful, suggests that "architecture" is one of the important ingredients.[1] The distinctive architecture that Lyons had developed over the years was the way information was passed from operations—manufacturing, selling, distribution, as well as the concomitant operations concerned with invoicing and payments—to the decision-making senior management. Each of the many businesses (tea, tea shops, ice cream, bakeries, kitchens, and so on) had its own groups of clerks and managers. The vast mass of transaction data stemming from these operations was summarized and compared with pre-set standards, forecasts, and budgets. The resulting information was analyzed by the junior manager in charge of each group, who would be responsible for explaining any important variances.[2]

A version of this story is included in D.T. Caminer, J.B.B. Aris, P.B.H., Hermon, and F.F. Land, *User-Driven Innovation: The World's First Business Computer,* McGraw-Hill, Maidenhead, U.K, 1996. An American edition of the book is to be published in 1997 under the title, *LEO: The Incredible Story of the World's First Business Computer.*

134

The junior manager had a direct line to the senior manager, often a Lyons director, responsible for that activity and had to explain the functioning of that activity. At the same time the senior manager could ask the junior liaison manager to undertake "what if" investigations: suppose we wish to increase the production of Swiss rolls by 10 percent and reduce the production of cup cakes by 3 percent, what would be the effect on gross profit? The arrangement ensured direct access by senior management to information originating at the operating level and bypassed the more usual filtering through layers of middle management.

This architecture provided the company, long before the advent of computers, with both an almost real-time management information system and a decision support system of considerable sophistication. In addition, the architecture and system provided senior management with a detailed picture of the week's trading on the Monday of the following week.

The management had seen the need to innovate not only in new products and services but also in "business processes" as early as the 1920s when they had engaged a senior wrangler from Cambridge to oversee the office functions that already then were seen to be the source of information for management.[3] They established a systems research office whose function was to analyze primarily office operations in order to see how processes could be improved to provide better control and to reduce costs.

The systems research office working with line managers produced a stream of business process innovations from the time of its establishment. Examples include the notion that each sales representative, each having a customer group of many small retailers, would be not only responsible for selling to their customer group, but would be totally responsible for the accounting, credit, and payment functions conventionally carried out at arms length by a separate accounting office. The introduction of "traveler covered credit" was a radical business process innovation that increased efficiency and the effectiveness of the representative.

Yet in many other ways the company was deeply traditional and conservative. It operated on a strictly hierarchical basis. At the top were the owners, the founding family. They ran the company with the help of a very few employee directors. Each grade of management had its own dining room. Separate toilets divided managers from the rest. Trade unions were discouraged, though the family took a paternalistic interest in its staff.

This was the company I joined in 1952 as a recent graduate in economics. My first job was as a clerk in the statistical office—one of the major offices compiling and checking transaction data for posting to the cost accounts of the various operating units. I was responsible for keeping the cost accounts of the Provincial Bakeries and the Lyons' laboratories for further analysis and interpretation by the junior manager Alec Kirby. I learned then that the laid-down routine for almost all staff down to the lowest clerk covered only a portion of the time available. Much time was spent on tracing errors and various forms of troubleshooting. The more senior clerks and junior managers seemed to spend most of their time in that kind of activity. Like in much of the U.K., "progress chasing" by the manufacturing industry kept the wheels turning.

At that time Lyons had already embarked on its pioneering adventure with computers. In retrospect the move into computers is not so surprising. The systems research office had investigated the possibility of coping with the mass of transaction data by some kind of mechanization or automation for many years. They had started to investigate the possibility of devising a document reader for transaction data before World War II. They had researched the possible application of unit record systems based on punched cards, but rejected these as too localized, too constraining, and too costly. Lyons had only one punched card installation, and that had a very limited application. Instead they had installed alternative types of office mechanization based on accounting machines and calculators.

In 1947 two senior company executives, T.R. Thompson—another Cambridge senior wrangler recruited by the company in the late 1920s—and Oliver Standingford, visited the United States to see what developments in office equipment had taken place since the start of World War II. They found little significant change in office equipment. But they did hear about experiments with "electronic brains," such as ENIAC used exclusively for military, scientific, and engineering calculations. They visited a number of the pioneers and were told that in England Cambridge University had started work on the EDSAC, the first stored program computer. They wrote a report for the Lyons' board of directors that foreshadowed many later developments (including, for example, word processing) and recommended that Lyons obtain a computer.

The board accepted the recommendation but found that they could not simply purchase a computer. Instead, they helped finance the work of Cambridge University with a grant of £3,000 and in return received advice from Cambridge for Lyons to design and build their own computer, later to be called LEO (Lyons Electronic Office). LEO differed from EDSAC in that it was designed specifically for large-scale data processing with multiple buffered input/output channels capable of being linked to a variety of input and output devices. By 1951 the LEO team had built the computer, and the first regular business application was being run for the bakeries.

I knew nothing of the experiments going on with the LEO computer. But as the LEO group expanded, the company trawled for possible recruits from its offices. It was suggested that I might like to learn about LEO to see if I was interested and fitted their requirements for computer programmers. I was put on a one-week LEO "appreciation" course. The course taught us the rudiments of binary arithmetic, programming, and how the computer worked. It was tough. Each evening I would go home, sometimes in despair, and together with my wife work on the homework and master the exercises. By the end of the week I was still in a fog but felt that joining the LEO group would be a most exciting challenge and certainly an improvement over the by then rather boring Provincial Bakeries.

In 1953 I was selected to join the LEO group. At that time the first LEO (LEO I) was being commissioned in its final form. Magnetic tape, though still around, had been abandoned for the time being. Punched card and paper tape were the main input devices, though it was possible to intervene directly from the console to change the program or data, or to single step one's way through a program when debugging. Output was also on punched cards and paper tape but also in printed form directly onto a line printing tabulator. By present standards the computer was very unreliable, and the combination of programming errors, data errors, and an unreliable machine made the log entry "passed point of previous stoppage" a particular joy for the operators and programmers. Nevertheless, a substantial amount of work was being carried out.

The first application to provide experience of what was involved in running a live, time-critical office job that had to meet a precise weekly schedule had gone live three or four years earlier. Now the team was working on the various Lyons' payrolls (L1) and beginning to plan the tea shop ordering job (L2) and the reserve stores allocation job (L3). In addition the machine was being utilized as a service bureau with work, principally of a scientific nature, being carried out for a number of external organizations. Some of these involved programming on the customer specification by a member of the LEO team, but others were programmed by the customer's own staff, with LEO merely providing machine time.

Although the Lyons' applications were some of the earliest business systems on a computer, a pattern of planning and development had already been established, and for any application a kind of standard of "good practice" had been laid down. Many of these standards are as relevant today as they were in the early 1950s.

Selecting and planning the use of LEO for business processes that might benefit from the use of computers was in the hands of the senior LEO management (T.R. Thompson and David Caminer) and the Systems Research Office,[4] working with senior Lyons managers—often directors—and line management from the business area affected. To be selected, an application had to provide clear cost savings over conventional methods or had to make the business process more effective as well as show cost savings. The planners would look for opportunities to improve the business process in a way that would have been impossible with alternative methods.

There are many examples of such improvements. These included the development of standards, such as standardizing menus in tea shops, which added value by reducing the workload of the tea shop manager, who, as a result, could pay more attention to such matters as the presentation of the food and staff management. The standard menu provided the production management with the means of planning production and a way of dealing with emergencies. It also gave time to the tea shop managers to think about what an appropriate menu should look like. At the same time the use of LEO enabled changes (for example, in deliveries) to be made closer to the business situation that gave rise to the changes. In other words, the response to market conditions became closer to real time. The tea shop ordering job made possible a major business process innovation.

Another early application illustrates the focus on using the computer to achieve extra value. In 1953, rationing of foodstuffs was still in force, and Lyons as manufacturers of food had to rely on a great variety of materials, including substitutes for the natural raw materials. For example, in the bakeries sweetened fat was used as a substitute for sugar. The substitute materials were held in so-called reserve stores. An application was planned and developed for maintaining the inventory records of all the material held in the reserve stores and allocating these to the manufacturing centers, bakeries, ice cream plants, and kitchens on the basis of orders received and manufacturing schedules. The computer received manufacturing schedules as data and consolidated and allocated material from reserve stores according to the availability of transport in order to keep distribution costs to a minimum. As with all LEO jobs, the automatic procedure could always be overridden by management action. Costs were calculated for each store and charged out to the manufacturing departments. The reserve stores allocation job ran successfully only for a short time—it was abandoned once rationing ended and material could be ordered from suppliers on something close to a just-in-time basis.

Whereas the focus of the more senior LEO management was on business processes and the selection and planning of applications, those of us involved with getting the work onto the computer lived and dreamed of the technical problems of getting the programs to work. Each job presented major problems of fitting the tasks required into the small computer store and at the same time getting the job to run efficiently. The trade-off between saving instructions by tight programming and saving time in execution was a constant problem. Saving the execution of one instruction in a loop was a triumph and reported on and discussed at meal times and refreshment breaks. Programming so that a transaction could be fully computer checked within the time it took to read a punched card was good, whereas missing the cycle by a fraction of a second could double the execution time of a job with thousands of transactions to be dealt with. Every day produced new tricks of programming and avid discussions on how each trick was accomplished.

At the same time, the standards of good practice already in force were maintained and supplemented. Senior management kept a tight discipline, which ensured high quality and safe applications. No program was allowed on the computer for debugging without its having been desk checked by a colleague. This practice helped the learning and the spread of best practice among the team. All applications had built-in reconciliation procedures that were based on good accounting practice and not only ensured accurate work from the computer, but helped to pinpoint mistakes when they occurred and demonstrated to the business user the integrity of the work done on the computer.

In the year I joined the LEO group the Lyons payroll and tea shop ordering jobs were rolled out and became jobs routinely carried out on a daily or weekly basis. Having routine jobs required the computer to be run by a cadre of professional operators. Hence a new operating section with initially two computer operators and a number of data preparation staff was set up.

By now what had been regarded by the outside world as a perverse experiment was reality. Knowledge about what was happening at Cadby Hall began to spread largely through the Office Management Association of which John Simmons, a Lyons employee director, was president. A frequent occurrence was to take visitors around the computer and to talk about the applications. As a result inquiries about the possible use of the computer for their own businesses began to arrive. For LEO and Lyons management this suggested the possibility of making LEO an independent business, manufacturing and selling computers and running computers as a service bureau for other companies.

The requirement by Lyons management to continue to develop applications for the Lyons group and to provide for the planning, development, and implementation of applications for an outside market increased the need for programming staff, and a period of recruitment and expansion followed. For the group already in place it meant that the lessons learned from the successes of the Lyons' applications and the standards of good practice that had been absorbed into the way of working had to be rapidly applied to a range of new jobs on behalf of outside clients. Of these, the biggest to be carried out on a regular basis was the weekly Ford Motor Company payroll for over 20,000 workers. In terms of developing operational practices, providing regular secure delivery of outputs to a host of service customers provided a major challenge, which the LEO team met successfully.

To some of us the real challenge was understanding and mastering the business need of a very diverse group of customers covering almost all sections of British and, in later years, East European business. The fact that this offspring of a food business could sell systems to a wide range of blue chip companies and government departments is an outcome of the quality of the team recruited by the LEO management and of the good practices this team had inherited from the Lyons pioneers. Many of those involved in those early days have risen to high ranks in industry and also in academia, reflecting the important role of the LEO venture as an educator, almost as a business school.

My own progress was hesitant at first, but under the tutelage of my peers I began to acquire some skills as a programmer. At that time all of us worked on a wide range of applications. Some of these involved systems programming. One of my earliest jobs, working under Derek Hemy, was to make some small alterations to the LEO I initial orders. Later I helped to prepare the routines for the calculation of tax tables for the Inland Revenue. The application was carried out once a year only—immediately after the Chancellor of the Exchequer gave his budget speech to the House of Commons. We waited at Elms House for the courier to come with the data describing the tax changes to be incorporated into all the tax tables. We had no idea what the Chancellor would propose but hoped that our system was sufficiently flexible to cope with any changes he might bring in. The programs could easily cope with tax rate and allowance changes, but if the Chancellor wanted to make basic changes in the tax structure, we could have been scuppered. Of course, the civil servants who briefed us had a fair idea what was likely to be in the chancellor's package. Nevertheless, budget day had a rather special frisson for those of us involved with the tax table production.

The first job for which I was primarily responsible was a service bureau job carried out for a Liverpool clock manufacturer, J.D. Francis. The job entailed a weekly calculation of production costs using standard costing and computation of variances of the rather complex product—complex when compared to an equivalent task for, say, the Lyons' bakeries. This required the breaking down of production orders for the end product (clock and watches) into the parts and subassemblies needed to complete production. With the very limited computer store available, this involved a very ingenious design of the computer program in particular, because the job also had to do the reverse process of building up actual product costs.

The requirements for the job were specified by Oliver Standingford, who by that time was working as a director of J.D. Francis. [5] The job broke new ground in providing management information for a complex group of products. I was helped in bringing the job into operation by Betty Newman, then a quiet, unassuming woman, who became a first-class programmer. The J.D. Francis job appeared to achieve the objectives set by Oliver Standingford to bring the manufacture of clocks under rigorous control. However, it could not save the company from eventual bankruptcy, illustrating the important lesson that however good and effective the support activities of an enterprise are, they cannot save the enterprise if the core operations—in this case the manufacture and marketing of a range of clocks—are not equally well-managed.

Gradually the emphasis of our work changed. From primarily programming applications designed in essence by someone else, I became involved, first, in designing the system as a group of linked programs and, later, in establishing directly with users what the system as a whole should do and what part the computer could play.

My first major application in the first sense was the Lyons Tea Blending job. This was largely specified by members of the tea management working in conjunction with the Systems Research Office and senior LEO people. But I came to the job at an early stage in its specification.[6] The job concerned tea purchased by the company each week at the Mincing Lane tea auctions and tea that had been contracted for directly from growers in India and Ceylon but not yet allocated to the Lyons' Tea Blends; the job also involved valuation of the stock according to an average price formula and the charging of costs to forecast and actual tea blending programs. The application commenced working in 1954 and continued very much as specified for the next 25 years. As with all other LEO jobs it combined information relevant for the efficient running of the tea business at the operational level with management information to help in the longer term planning of that business.

The tea blending application was the first of a number of jobs I worked on that had stock control as a central feature of the application. These applications varied enormously in scale and scope. At one extreme was the spare-parts ordering system for the Ford Motor Company, who acquired a LEO II computer for the task. The number of spare-part items stocked was vast—well over 40,000 discrete items. They ranged from parts originally used in the Model T to the newest release of a component for the latest

Ford model. Model T engines were still in use the 1950s—not in cars, but in old pumping engines. The number of transactions to be handled on a daily basis was also vast—primarily orders from the thousands of Ford dealers plus the deliveries from Ford's own factories and suppliers, like Lucas. The objective was to turn around orders quickly—to prepare picking and packing documents for the Aveley warehouse within 24 hours of the orders being received and to deal with emergency orders, that is, orders for immobilized vehicles, almost as soon as they were received. At the same time the application warned stock controllers of items that were at risk from stock-outs and suggested reorder quantities.

A number of LEO people worked on the design of the application, cooperating with Ford's own staff. I took over the LEO liaison with the Ford staff from John Gosden. On the Ford side the senior man in charge of managing the implementation was Stan Woods, who had previously been responsible for a very large punched card installation at Aveley. That experience enabled Woods to understand and manage the huge task of preparing the data that had to be ready for LEO each day. The designated method was to use a very large pulling file.[7] This permitted much of the data to be prepunched, thus avoiding the problem of having to prepare the vast volume of fresh data each day. However, Woods found it more difficult to appreciate how the computer could do tasks that were impossible (or impractical) on unit record equipment. Hence we were faced with many battles on how best to exploit the LEO.

The situation at Aveley was eased by the arrival of Peter Gyngell, who became Stan Wood's systems manager. Gyngell was a somewhat larger-than-life figure. He had arrived at Aveley from his native Wales, having studied philosophy, playing Rugby, and having narrowly decided to join the world of business rather than becoming a preacher. He rapidly saw what could be done with a computer and was willing to work very closely with the LEO people. The success of the Aveley project owes a great deal to his skill. Later Gyngell joined LEO and became the manager of LEO in Australia.

A very different stock control application with which I was involved was a service job carried out on LEO III on behalf of Lightning Fasteners, a subsidiary of the ICI (Imperial Chemical Industries) company Imperial Metal Industries (IMI). Lightning Fasteners was then the major supplier of zippers in the U.K. The company was facing increased competition from abroad and had to improve its efficiency to survive. On the one hand, it needed to reduce costs by reducing its inventory of finished goods; on the other, it needed to improve its service to customers by reducing the incidence of stock outs. Both requirements might be met by finding a way of more accurately predicting the demand for fasteners. The LEO application was based on recording all stock movements each week and then using a statistical technique only recently developed—exponential smoothing—for predicting stock movements. The application appeared to be a success, achieving the goals set by IMI management. It could not, however, save Lightning Fasteners, who found the competition from the Japanese fastener company YKK unbeatable, and rather rapidly IMI, by then demerged from ICI, decided to abandon the zipper business.

The job that taught me the most about stock control as a business process was a pilot service job developed for the central stores of the North Thames Gas Board, the gas supply utility in the South of England. The Gas Board ran a central stores to supply its service departments with items needed for construction and maintenance. Items of stock ranged in value from a few pence to thousands of pounds. Some were highly specialized, manufactured only for the Gas Board. For others the stock held was a life-time stock. Many items were issued to user departments on a fairly regular basis, whereas others moved only occasionally and erratically.

The business problem was the classic one of achieving a high level of stock service with a minimum investment in stock. The operational problem was to deal efficiently with a large number of very varied transactions in a sufficiently reliable way for the book stock to be a good indicator of physical stock. The North Thames manager responsible for central stores was a Mr. Ryan. He had worked with central stores for many years and knew what went on—both the formal rules for operating the stores and the informal short cuts that are used to make any system work. Ryan saw the possibilities of using the computer and strongly supported the notion of setting up a pilot system to evaluate possibilities. We established an excellent relationship and as a result were able to specify a comprehensive description of what had to be done.

In practice we were forced to make some compromises. The timetable for getting the pilot running was tight. As a result we decided not to implement some of the less frequently occurring transactions. This is a course of action frequently advocated under the guise of invoking the Pareto principle. Pareto had shown that in many situations 20 percent of the possible types of occurrence account for some 80 percent of the activity. Hence if the computer system could cope with the right 20 percent of transaction types, it would cover a very substantial part of all the activity. The advocates of following the Pareto principle point to the large difference in costs between implementing a system based on the most active transaction types and implementing one that is comprehensive and accounts for 100 percent of activity.

In the case of the central stores for the Gas Board we were able to deal with many of the possible transactions. However, where the system could not account for all transactions it became necessary to develop independent noncomputer systems to cope with the residue. Inevitably this would lead to synchronization and reconciliation problems. The practical outcome would be that even if the fraction of transactions dealt with outside the computer system were very small, there could be differences between physical stock and book stock on some stock items each day. It would not take long for the central stores staff to distrust the computer-based system and to start keeping their own manual records.

In many ways the pilot was a success. It showed that a computer system could cope with a large number of stock items and stock movements and produce valuable management information, enabling the stock controller to keep a good balance of stock. However, the North Thames Gas Board decided against a full-scale implementation of the system at the time.

As the emphasis shifted from serving the parent company to doing jobs for prospective users of the service bureaus and prospective purchasers of first LEO II and later LEO III computers, the content of our jobs changed too. Our role was still to understand and interpret the needs of users, but the object was to sell LEO computers. The transition from a primary emphasis on systems analysis in order to develop computer systems to systems analysis designed to demonstrate to potential customers the merits of buying into LEO was gradual. Our marketing strategy was based on our ability to convey to potential customers that they would be buying into an organization that could understand their needs and leave no stone unturned to help them launch their computer systems.

At the time, persuading senior management to accept the use of computers required strong championship, usually from one individual. Later, as the 1960s advanced and the use of computers became more widespread, the procedures for acquiring computers became more formal, with calls for tender and formalized evaluations of the tenders. In the early years, selling the usefulness of computers required enthusiasm and willingness on the part of the champion to overcome obstacles. I believe one of the strengths of the early LEO team was their ability to work closely with and to support these champions. Sometimes, however, this led to trouble. In practice, the champions were very different from each other. Some had vision but also saw the need to prepare carefully and above all to keep the rest of the organization in the picture and to work at the pace the organization could take. Others could not foresee possible difficulties and opposition from counter champions. A number of the failed projects that we had to accept involved champions of the latter kind. Their enthusiasm carried us with them, and sometimes we saw the dangers ahead, but we allowed the champion to block access to others in the organization who might have provided needed balance. Perhaps we should have seen that we were building on sand.

Of course, the LEO team also made mistakes. We assumed that all companies could change at the pace of the fastest movers. We also assumed that we understood the needs of organizations and the business problems they faced and, therefore, developing and implementing a system would be straightforward.[8] On the other hand, a 1958 article in *Computer Journal* by David Caminer points to the difficulties of putting applications into operation and provides guidelines as relevant today as they were then.[9] Our confidence in our abilities to understand what a company needed sometimes made us appear arrogant. Clearly, we too misunderstood requirements and misjudged situations.

Over the course of many years working as a consultant with LEO, I had the opportunity to visit and study a large number of companies from many industrial sectors. Some decided to come to LEO and acquired LEO computers or used the LEO service bureaus. Many others went elsewhere. Competition in the late 1950s and throughout the 1960s was intense. As consultants we not only had to understand what potential customers needed, but what hardware and systems advice our competitors would offer. Some of the hardware features offered by competitors were difficult to match—in particular, random access storage—and it took LEO some time before we could match competitors' capabilities. Thus I could claim to have a better grasp of how, say, NCR would use their random access store than the NCR sales rep I was in competition with. In the meantime we had to demonstrate that we had a clearer understanding of what was needed and that we knew better than did our competitors how to translate requirements into effective systems.

The opportunity to see so much of British industry—private and public—provided an unrivaled insight into the strengths and weaknesses of the U.K. economy. Perhaps the weaknesses left the more lasting impressions. The most obvious weakness, for someone trained in the Lyons tradition, was the widespread failure of senior management to acquire any detailed knowledge of how the business processes—in particular, the support processes on which the effectiveness of the business depended—actually worked.

There are many examples. A potential customer of Lyons was one of the U.K.'s premier machine tool companies. It had a worldwide reputation for the advanced design of its products. I was shown around the company by the chief executive. He talked at length and with enormous insight about their product line and new product developments. These were clearly his interests. But a visit to the works showed very quickly that the production management system based on punched card equipment was not in control because it was being bypassed by a variety of informal procedures. Only the ingenuity of the "progress chasers" kept the factory going at some level of effectiveness. Overhead costs were high and schedules were not kept to. The management staff of the support procedures was poorly paid and held in low esteem. Senior management did not seem to be aware of the problem. The company decided to go to IBM. Computer systems, however, could not save them, and soon afterward the company went bankrupt.

Another company, an important steel maker, later a LEO customer, ran its offices almost as an independent division, working at arms-length from the manufacturing division it was supposed to serve. Considerable rivalry existed between the engineering division, also responsible for supporting the steel-making functions, and the office division, which was more concerned with the accounting functions. Some support functions, such as payroll, were divided between the two divisions. The engineering division and the office division independently requested bids for computers to carry out, among other tasks, payroll. Each of the divisions favored a different supplier. LEO was chosen by the engineering division, whereas the office division chose ICT (International

Computers and Tabulations) as its supplier. In business terms this made no sense. But senior management seemed to be scarcely aware that a problem existed.

One company we studied, a multinational, was the leading brand name for a class of white goods (washing machines, vacuum cleaners, refrigerators, and so on) that owed its dominant position in the marketplace to soon-to-expire patents. However, its lead position had made it complacent. I visited the company with Ninian Eadie. We were astonished to find that the manufacturing site was like a museum of the industrial revolution. The production process utilized banks of belt-driven, old-fashioned machine tools. The factory was totally vertically integrated. They produced everything themselves, including hardware items such as screws, nails, and bolts, lubricating oil, and the oil cans delivered with the product to the consumer. We were shown around the works by a young man—the first and only college graduate the company had ever employed. When the patents expired the company could not match the new competition from Japan.

German manufacturing companies that we visited underlined the problem of management not understanding basic processes. The basic support services in German manufacturing companies were not very different from British companies. However, senior management in the German companies appeared to have a very thorough understanding and interest in the operation of their support services. Hence they spotted weaknesses much earlier and seemed to be ready to invest in providing solutions.

I worked for LEO between 1952 and 1967. I started as a naive recruit scarcely understanding how to make computers work. I finished in 1967 with the title of chief consultant, responsible for the company's regional offices and much of the U.K. marketing organization. By that time the LEO subsidiary had become part of the computer division of English Electric to form EELM (English Electric, Leo, Masconi), and the joint company disputed the title of premier British computer manufacturer with ICT. In 1952 there were only a handful of computers worldwide intended for business use. In the U.K., J. Lyons, with its LEO, was without doubt the pioneer. A few more computers began to be used in the control of industrial processes, but the majority—still only a tiny number— were used for scientific and technical calculations.

By 1967 only a few major companies and government departments in the industrial world were not using computers for some business functions or at the very least not planning to use them. Companies that had in the early 1950s scoffed at the idea of computers playing any major role in business were now planning ever wider use of them. It had become fashionable for computer managers to have vast block diagrams papering the walls of their offices with an often detailed master plan for achieving the totally integrated management information system. The number of computers in use had risen to thousands. The number of personnel engaged in computer work of one kind or another had risen to hundreds of thousands. The business machine companies that in the 1950s had entered the computer business reluctantly and doubtfully now competed for the growing market with the utmost vigor. The largest of them, IBM, was on course for becoming the largest business enterprise in the world. Governments were beginning to use computers on a large scale to support and replace the work of civil servants. At the policy level the computer industry was regarded as an important national asset that had to be strengthened through direct governmental intervention. In the U.K. at the end of the 1960s the once fragmented computer industry was united into first two and then one major group called ICL (International Computers Limited).[10]

Over these years our own perceptions and style of working changed. When I started in the field the Lyons' tradition of systems research was the dominant influence. The Lyons' tradition focused on the whole business, and the function of planned change was to improve the business as a whole. This required an intimate feel for and understanding of the relationships and interconnections and power bases in the company. However, without John Simmons—the powerful champion who had won the esteem of his peers at the highest level—it would not have been possible to win over the line management of the productive parts of J. Lyons to the stream of radical changes that the introduction of LEO and some of the key applications brought about. Interestingly, many of the ideas we put into practice at that time are now trumpeted as the latest solutions to the problems of intense business competition.

As interest in LEO and the potential value of computers to business rose, we increasingly became involved with the outside world. At first those who approached us were themselves companies with good organizations and an innovative spirit. We were encouraged by at least some of them to behave as "experts" and to provide advice on how a LEO might be used within their organization. This gave rise to the term *consultant* for the group of senior programmers and systems analysts who gradually took over the role of selling LEOs or LEO service bureaus to the outside world. Nevertheless, we soon came up against restrictions that in Lyons we would have had encouragement to overcome. For example, while working with Dunlop (a premier rubber company), it seemed out of bounds at the time to suggest that the tangle of sales terms that had grown up in their organization were counterproductive and that simplification would have served the business as well as eased the implementation of the computer system. Any such suggestion would almost certainly have raised the suspicion that we wanted simplification because we could not cope with the complexity of the pricing system.

Throughout the early years of LEO II and LEO III, the way we worked changed slowly. For many potential customers we still carried out first-hand systems studies and provided them with detailed job plans. But as the number of customers that each of us had to deal with rose, the pressures on us became greater and we allowed ourselves to accept without question more of what the potential client described as the needs of the business. After all, we received no payment for work for which management consultants now charge large sums. In any case we were most frequently only one of many competitors tendering for the business, and our competitors' sales reps worked to a very different pattern. More and more we were expected to respond to a defined specification, and from the point of view of the customer it was easier to evaluate tenders when each contender responded in an identical form. In other words, putting our own gloss on what we thought the business needs were was not always welcomed.

Some of the people we worked with from other organizations thought that as vendors of computer equipment our style of selling was amateur. Our enthusiasm for understanding the business and using computers in a radical way to improve the business may have seemed amateur compared with the hard-nosed sales reps from our competitors whose efforts were solely confined to selling boxes using whatever means were necessary to get the order.

The merger with English Electric underlined the differences in selling styles. We joined up with a group of people whose culture was completely different. English Electric's approach was based on a divide between the sales reps, who fronted all negotiations with a customer, and a backroom systems analyst, who provided a service to the sales rep and worked under the sales reps' control; however, the success of the LEO III range and its sales were largely based on winning approval from our customers by means of our application-led mode of operation and our attempts to understand the way computers could help to improve the running of their businesses. The conflict between the cultures was never completely resolved.

For me the years 1952 to 1967 were largely exhilarating. We often worked at a frantic pace, and at times the pressures became immense. We felt that we were leading the world in the application of computers to business, and for a time we were in the forefront in technical developments. By 1967 the world had changed. The pace of work and what was expected of individuals was, if anything, still accelerating. But by that time we had become bit players in the global computer business. We had had little time or opportunity to reflect on what we were achieving. I left the company in 1967 to set up the study of computer applications at the London School of Economics, partly because I felt the need to think more clearly about the way computers should be used .

The current orthodoxy is that the way to achieve competitive success is through business process reengineering (BPR). Most of the management consultancies now have teams of consultants advising companies on ways to reengineer their businesses. The methods suggested are often brutal in their operation. A recent survey suggests that over 60 percent of companies are currently engaged in BPR. The failure rate of reengineering efforts is said to be about 70 percent. Much of what J. Lyons preached and practiced, but without the brutality, would now be called BPR. It is ironic that the current rhetoric suggests that the way ahead lies in following the precepts I learned over 30 years ago while working at J. Lyons and which we implemented with our LEO customers.

ENDNOTES

1. John Kay, *Foundations of Corporate Success*, Oxford University Press, Oxford, 1993.

2. In the Lyons grading structure, these people were placed in the "F," or supervisor, grade and not deemed managers. Many of them rose to manager rank in their subsequent careers, and some reached the very top of the organization.

3. The company engaged John Simmons, who subsequently played a major role in the development of the J. Lyons style of management and who backed the LEO venture and gave it direction.

4. The Systems Research Office was renamed the O&M Office when it became fashionable to have an O&M function in an organization. The manager of the O&M Office at the time I joined the LEO team was Frank Blight, who when he left Lyons was succeeded by George Robey.

5. Oliver Standingford was the Lyons manager who went with T.R. Thompson to the United States and later to Cambridge University in 1947 and wrote the report advocating that J. Lyons should themselves develop a computer for business data processing.

6. I still have the specification, entitled "L4. Tea Blending, Draft Job Specification" dated Oct. 18, 1954. Other correspondence suggests that by that time the L4 job was already working, although some requirements had not been fully implemented. An earlier note dated August 1953 from David Caminer sets out a number of questions regarding the tea blending requirements. An outline of L4 must have been clear in his mind.

7. A pulling file is made up of prepunched cards, set out in boxes, with a set of cards for each item in the inventory. A data-preparation clerk selects the cards required to fulfill a dealer's order—some hundreds of items—and takes them to a card puncher for entering the order quantity.

8. I remember vividly a meeting with T.R. Thompson. David Caminer and I had been working for a number of weeks with the Ford Motor Company at Dagenham trying to come to grips with their production planning and control procedures. I had finally reduced the complex procedures to a series of block diagrams that I believed to be a fair but rather simplified representation of Ford practice. At that stage we had to admit that we did not yet see how the job would be organized on the computer. To us, this served as a first step toward getting the understanding necessary to start eliciting detailed requirements. We were summoned to explain the situation to Simmons and Thompson. I walked them through the block diagrams. Thomson congratulated us and

assumed we had provided a solution rather than a way of describing the problem. All that was now needed was an implementation of the systems. In the end we decided not to make a bid for the Ford contract.

9. D.T. Caminer, "———— And How to Avoid Them," *Computer Journal*, Vol. 1, No. 1, 1958.

10. In practice the 1969 rationalization was only partial. The computer suppliers working primarily for the Ministry of Defense held out against the formation of a single all-embracing computer company. As a result the defense computer divisions of English Electric (Marconi Computers), Plessey, GEC, and Ferranti, remained outside the new company ICL (International Computers Limited). A great deal of expertise at the frontier of computer application and design was lost to ICL. I believe that this held back the progress of ICL for a considerable period.

COMPU-THEN: BEFORE MEGABYTES

Ben G. Matley

The year was 1956. The IEEE was ten years old. I began my first job in what was then termed "data processing" and later termed "computing." Subsequent years and jobs would bring feelings of exhilaration from being in a new industry; feelings of frustration from performing interesting and new activities that proved marginal; and feelings of disappointment from other efforts that seemed so successful at the time but proved in retrospect misdirected, though unfortunately, quite well accomplished.

For the purposes of perspective, the reader must first know that the reflections here relate only to the commercial era of digital computing, not to earlier R&D projects and not to the very early inventions. I was simply one person in a small army of workers in the commercial digital computer vineyards. We were relatively few workers of the time attempting to apply electronic digital computers in economically useful ways, without benefit of prior knowledge or training. There simply were no courses in "computing and programming" generally available. For example, my first lesson in hardware logic came from an advertising brochure by a firm named Computer Control Company. The brochure explained the mechanization of AND and OR logic, and the implementation of de Morgan's theorem. Similarly, my first lesson in programming was from another programmer's notebook. That notebook contained a 15-instruction computer program in numeric language that had been presented in an engineering magazine. Little did that programmer suspect that his personal notebook would become a departmental textbook.

In my experience, all emerging industries begin in a similar manner: work precedes organized curricula. On-the-job learning precedes in-school learning. Such are the working conditions that lead to moments of exhilaration, frustration, and disappointment.

154

Exhilaration

I felt exhilaration just from being in a new industry and being there when the founders were still defining that industry; exhilaration from working with an eclectic labor force, where no one had pre-employment training for that industry; exhilaration from the sheer chaotic nature of that infant industry. Not everyone reveled in those conditions. It was no place for employees who thrived on stability and predictability.

I was early impressed by the notion that we were performing tasks not done by prior generations of workers. That view was evident to me by the lack of formal job titles in computing. Titles such as "computer programmer" or "computer data analyst" or "computer systems analyst" were not in the Dictionary of Occupational Titles, nor in the help wanted ads. Some employers used titles such as mathematician I and mathematician II, or other borrowed titles. The mathematician I workers wrote numeric programs for the "large 2K mainframe" computer (no, not 2MB—that's 2K).

We were also privileged workers—privileged to witness first hand the founders of our industry, through their writings and conference presentations. True, we had to wade past the inappropriate analogies such as "giant brains" and "machines that think," but those references were mere whims of the times. [1] A more accurate analogy was at hand, in my perception.

Often, I reflected that we must have been reliving the roles of early aircraft engineers and technicians who worked in the Southern California aircraft industry when founders like Donald Douglas, Jack Northrop, and Claude T. Ryan were still directing that industry's development. Early on, pre-employment training was not available in that specific industry. So, too, was the case for the computer industry. Because there were no computer majors available for employment, we came from varied backgrounds.

Our co-workers in the early commercial computer period (1950s and early 1960s) presented an eclectic labor force. The setting was indeed exhilarating. I remember one man who held a master's degree in aeronautical engineering; he had written his masters thesis on wing tip design. When I knew him, he was project manager for writing and installing the software for a computer-based accounting system. Since aircraft were on the wane (at that time) and missiles on the rise, no one needed better wing tips designed. He sought technical employment in the computer field. Since no computer classes were available, he was as well prepared as anyone. As to accounting, he would often muse, "Some day I just have to take some accounting classes." I recall thinking that the educational systems must have been working. All around me were people performing jobs for which they had no training. Transfer of learning must have been working as well. Apparently, people had learned not merely specific facts but *how* to learn. That applied to other persons with whom I worked—the foreign language major, the music major, and others seemingly less likely to become computer specialists. I found all of this profoundly stimulating.

Moments of mirth were not lacking amid the turmoil. I recall an employment interview wherein I presented my experience on four jobs as "diverse and in-depth" over a ten-year period. The personnel manager who interviewed me was originally from Detroit. He chuckled at my presentation and then explained his amusement. In his experience (with three auto manufacturers) any worker who spent less than 20 years with one firm would be considered unstable and lacking allegiance to the employer. But, in the Southern California computer industry, four employers in ten years represented "diverse knowledge," and six months of work qualified as "experience" in the business.

That migrant nature of our workforce came to haunt us as well. Later, as project managers and department heads, we, too, had to consider the puzzle of the day: Does this applicant have ten years of experience, or just two years of experience, five times over? (That is, did he or she write a payroll program for five different employers?)

A most fascinating case, to me, was that of an English major. He wanted only to teach English composition in the public schools; to teach kids to write. He wrote computer programs because it paid well, and so he could raise his family while finishing his graduate degree. Once all tuition had been paid, and the master's degree completed, he would take the pay cut and teach English composition. If that ambition seems strange in retrospect, it was no more strange than was the general chaotic nature of the industry itself.

The chaotic nature of the early commercial electronic computer industry was itself exhilarating. For every four firms that entered the industry, three others went broke. That meant that one's employer might be quickly among the missing—a condition not offering stability nor predictability. I recall the near-humorous admonition of the time: "Don't go to lunch until you've updated your resume." As more computers were installed, the stock market not only rewarded the manufacturers of computers, but rewarded as well the manufacturers of commercial air conditioners. Those behemoth mainframes were built of vacuum tubes that were heat sources in the extreme. Only massive air conditioning towers could cool the working areas.

Chaotic was the industry, indeed. We saw some computer firms, like Raytheon, enter and exit more than once. We saw General Mills (yes, the cereal company) enter and exit only once. When RCA entered the industry, its stock price rose on the optimism. Then, when RCA exited the industry, its stock price rose on the relief from the massive cash flow needed to support computer manufacturing operations. Through it all, IBM sustained 65 percent of the mainframe business and 90 percent of the industry's profits. Little wonder that firms lived a chaotic entry-exit pattern.

If the industry itself was chaotic, so too was the work pattern of computer programmers. Programmers spoke in the possessive about their work: references to "my program" were commonly heard.

FRUSTRATION

The practice of programming as personal art led to the realization that standards in programming were imperative. Programmers were producing thousands of lines of code in a single program, and those programs increasingly had to mesh with other programs. Certainly, files were common to many programs, thus refuting the notion of personal possessions in software. That need for software standards and "auditable" software systems led to the notion of quality control in software (QCSW).

Quality and reliability requirements included in hardware engineering design had been around for a long time. The imposition of quality standards (though certainly not reliability) in software was simply not part of the mind-set among programmers who adhered to the notion of software as personal possession and personal art. Thus, QCSW offered a clash of cultures—and considerable frustration.

In the period 1962 to 1963 I was aware of three firms that had established formal departments of QCSW. Not to say there were no others. In searching for background material at the time I did find a U.S. Air Force publication of 1961 entitled "Auditing ADP Systems," which referred to the pre-computer punched-card systems. In the *Journal of the ACM*, July 1962, a paper entitled "Management Techniques for Real-Time Computer Programming" was offered. The paper addressed the basic issue of QCSW, though not proposing such an organizational department. Later, in March 1964, the magazine *Data Processing for Management* (long since out of print) published a paper entitled "Quality Assurance in Programming," which did address the matter of organizational departments for QCSW.

I was department head of one such QCSW unit. We sought to define the software development cycle and to identify audit points. We sought to define documentation requirements at each audit point, and to develop procedures. Finally, we sought to define independent program testing prior to release and postrelease change control procedures. We drew heavily on quality control (QC), final testing, and change control models used in hardware. But hardware designers were trained to the idea of external controls through quality and reliability requirements. Programmers were not so inclined. Many programmers resented the imposition of external controls on "their" work.

Implementing QC was a supreme test of skills in personnel relations—and was not well demonstrated. To the extent that we were seen as "imposing standards" there was resistance and resentment. As hardware QC models were evident, programmers were indignant. The very choice of the words *quality control* cast programmers as mere manufacturing, production-line workers. Ergo, Ego!

Without doubt, we failed in every aspect of personnel relations. In a day when programmers were simply not unemployed and available in the labor market, we experienced more than a 100 percent turnover in programming personnel in a six-month period. Some working conditions were simply not tolerable among crucial workers who could find a new job during their coffee breaks.

As QCSW began to function, even the doubters began to see some benefits. When programmers left suddenly or were taken from the building by paramedics (heart attack, ulcers) the documentation from the prior audit points were available in the program library. That documentation invariably proved more plentiful than the contents of the programmers' desks. Imperfect though such QC efforts proved to be, they were a start. And certainly, all such results were most frustrating.

In retrospect, it was somewhat consoling during the 1970s and the 1980s to read in the literature that people still struggled to define the software development cycle, documentation standards, certification testing, and audit procedures. Of course, that struggle had to be an ongoing process, as both programming practices and the programming environments changed from decade to decade.[2]

As exhilaration in early years had given way to frustration when better management techniques (such as QC) were attempted, so too simple frustration gave way to abject disappointment (for me) in the next phase of software progress—that of computer education. That phase also began with exhilaration, before succumbing to disappointment.

DISAPPOINTMENT

In my personal view and experience, computer specialty education began well and was successful as post–high school vocational curricula in the community colleges. In my view, computer specialty education became a disappointment when we transferred those curricula to the senior institutions. That was our error: we literally transferred community college vocational curricula into the university rather than design entirely new professional curricula for those senior institutions.

An additional historical perspective is of interest here. The term *data processing* (not computing) was used during and prior to the 1950s commercial era and well into the 1970s. The term was at first a hand-me-down phrase from the era of the punched card machines, dating from Herman Hollerith's machines of the 1890s. Those precomputer devices were referred to as automatic data processing (ADP) systems, later shortened to DP. Then, during the 1950s, electronic computers were introduced into these "DP centers" in the role of calculators. As the computers increased in main storage capacity, additional data processing functions beyond computation were programmed for the computer to perform. Gradually, the DP centers became electronic data processing (EDP) centers; however, the abbreviated reference "DP" was retained.

Well into the 1960s, computer centers were labeled "DP centers," and computer curricula consisted of "DP" courses. The reason for this antiquated terminology was related to federal legislation that funded "data processing education and training" in the colleges. At the time, computers were too expensive to be had by individual schools or colleges. The U.S. Congress realized, however, that the computer industry could advance only with an available, trained labor force. So, in 1958, Congress modified the Defense Education Act to fund DP training. Consequently, schools titled courses "DP" to qualify for funding. Thus, "data processing" was retained as the label for computer classes even into the 1970s.

In 1963, while still working in industry, I was invited to teach an evening class in FORTRAN II, using the IBM 1620 computer, at Orange Coast College (Costa Mesa, California). In retrospect I have considered that invitation an honored one, and it provided an unexpected turn in my professional life, even leading to university teaching positions later. At the time, Orange Coast had already established itself as a national leader in providing community college post–high school vocational training in computer programming and in machine operations. Orange Coast had been one of three community colleges (then called "JCs," junior colleges) funded by federal legislation in 1958 to teach "data processing" on an experimental basis. By 1963, Orange Coast was well established in college computer training. I was delighted to participate in such success.

My first class was, in fact, not of community college students. Rather, most of the students in a class of 30 held bachelor's degrees. These graduates worked for firms that had installed computers but had no computer programs related to their specific work. As undergraduates, the universities had offered these students no courses in computing of any kind (a condition common at that time). Now, as employees, these people were told to "do something" with the computer and to "make it useful to us" somehow. So the local community college filled a role it had not imagined—that of postgraduate computer classes for employees. I later found that pattern repeated at other community colleges long before the universities were able to fill that void for their undergraduates.

The community colleges provided vocational training in computing, from then until now. Always, the orientation of curricula was "current industry practices" to assure employability of graduates. Federal funding required "industry advisory committees" to the colleges to assure that "current industry practices" were taught. And the thrill of being associated with those curricula was to see those graduates quickly employed. (As I used to tell my students, "Get out there and help me pay taxes." That may have been evidence of a selfish motive!)

The four-year colleges and universities began moving into computer classes for undergraduates by first requiring one or two support courses for business majors and for engineering and science majors. By the mid-1960s that curricular pattern was common. Typically, the business major completed one survey course in computing and one introductory course in COBOL programming. The engineering and science majors completed either one or two courses in FORTRAN programming. Since the community colleges already offered those courses within their vocational curricula, the university transfer students could complete those requirements within the community college offerings.

The native university students then needed those basic programming classes. Therefore, some universities implemented those same programming classes. That was best done, and most quickly done, by using community college faculty as adjunct faculty at the universities. As a consequence, the universities inherited programming classes as foundation for later full curricula in computing—both management information systems and computer science. By default, the vocational community college curricula had thus been transferred into the university academic curricula.

Why was programming considered a foundation subject in the first place? The reader may not realize that in the 1950s and early 1960s, we who wrote curricula honestly believed that writing programs was basic to "understanding" computers. In fact, that perception was valid for first-generation electronic computers of the 1950s and for second-generation computers of the early 1960s. At the time, each instruction written by the human programmer did directly control the machine. Even input/output (I/O) instructions directly controlled external devices (such as the reader and printer). That relationship between the applications program and the machine remained into the second-generation machines. But, by third-generation machines (1964), that relationship no longer existed. The sequential nature of COBOL and FORTRAN programs in no way reflected machine architecture of third-generation and later machines. This changing relationship was one reason for the later disappointment among educators about computer curricula in colleges and universities.

Computer programming (a vocational subject) became the core and foundation for university (academic) computer curricula. Yet, there were no agreed on principles of programming—no agreed on standards. This condition was not the foundation of typical academic curricula at the universities.

Reservations about the nomenclature and content of computer curricula have persisted since the 1970s. Those discussions were recalled in the March 1996 issue of *Communications of the ACM.* But by whatever label, those computer curricula did advance to become computer science, information systems, and software engineering. And whatever the nomenclature for present-day software workers, a recognition seems due for those earlier software workers who did so much with so few Ks (yes, Ks, not MBs or teras).

A TRIBUTE

Recollections bring reflections. Software workers of that early commercial computer era can now reflect with wonder at the amount of useful work they accomplished with rather primitive tools. Using machines described variously as 2K and 4K, then 8K and 16K, those early software workers actually accomplished economically useful work. That era can be characterized as one of persistent "overreaching"— we attempted applications that would now seem, in retrospect, unlikely given the minimal capacity of computers at the time.

Unfortunately, the overreaching offered results that were also over budget, over deadline, and under performance. Some critics still see computer folks in such light—selling "cyber snake oil" as it were. I lived a more positive and fulfilling experience.

The software workers I saw were *driven*—overly enthusiastic, not overly promotional; *consumed*, not workaholics. And always, those software workers saw that their programs could do even more—never acknowledging that machine capacity did not expand with their personal enthusiasm. As a consequence, sheer human effort and hours had to make up the difference.

Programmers invested massive hours to "break up" programs into "parts" that could fit into main storage and execute. (The techniques and terminology of "segmentation" and "paging" were then not known to mere applications programmers in business and industry.) The intermediate data values from one "part" of the program were stored or written to an external device. The next "part" of the program would be "loaded" from an external device—all a manual procedure, since operating systems were not then common to commercial computer systems. Thus, human work hours by both programmers and users substituted at steps that were later automated. It all made for long days and nights, but not without humor.

One example of an "overreaching" application, attendant with excessive human work hours by the user, was demonstrated to me while in evening graduate school. In the early 1960s, computer programs to "simulate" competitive business activity were all the rage at universities. Our management class was divided into five "companies" in competition. Each week was a "quarter" of business activity, when each "company" made "decisions" on production, inventory, prices, market research, advertising, and the like. The simulator program was on a 12K machine in the basement. Each "company" had to "make runs" that would register decisions and write results to tape. The next day, the professor would make the "final computer run" that set dollar results to the "decisions" for each "company" in the "industry" represented.

One week, my "company" was the last to make the preliminary computer runs. We finished about 1:00 a.m. When I arrived home about 2:00 a.m., my wife greeted me in the hallway, worried at the late hour. I explained about the computer runs and about the make-believe companies. She responded, "Oh, wonderful! I am a corporate widow to a nonexistent corporation."

Sometimes, the hardware workers were also overzealous—practicing overreaching. For example, in the period 1958 to 1962, three firms marketed a "microprogrammed" computer (Packard Bell, with the PB 440; Ramo Woolridge, with the AN/UYK-1; and Collins, with the C8400). Those machines were an attempt to implement architecture suggested by M.V. Wilkes in 1950, also termed "stored logic" or "programmed logic" machines. The microprogram was stored in "micromemory" (that is, read-only memory, ROM), which might weigh as much as 40 pounds at that time—some 20 years before mass production of the microprocessor chip. Here was an example of "overreaching" in hardware, to match overreaching in software, represented by business simulation.

The pattern of overreaching in the early commercial computer era is what bore the seeds of the information society to come. Those early commercial information workers are to be saluted for their missteps and frustrations, their misdirections and disappointments. They are also to be lauded for their tenacity and enormous vision.

ENDNOTES

1. Such historical whims were reviewed in *Technology and Society*, Winter, 1995–96.

2. Special issue on "The Quality Approach: Is It Delivering?" *Communications of the ACM*, June 1997.

ACADEMIC COMPUTER CENTERS

Academic courses in computing did not arrive on the scene until the late 1960s, more than ten years after a thriving computing profession was under way. But that does not mean that computing had no presence on campus.

Just as there were applications of computing in the aerospace business and the information processing field, there were applications of computing in academic computer centers. Typically, in fact, two kinds of centers existed—one for administrative applications, mostly information systems; and one for academic needs, mostly for student and class scheduling and faculty research support. It seems ironic, in retrospect, that campuses were using computing before they realized that it was a subject to be taught. But those are the kinds of things that happen in the earliest days of any discipline. Practice precedes and helps to shape theory.

Harold Joseph Highland's story speaks for itself, and I will not try to abstract or elaborate it. However, he brings up one subject about which I cannot resist adding a story of my own.

The predominant computer used in his computer center, as you will see from Highland's stories, was an IBM 1620. The 1620 was a peculiar machine in many ways. Back in the days when scientific machines operated in binary and business machines operated in decimal, the 1620 was an anomaly. IBM marketed it as a scientific machine (you will note Highland's discussion of the use of FORTRAN), but it did decimal arithmetic. In fact, the way it did arithmetic was interesting. Rather than having intrinsic arithmetic capability, the 1620 did all of its arithmetic by table lookup—for example, to add 2 and 3, the computer "looked up" the numbers in an addition table, where the result, 5, was prestored. At one time IBM called the rather small machine the Cadet. Some wags of the time said that Cadet was an acronym, standing for Can't Add—Doesn't Even Try!

But enough of my stories. Highland has some wonderful ones of his own to share.

Four Anecdotes

Harold Joseph Highland

The computing field of the late 1950s and early 1960s was fairly primitive, and things happened then that today would seem exotic and bizarre. I offer four examples from my experiences at the Long Island University Computer Laboratory.

Neither Rain nor Snow nor Ice

The university received its first computer, an IBM 1620, in 1958. My colleagues and I from the Graduate Business School took over the former interior kitchen of the school's cafeteria and converted it into a space for the computer. The computer's massive air conditioner was mounted on the roof three flights up, with ducts down to the first floor.

A week after the computer was installed I was having trouble with the FORTRAN compiler and asked a graduate student to join me on a Saturday morning, 8:00 a.m., to see if we could get the compiler to work before school started on Monday. We had had a severe, wet snow storm, such as you find along the East Coast, but we both arrived. I opened the door to the computer laboratory (that word made it more respectable to our science faculty—*center* was too elegant for our provost; however *center* was associated with the student center). As I opened the door the student and I were struck with what appeared to be wet snowballs. He worked his way across some ten feet to reach the light switch. When the lights went on we both realized that we were standing in almost two inches of water. The ice was flying at us from the air conditioner vent that was hanging down from the ceiling just over the computer. The powerful air conditioner that had been installed on the

roof was operating at full blast. With the wet snow that was falling the air conditioner had formed ice and was blowing it down the two stories and out the vent into our room.

Since our card file cabinets had not yet been delivered, all the boxes of cards (punched and unpunched) were stored on the floor. We did not have a dry card; furthermore, all the machine cables were under water. I had to battle the president of the college not to throw the damn machine out and forget "this needless piece of junk." I have always claimed that this experience led to the use of raised floors in computer centers.

LONG PROGRAMS

In the early 1960s when the IBM 1620 was the computer on the campuses, most programmers had to learn modular programming, although we did not think of it in those terms then. The limited computer memory required us to take a long program and divide it into several parts; the length depended on the amount of memory used.

I volunteered our university to test a prediction formula that had been developed by Educational Testing Services of Princeton, New Jersey. We prepared data cards for each of the students, noting the individual's verbal and mathematical SAT scores along with the individual's high school average and standing in the class (a discreet series ranging from 1 to 5).

The first step was to determine percentiles based on each SAT score. This would be followed by additional data manipulation. At the time we had an IBM 1620 in our computer laboratory. The procedure necessary to compute the percentiles was exceedingly lengthy. It was necessary to prepare one program to compute the verbal percentile. We reloaded the program, the percentile base, and all the freshman student data cards. The output was on punched cards, each of which included the original data and the verbal percentiles listing. The first set of data cards were stored, and then phase 2 of the program was loaded. At this stage, the program was reloaded, followed by the math percentile data and the new set of punched cards. The output consisted of a copy of the original data to which the math percentile was added. We added an entering class of 250 students. The final program required that we reenter the data in the computer 13 times before the final analysis was obtained.

I recall that the 13 different programs contained over 2,500 punched cards. The percentile basis ran about 500 cards. The original 250 student cards were reproduced with one figure added in each pass, so about 3,500 cards in all were used in output data.

Because this was a learning experience for the graduate students who worked with me in the laboratory, we did the processing on a Saturday. We started at 8:30 a.m. and kept the machine busy until 7:00 in the evening. The final set of cards was used to obtain a printout on the 407. I did use part of the computer laboratory budget to buy my eight graduate students and myself lunch and after all was completed, a well earned dinner.

The project taught me that we either needed to find a bigger computer or give up such extensive esoteric jobs.

WHEN THE TRUCK HIT THE POLE

Back in the 1960s, IBM eagerly cooperated with a number of universities in developing a student class scheduling program. I and several of my colleagues who headed computer centers at other universities in the New York City area were invited by IBM to observe their latest workable program.

Three branches of a midwestern state university were used for the experiment. At each school the students filled out mark-sense cards to indicate their course choices. These cards were then run through an IBM 514 so that hand punching was not necessary. Each school's cards were run through the program along with faculty availability cards and students assigned to specific classes. The final result would be a printed schedule for each student and student list for each class section.

The schedule was somewhat ambitious because the three schools did run some courses that were available to all students but only on a particular campus. It was not a question of budget cuts but of availability of qualified teachers.

The experimental run was started on Friday after lunch. As observers, we watched the cards fitting into the reader and the machine blinking its lights and chugging away. Several large matrices were developed and the machine was still pumping away when at 1:00 a.m. Saturday morning, it was decided that we should all go back to the hotel, get some sleep, and come back for breakfast. Because of the extensive job, the computer at the campus passed off data by telephone to the computers at the other two campuses. There was a periodic exchange of information between the main computer and the other two.

Saturday morning I arrived at the computer center by 8:00 a.m. and found that three of my other colleagues were already there. The scheduling program had still not optimized the master schedule. We all relaxed in the conference room hoping that here might be a program that would show the value of a computer on our campuses. Three of my colleagues and I still had IBM 1620s and were unable to convince the administration to upgrade to an IBM 700.

As we were heading out to lunch, we visited the computer to see how many bases in the matrix optimization had been made. We were shocked to find that the lights on the computer were all off and the room was in darkness. There was only the sunlight through the large windows that had fooled us earlier into thinking the computer was running fine. We had lost all electrical power. We discovered that a truck on a campus road had lost a wheel and brought down a light pole. Not only had we lost power but telephone communication as well. By the time we discovered the power failure , we had chalked up almost 24 hours of operations with no results.

A hurried conference revealed that the programmers had not included any restart procedures. Unfortunately, as a result the school administration was not optimistic about computerizing registration and ordered a return to manual registration procedures starting Monday morning. All three schools opened several days late for the fall semester.

Lesson learned: Always include possibility to restart a program at critical points, and make certain that you have power back up, especially if you are handling critical data.

IVERSON NOTATION

Back in the early 1960s the Ford Foundation supported special computer programs to assist in teaching noncomputer faculty members how the computer could be used in teaching their courses. One program was set up in 1961–62 in the University of Toronto under the direction of Professor Calvin (Kelly) Gottlieb. He assembled an array of leading individuals in the computer field to lecture to a very specialized class.

The class consisted of about 30 college professors who taught in schools of business across Canada. To make it international, some (about five) members of the class were from the United States. At the time, I had been director of the computer laboratory at Long Island University for about three years. We had an IBM 1620 supplemented by a large array of tabular equipment. As Dean of the Graduate School of Business, I received notification requesting applicants for the Toronto program. I applied and was accepted.

There was an assortment of lecturers each day, including Peter Sandiford (who two years later became Dean of McGill University), Dan Teichrow, Bernie Galler (who was then president of ACM) and of course, Kelly Gottlieb. Kelly lectured for one hour every morning prior to lunch. To an audience who had no knowledge of programming or even an understanding of how computers worked, Kelly taught a crash course in flow charting. After one week he switched to Iverson Notation. These were the days before APL, and Ken Iverson at IBM was looked on as eccentric. Personally, I found Iverson Notation exceedingly interesting and useful. Unfortunately, most of my classmates, even several who had Ph.D.s in mathematics, were absolutely lost.

When my classmates realized that I had some understanding about what Kelly was talking about, they suggested we bring our lunches to the classroom and I could attempt to translate the earlier lecture by Kelly. Jokingly, the course became known as "Highland's translation of Kelly's translation of Iverson Notation."

This continued for about three weeks until one day, as I was lecturing at lunch, Kelly came into the classroom (he generally disappeared to work in the computer center every afternoon). When he became aware of what was going on, it was difficult for him to understand how such a simple subject was not obvious to this highly educated audience. His remaining lectures in Iverson Notation and application were presented at a slower pace.

Several years ago while attending a Canadian conference at which both Kelly and I spoke, we had a good laugh about the early days of teaching Iverson Notation. I told him that I really understood his problem, since I was still teaching Iverson Notation to my students rather that teaching conventional flow charting. I admit that I probably did not get any farther with my students than he did with us although it was 20 years later.

CONSULTING

Consultants are not born, they are raised. They usually begin by working for someone else, only later evolving into consultants. That is certainly the case for Robert L. Baber. His early post-college experiences, as you will see from his stories to follow, were at a famous U.S. military installation, where as a young serviceman he was engaged in information systems applications. His story of the transition from a card sorting process to a computer sorting process is typical of the events occurring in the field at the time.

Before long Baber was on his own. The stories he tells are largely those of the active consultant, tackling a diversity of software applications at a variety of client sites. Throughout the enormously varied experiences he recalls as a pioneering consultant, there is one dominant theme: the importance of mathematics and formalism in doing good software work. We see success stories of his philosophy in such varied applications as

- a program for eliminating name misspellings by transforming all names into a common abbreviated form ("I recommended constructing . . . a table and writing one program that, given any table, would perform the corresponding name transformations.");

- a program for optimal cutting of metal rods to required lengths from stock material ("I discovered simple heuristics that almost always computed an optimum cutting schedule . . . and always gave better results than the previously used manual method."); and

- a system for inventory control ("I proposed defining the communication process between the human user and the machine system in terms of a finite-state machine.").

Baber is a convincing advocate for his concerns. In his stories, he confronts the opposition to his ideas (opposition to such ideas remains strong in practice): "Marketing the seminar [on the topic of mathematical, formal approaches to software] has been difficult; potential participants appear to be skeptical of the very idea of a mathematically based approach to practical software development, even to the point of complete disbelief." But he sticks by his guns:

> I have found that mathematics frequently enables me to think effectively about and solve problems I could not have come to grips with in any other way . . . The elegance and simplicity of mathematics and the elegance and simplicity that the application of mathematics imparts to the problem in question and its solution can be enjoyed in their own right. . . . In short, mathematics has been my genie in the wonderful, magic lamp.

Sometimes during his story, I found myself wondering if Baber were speaking directly to me. After all, I have gone on record in many places and on many occasions as decrying the importance of mathematics in the software field. His view and mine could not be farther apart on this subject. And yet I found it exciting to read his strongly constructed, practice-based advocacy/defense of his belief system. I hope you will find it so, as well, as you enter the world of Robert Baber, pioneering international software consultant.

THE PROLONGED METAMORPHOSIS
OF A SOFTWARE ENGINEER

Robert L. Baber

MY BEGINNINGS

My interest in computers was initially sparked as a child in the mid-1940s by occasional articles in the press about "electronic brains." I remember reading some simple descriptions of the biological functioning of organs and muscles in animals and concluding that such physiological processes could, at least in principle, be completely understood. However, the brain and thinking, consciousness in general, consciousness of one's self, the very process of understanding, seemed quite different and mysterious in nature, and it was not at all clear to me whether one could understand them or not, even in principle. But if an "electronic brain" could be built—and the articles I had seen described operational ones—it should be possible to understand such a machine and hence, by extension, the human brain and its functioning also. So understanding the "electronic brains" seemed to me at the time to be the key to understanding the brain and its thought processes. I was therefore very interested in finding out as much as I could about these machines, but alas, the articles I could find contained no substantial detail. Eventually, though, I became preoccupied with school and other aspects of growing up, and the subject of "electronic brains" was relegated to my subconscious

---

Much of the material in this recollection is taken from my book *Software Reflected: The Socially Responsible Programming of Our Computers*, North-Holland, Amsterdam, 1982.

174

archive and more or less forgotten. My interests turned more to electronics, whether or not because of the hardware implementation of those artificial "brains," I cannot say.

Some years later, when I was an electrical engineering student in college, I had the opportunity to see my first computer, the Whirlwind, at MIT. To an engineering student in the mid-1950s it was an impressive installation. Viewed from the standpoint of today and current computing technology, it was impressive in quite another way. I feel sorry for today's students of computing science who have never experienced the thrill of walking through a CPU or past racks of memory banks as high as themselves. Whirlwind was not just some piece of equipment inside a building, it *was* the building. One room was the CPU, another the arithmetic unit and registers, and still another the operating console. Most of the basement was the power converter. On the upper floor were a few office rooms, but most of the building (about as large as a good-sized house) was taken up by this "electronic brain." I do not remember many technical details, but Whirlwind's computing and memory capacity was certainly quite puny by today's standards. The main input device was a paper-tape reader. An important output device was, if I remember correctly, an electric typewriter or teletype printer, and a CRT (cathode-ray tube) display (black and white, not color) was also used. Our host ran two demonstrations for us: finding the roots of a polynomial and determining a suitable initial horizontal velocity of a ball so that it would fall through a small hole in the floor of a room after bouncing off the floor and the walls a few times. Both demonstrations included attention-getting displays on the CRT.

My career in computing really began with a course in digital computation in my fourth semester of college in the spring of 1956. I do not remember the exact title of the course, only its number: 6.538. (We usually referred to all of our courses only by number, and these numbers became affectionate nicknames indelibly engraved in our memories.) I wanted to take an elective in my major field but lacked the prerequisites for all other elective courses. 6.538 had a prerequisite, too—a course that I planned to take at the same time. There was a major hurdle to overcome, however: 6.538 was listed as a course for graduate students, and I was only a sophomore, so I had to get permission of the professor giving the course to register. In our first meeting, I had the distinct impression that he was somewhat put aback by the idea of a lowly

sophomore taking his very specialized, advanced graduate course. Apparently, though, he could not think of a good rational reason for denying my request and agreed to my registering for the course. Later, I wrote my masters thesis under his supervision. Subsequently a warm and long-lasting personal friendship developed between us.

The course 6.538 included a brief history of a few lines of computing and computers and a good introduction into EAM (electronic accounting machines, that is, punched card equipment), but primarily we learned to program the IBM 650 computer, a decimal, two-address machine with a word length of ten digits and a sign. We programmed in machine language in those days. The only language support we had was an interpreter that effectively extended the instruction set to include floating-point arithmetic operations and trigonometric, exponentiation, and logarithm functions. Toward the end of the course we heard about a new and advanced technological development, the Symbolic Optimizing Assembler Program (SOAP), but we were not so fortunate as to enjoy the benefits of that new programming support tool.

From my work on my 6.538 term paper I learned an important lesson in digital computation: accuracy is quickly lost in the lengthy sequence of arithmetic operations typically arising in computerized calculations. Another aspect of my work on that term paper stands out clearly in my memory: walking home across the Charles River very early in the morning, bleary eyed after spending the whole night with the computer, with a box of punched cards under my arm and watching a very pretty sunrise reflected in the river's wavy surface. Do you know that there were 2,000 cards in a full box? And that each card contained 80 characters of information? That 160K of data weighed a few pounds. Today a disk drive weighing less can store more than 1 GB, a quantity of information unfathomable to us then. Probably the entire memory capacity of all the world's computers together then was less than 1 GB. That amount of data would have filled 12.5 million cards, that is, 6,250 boxes of cards, which would have weighed several tons. My newest streamer tape (an inexpensive one not at the forefront of current technology) stores 800 MB (which would equal 5,000 boxes of cards) and weighs 113 grams. That works out to 22.6 milligrams per box of cards. Hardware engineering has progressed very much and very impressively—in engineering jargon, four to five orders of magnitude—in the intervening years. (The increase in speed from walking to flying in a civilian jet airliner is less than 2.5 orders of magnitude.) Software development has progressed very similarly in the sense that we are able to fill the enormous memory capacity provided by hardware engineers with program code and data, but I do not consider this to be a reasonable measure of progress in the software area.

At the end of 6.538 I commented that the fundamentals of the subject could be presented to any student and that prerequisites were needed only in order to understand the examples and problems selected as programming exercises, not programming itself.

Therefore, if the examples and exercises were suitably selected, it would even be possible to give such courses to freshmen. About two years later the professor in charge of 6.538 mentioned to me that a programming course had just been offered as a freshman elective with catastrophic consequences: Some 200 freshmen had come to the first meeting, many more than even the most optimistic forecast. He would have considerable trouble finding enough instructors—and rooms—for so many students.

SOME EARLY EXPERIENCES

In my early work in computing I was exposed to a number of experiences, some of which represented advanced developments, whereas others represented clear steps backward. Mechanisms for transferring new knowledge, ideas, and concepts to others working in the field appeared to be sorely lacking. Although we have made much progress in this regard in the intervening years, I believe that this shortcoming still exists and is hindering our achieving a state of affairs characteristic of professional (in particular, engineering) fields.

One illustration of this point was the Autocoder assembler for the IBM 705 computer with which I worked as an engineering student in 1958. The Autocoder assembler was the first assembly program I used extensively; it had what seemed to me then to be an ingenious and well-developed feature called "macros." It would replace one assembly line of code with many lines of in-line code and would even include called subroutines as needed. It came with an extensive collection of macros for magnetic tape operations (with error routines), for various numeric functions, and so forth. However, the efficiency with which it searched the macro library tape left something to be desired. After assembling one macro and before assembling the next one, it rewound the macro library tape and searched for the next macro from the beginning. Most of the assembly time appeared to be spent rewinding and reading over unwanted macros. A simple modification would have about doubled the searching time on average: rewinding the tape only if the next macro needed was located before the current tape position instead of unconditionally. The idea of analyzing the efficiency of such algorithms was not yet widespread.

I thought about this shortcoming in that system from time to time until several years later when I finally had the time to analyze mathematically a somewhat generalized form of the search algorithm involving a conditional rewind operation. I wrote my first scientific paper on that subject and submitted it. It was accepted and published in the *Journal of the ACM*. My first impression of scientific publication—that any reasonable idea reasonably well written will be published—turned out later, of course, to be rather naive.

Several years after my contact with the IBM 705 Autocoder assembler I programmed a large IBM 1401 system, which also had an Autocoder assembly system, obviously patterned after the 705 Autocoder assembler ("copied" is probably a more accurate term). But the system for the 1401 included only a few macros, none of which were of any use to us. I missed the macros for tape operations that I had so often used several years before. I wondered why the macro library had not been copied along with the rest of the Autocoder system. The 1401 Autocoder system was only an amateurishly plagiarized version of the earlier 705 Autocoder. Finally I felt compelled to write a set of tape macros for the 1401 myself.

This Autocoder assembler for the IBM 1401 once gave rise to an error message that we could not understand. For the error message number in question the supplier's internal documentation for their system specialists contained only the explanation "System error. This error should never occur." (The documentation for the programmer using the assembler did not mention this error at all.) I discovered that the error occurred regularly when we assembled a particular program with a particular tape in a particular tape drive. When a different tape was mounted in the drive in question, the error no longer occurred. Suspecting an error in a tape error routine, I examined the assembler program itself. It contained a different tape error routine for each tape read and write command in the program, and the program contained a large number of these commands. At least one of those error routines was faulty. The concept of calling a subroutine appeared to be unknown to the authors of those parts of the 1401 Autocoder assembler. Many users of the IBM 1401 system were presumably not aware of this retrograde advance represented by the 1401 Autocoder assembler.

WHERE IS THE THEORETICAL FOUNDATION FOR PROGRAMMING?

When I studied electrical engineering in college we were taught to design our circuits and systems based on mathematical models and principles appropriate to the objects we were working with. When designing a circuit, for example, we always applied Kirchhoff's voltage and current laws as well as the laws relevant for the resistor, inductor, and capacitor ($e = iR$, $e = L \, di/dt$ and $i = C \, de/dt$, the latter two being special cases of Maxwell's equations) when calculating values for the components and when verifying the correctness of our designs before building them. As a result, our designs normally worked as expected when they were built. We used theory to predict the behavior of circuits, not just to explain observed behavior afterwards.

One example of such a priori predictive use of theory was a situation that arose in my first term as a student engineer in a computer hardware design group at IBM. The problem (a small part of a larger design task) was to calculate the values for a resistor and a capacitor to connect across a relay coil so that when the current to the relay coil was switched on and off, minimum damage was done to the switch contacts. When the contact was opened, the inductance of the relay coil would generate a high voltage across the switch contacts that would cause sparking and burning of the contacts. When the contact was closed, the capacitance would result in a current surge that would also tend to burn the contacts. The problem was to balance these two effects. I remembered a lab instructor's casual comment the previous semester, that when the time constant of the inductor-resistor combination was the same as that of the resistor-capacitance combination, the entire circuit would exhibit the same external behavior as a single resistor. Both the peak current through and the peak voltage across the switch contacts would then be equal to the steady-state values, clearly resulting in minimum possible sparking and peak current and, hence, minimum wear on the contacts. Thus one could calculate values for the bypass resistor and capacitor on the basis of theoretical considerations, without resorting to trial and error.

Because of my education, I was accustomed to basing designs on theoretical and mathematical models of the artifact being designed. However, in my experience, writing programs, both as a student engineer in programming groups and later at the IBM 1401 installation, seemed to require just the opposite. No mathematical models existed for programs or for designing programs. Obviously, programs had mathematical, logical aspects, but the theoretical-mathematical foundation for programming as a whole was missing. I wondered why this was the case and whether this lack of models was due to the nature of programming or whether such a foundation and such models were possible but had simply not yet been discovered. The commonly observed high error rate in the programming activity clearly made such a mathematical foundation for programming very desirable, since it would presumably lead to design error rates comparable to those in the engineering fields, that is, much lower. These thoughts did not lead to any concrete results then but I was on the lookout for such a mathematical foundation for programming should signs of something along these lines appear at some point. Years went by before models were developed and still more years went by before I became aware of them and recognized their usefulness in practice. In the meantime, the trial-and-error approach to software development dominated. Faulty software was the rule, not the exception. Software developers produced much software of considerable value and impressive results were obtained, but all this work, all these achievements, were bug-infested.

Loading the Database at the Rock

After graduating from college I went into "voluntary obligatory" service in the army. This was army double-talk for ROTC students who would be taken into the army involuntarily if we refused to go voluntarily. After officers' basic training and a brief sojourn at the Pentagon I was assigned to a computer center at a nuclear bombproof installation in the middle of a rock mountain. This military installation was, therefore, affectionately nicknamed "the rock."

Shortly after my arrival at the rock preparations for the monthly exercise took place. These preparations consisted of "loading the database." A newly arrived deck of about 25,000 cards was first reproduced. Each deck was then sorted, using a standard electromechanical card sorter. The two decks were sorted into different and complicated sequences, ascending on some fields, descending on others, and ascending or descending on another depending on the data in some other column. Three to six shifts of several people were required to complete the sorting, during which time both our computers, an IBM 1401 and a Control Data 1604, were idle. After the cards were sorted, they and a small deck of constant data were fed into the IBM 1401. The first pass checked that the decks were in proper sequence. This test typically identified sequence errors, which were manually corrected repetitively until the decks were in proper sequence, a process that lasted an unpredictable and sometimes fairly long time. Then a sequence of programs designed for a completely different purpose was run. If one stopped these programs at the right places (by turning certain tape drives off-line or by pressing the computer's stop button when the lamps on the computer control panel blinked in a characteristic way) and mounted different tapes on the drives at these points, a properly loaded database would be created on one particular tape. During these preparations our parent office in the Pentagon was kept informed of progress, and shortly before completion of "loading the database" a number of people would drive to the rock for their monthly exercise, the closest these office-bound military officers would get to the "field."

Remembering the words of our instructors at basic officers' training that the junior officer (that is, me) was typically assigned the most distasteful tasks to supervise (that is, this sorting operation), I was struck by extreme fear at this prospect and panicked accordingly. I knew how to sort cards and understood the process well, but I had no confidence in my ability to supervise this operation in which small decks of cards in various partially sorted states were scattered chaotically all over our offices and rooms and the hall between them. Especially problematic to me was handing over the sorting operation from one shift to another.

Out of fear and a classical reaction of self-protection and defense, I decided to program this entire operation on one or both computers before any of my superior officers got the idea of assigning supervision of this task to me. I had noticed a deck of cards labeled "IBM sort program" in one of our computer rooms and found a manual on how to use it. I also found a description of the format of the records in the final database file in a document on one of the programs used in the operation. The variety of sorting sequences went beyond the capability of the standard sort program, but this posed no real problem: I wrote a program that duplicated each record, calculated the nines complement of those fields that had to be sorted in descending sequence, altered the contents of certain other fields appropriately, and grouped all sort fields together. The standard sort program then sorted on one field and in ascending sequence. Being lazy, I wrote the field conversion program so that it was its own inverse, that is, so that it would also convert the contents of the complemented fields back to their original values. Another new program read the sorted records and wrote the database file in its final format. I set up the deck of program cards so that the several programs would execute one after another without operator intervention. Manual intervention was required at only one place in order to change tapes in one drive. That manual intervention was initiated, monitored, and verified under program control. I estimated that my new system would load the database in about four hours.

I had almost finished writing the programs when the Cuban missile crisis arose and a "Cuban database," much smaller than the normal deck of cards, arrived. That solved my only remaining problem: how to put together a small set of data to test the new database loading operation. I tested the system with this database, corrected a few errors, and announced that in the future we would be able to "load the database" in about four to six hours, with no scheduling uncertainty due to the manual card sorting errors. The system was used successfully thereafter, and everyone was happy, especially me because I never had to supervise the manual card-sorting operation.

I never did find out why this simple approach had not been taken originally by the software house that supplied the system or why none of the computer experts in our parent office had implemented it earlier. One of them was convinced that the standard sorting program could not do the job until I explained to him how it worked.

Months later and after the database had been successfully and uneventfully reloaded many times, we noticed that the sorting program once reported more records present after one phase than after the previous one. Apparently the Autocoder assembly system was not the only program with an error in a tape error routine.

TOP SECRET BLANK PAGES

One of the several program systems used at the rock printed a long, classified report. A security legend was printed at the top and bottom of each page, and the pages were numbered sequentially. The report was printed by a sequence of more or less separate programs, each of which printed one section of the report. Because of logical flaws in the programs, occasionally a page would be printed that contained one or both security legends but no data. Such pages could not be deleted from the report because doing so would introduce a discrepancy in the registered page count, resulting in a serious security violation. Thus the blank pages were classified "Top Secret" and were registered accordingly. I wondered if this implied that the program errors causing this situation were themselves top secret.

Over 20 years later I encountered the same type of error in a commercial data-processing center. At the end of the report the line "End of Report" was printed. When this line appeared by itself on the last page of the report, that page was usually thrown away. In these cases auditors could not know whether or not part of the report with data had been thrown away. One would think that such a basic and common function as printing reports would be, after 20 years, mastered by software developers, but this had obviously not happened.

COMPROMISED CONFIDENTIAL DATA

Several years after leaving the rock and back in civilian life, I submitted a job to a commercial computer center and received a long printout back. Appended to the output from my job was a partial listing of the employees of the computer center, their salaries, and other similar personal data. Apparently my job did not write an end-of-file marker on the tape, which had previously been used by the computer center's payroll system. Data security was not as important a concern as it is now.

THEORY FACILITATES PRACTICE

One of the useful pieces of information I learned in college was that there can be no such thing as a "blivit" (for example, ten pounds of material in a five-pound bag). We did not learn, however, how to recognize when a specification might be for a blivit. Later I learned that theory can help considerably in recognizing a specification for a software blivit.

In the late 1960s I was a member of a small group of consultants who were advising the data-processing manager of a broadcasting authority in a European country on various aspects of his operations. In one of the systems, data relating to individual persons was indexed by name. A method was required for locating data on a particular person even when the name available to the searcher was misspelled. This was to be accomplished by transforming the available name into an abbreviation so that typical misspellings of a name would be transformed into the same abbreviation as the correctly spelled name and so that as few as possible different names would be transformed to the same abbreviation.

The data-processing department had obtained several different suggested rules for transforming names into abbreviations. One rule had been programmed and tested using a large collection of representative names. The program contained intricate logic and had a confused structure. Some suspected that it contained errors. A new programmer in the client's data-processing department was given the task of identifying and correcting any errors in the existing transformation program, programming the other transformation rules, and evaluating the several different rules. After about two months, he managed to find and correct several errors in the program but had otherwise made disappointingly little progress. Whenever he corrected the program to handle one test case properly, it failed on another that had been processed correctly before. When he estimated that some two months would be required to program each of the other transformation rules but could not predict when he could finish the project, his manager asked us for advice.

Observing that such a transformation process could be represented by a finite-state machine with a reasonable number of states and that a table of state transitions and outputs could be constructed in a more-or-less straightforward way from the given transformation rules, I recommended constructing such a table and writing one program that, given any table, would perform the corresponding name transformations. The program would be much simpler than the one already written and could be used without modification for all the transformation rules to be evaluated. The client decided to take this approach.

In attempting to formulate the state-transition table for the first rule for transforming names, it was soon discovered that the specified rule was ambiguous and contained inconsistencies. This had apparently led the original programmer to become confused without his realizing the true underlying reason. His attempts to correct specific errors as he discovered them resulted unavoidably in the introduction of new errors. The many iterations of this trial-and-error (always error in this case) approach to getting his program right led ultimately to the unsystematic structure of his program. His approach would never have led to success, of course, for he had unknowingly been trying to program an unprogrammable process. His specification called for a software blivit.

The transformation rule was modified in a way that appeared to be linguistically reasonable to obtain an unambiguous and consistent rule. In two to three months the proposed new program for transforming names was written, the state transition tables for all rules were constructed, and the analysis and comparison of all transformation rules were completed. Using the original approach, it would have taken much longer to complete the project, assuming that the attempt could have been successful at all.

After his first discussion with us, the programmer, who had had no previous computer science education, obtained from a local library several moderately sophisticated articles on finite automata and closely related subjects. During the course of the project, he became something of an expert in applying his newly acquired knowledge to practical problems.

INTEGRATED COLLAPSES

In the late 1960s "Management Information Systems" (MIS) and "Integrated Management Information Systems" (IMIS), even better and higher tech, became fashionable and much touted—until a few spectacular collapses led to absolute silence on this subject for some time. MIS reappeared years later, but IMIS did not as far as I know.

During these years I was a consultant on the staff of the Diebold Research Program Europe (DRP-E). We proclaimed the benefits of such systems just as much as anyone else and with good reason. Significant benefits could be and were achieved by providing more extensive EDP support to more and more of the operations of large and medium-sized companies. But with the larger, more integrated systems came not only larger, more integrated benefits and successes, but larger, more integrated collapses.

In each of the various conferences we organized for the sponsors of the DRP-E, there were always several talks on various aspects of MIS and IMIS and usually one primary presentation of one company's all-encompassing system. At first the larger systems were presented by speakers from U.S. companies, sponsors of the parent DRP in the United States. The DRP in the United States spoke only of MIS, so we in Europe, tired of being a couple of years behind in computing matters, overtook them with our IMIS.

One of our sponsors in particular had launched a major IMIS effort about which members of its management team spoke at our conferences. It seemed to me that the higher-level goals, objectives, and strategy made sense both in business terms and technically and that the lowest-level plans seemed to be reasonably well worked out, but I found the middle-level design confusing and unconvincing. In particular, it was not clear to me that the connection between the upper-level concepts and the lower-level details was adequately established. Because the entire system was very much larger than any I had ever worked on, I attributed my incomplete understanding of this great system to my inexperience, but I had uneasy feelings nevertheless.

With collapses of MIS and IMIS projects, those of us in Europe were not so far behind the United States as we had been in the initial development of large systems. Suddenly, at one of our conferences, our U.S. colleagues from DRP, who had turned completely against MIS in the previous month or two because of more than one announcement of catastrophic failures of MIS development projects in the United States, warned our DRP-E director to stop all mention of IMIS immediately. He was informed that the whole idea of MIS had been proven wrong and was completely out of vogue. U.S. DRP warned him that it would be damaging to our credibility to even mention these terms any more. We thought they were overreacting to a couple of setbacks (which, on a smaller scale at least, were not new). We softened our line a bit, but did not substantially change our policies and direction. A few months later, the failure of our showpiece IMIS effort was announced. The project, in shambles, was abandoned.

It was originally intended that this IMIS should contribute to the profitability of the company, support management's decision-making process by providing appropriate information, projections, and proposed decisions, and relieve people of routine, operational tasks. Subsystems were foreseen for sales forecasting, order processing, production planning and scheduling, materials management, personnel, finance and accounting, planning and budgeting, management control, and so on. Each subsystem was further subdivided into groups of closely related business functions and finally into individual programs. This system was based on a centralized computer system with several subsidiary computer centers at key office and plant locations. A data communications network was planned to link the various computers and users' terminals.

Several hundred man-years of effort had been invested in the specification, design, development, and implementation of the application software when the IMIS project was stopped. Colleagues of mine in a consulting project to determine how best to salvage the remains of the effort told me that many programs and subsystems were running, some of them well, but that they did not constitute a meaningful whole. The operational systems did not fulfill the high-level goals and objectives of the company. The functions and services provided to the system's users were somehow not quite what management wanted and had expected. Just why this situation came about was never really clear, but ineffective communication between management, the system's intended users, and the development team appeared to have been an important factor. I suspect that the euphoria accompanying the project blinded the participants to the fact that they were all progressing rapidly in somewhat different directions. Only a small fraction of the results of the IMIS project could be meaningfully salvaged. The EDP manager, the project manager, several key members of the project team, and certain members of the company's top management team were replaced.

About ten years later, I heard about a similar development in connection with a planned worldwide system for an international transport company. The system was intended to coordinate fleet operations and accounting worldwide. After collapses of individual system development projects on both sides of the Atlantic, the collapse of an even wider scale, transcontinental project came as no surprise.

Lest the reader get the impression that the concepts underlying these systems that failed so spectacularly were ill advised from the beginning, I should point out that those basic ideas and concepts underly many operational systems today, systems that are now considered to be normal, perfectly ordinary, and commonplace. We probably tried to take too big a step too often, but the basic tenets upon which those MIS and IMIS plans were based were viable (in the mid to long term at least) and worth pursuing.

THE $1,000 LOOP

In the early 1970s I was a consultant in the national office of an international management consulting firm. As the only member of the staff with significant computer background and experience, I was assigned to every project related in any way to computers or computing. I was also interested in inventory control, especially mathematically based optimization techniques. Our parent organization obtained a simulation program for inventory policy analyses and, after some application success, made it available to us. The only feasible way then to use it both in the United States and in Europe was to install it on an international time-sharing system, which was large, fast, and effective but correspondingly expensive.

This simulator was used successfully both for consulting projects and as a teaching tool in seminars. During its long and useful life we were, however, continually plagued by the many errors in the programs. The most expensive of these "bugs" was an infinite loop in one subroutine, which once consumed about $1,000 worth of computer time before I interrupted execution. Most errors discovered in the early years of its use were in those parts of the programs that simulated unusual inventory control strategies. Years later, when I translated the programs to run on a different computer, I discovered a series of errors that could result in division by zero. The original version of the programs contained a control statement that caused run-time error messages to be suppressed.

Who knows how many error conditions arose in our simulations that were never brought to our attention. The programmers probably never considered the potential consequences of their carelessness and oversights. Such lack of a sense of responsibility on the part of software developers severely limited and, in my view, still limits the potential application areas for computer systems, based as they are on software and its typical shortcomings.

"Fully Tried and Tested"— but Erroneous—Standard Software

In the early 1970s a consulting team of which I was a member assisted a client to conceive, plan, and develop an inventory-control extension to their order entry and processing system. For the sales forecasting subsystem the client planned to use existing programs supplied by the computer manufacturer. We were assured that these programs had been successfully employed in a number of other companies and that we could rely on their being fully tried and tested.

When the manager of the sales forecasting group complained that the test runs resulted in clearly unreasonable forecasts, I looked into the matter. The mathematical analysis underlying the programs' logic contained a rather fundamental error: It first calculated a linear trend from the raw data and then, after removing the trend, calculated the seasonal factors from the adjusted data. This was, of course, backward; the trend must be calculated from deseasonalized data (that is, the raw data will appear to exhibit a positive trend if seasonal sales peak near the end of the year, or a negative trend if they peak near the beginning of the year). I manually calculated the forecasting errors to be expected from the inappropriate formulas and presented them to the manager of the sales forecasting group. They corresponded quite well with his estimates of the forecasting errors in the test data.

In addition, a member of the client's staff had discovered an addressing error in one of the programs as a result of which one factor used in the calculations was effectively only one-tenth of the correct value. We specified a new forecasting program to replace the manufacturer's standard program. The client's EDP department programmed it and used it successfully for many years.

Some Software Systems Do Work— but Not by Chance

Another subsystem in the project I just mentioned optimized the inventory reorder parameters. For this function I derived a set of formulas that could be solved numerically by iterative approximation only. Concerned by the possibilities that the iterative method might not always converge, that it might sometimes converge to an undesired solution, or that problems of numerical accuracy might arise, I analyzed the relevant characteristics of the formulas. A rather lengthy analysis showed that no such problems would arise in this case, but that a particular kind of nonlinear interpolation in a table was required in one part of the computation.

In another subsystem, the possibilities of confusion resulting from delays in the man-machine communication in this batch system gave rise to major concerns during the early design phase. I proposed defining the communication process between the human user and the machine system in terms of a finite-state machine. We specified the various states and, for each state, which events would cause the system to generate which messages and recommendations, and which state transitions would occur. A number of discussions with the users were required to define the states, the transitions between them, and the desired behavior of the system in all combinations of states and events. During these discussions, a number of possible sequences of events came to light that no one had thought of before and that forced the user to think through in detail what he or she really wanted from the system.

The system was implemented successfully and employed profitably for many years. A few years after the initial implementation, the user decided that a slightly different behavior would be desirable. The state transition table was altered accordingly and the modification implemented quickly, inexpensively, and without complications.

If we had not taken this theoretically based approach, but had just programmed intuitively using seemingly appropriate procedures, operational chaos would certainly have resulted in the system test phase, after all software had been developed. The need to construct the state-transition table in detail led us to ask the right questions at the right time and to avoid very embarrassing errors.

It has been my observation that success often goes hand in hand with a symbiosis of theoretical and practical capabilities. In the less-successful situations, one of these two important ingredients tends to be lacking.

Keep Trying Until It Works

In response to a software house's request, I contracted to deliver a program for a specified purpose to be written in a certain dialect of BASIC. I was familiar with many versions of BASIC, but had never had any contact with this particular dialect or computer before, so I was given the name and telephone number of the software house's expert in that particular system, whom I was to contact when system-specific questions arose.

I wanted to use one aspect of the input/output commands mentioned in the manual. Because that aspect was described ambiguously in the manual, I turned to the software house's expert for clarification. When he did not know the answer to my question, I asked him what he did in such situations and he replied, "I just keep trying different possibilities until one works."

Being under some time pressure, I could not afford the luxury of squandering time in a "trial-and-error, mostly error" approach (which Murphy's law would predict to be futile anyway). Furthermore, I felt very uneasy about the risk associated with delivering a program that processed my test cases correctly but in which I could not have more general confidence that it would handle all cases that might arise later. I therefore assumed only that which was unambiguously stated in the manual and designed my program accordingly. My program was certainly not as elegant (whatever that may mean) as it could have been, but it was reliable, and I knew why I could have confidence in its reliability. In fact, no erroneous behavior of the program was ever reported after I released it. The same could not be said of the programs written by the software house's expert.

A Tale of Two Operating Systems

When the Tandy TRS-80 microcomputer was first introduced, I was surprised that the manufacturer had the courage to place the operating system and the BASIC interpreter in ROM. It seemed to me that correcting errors in this software could prove very expensive and logistically difficult to carry out. I was, however, later surprised by its quality. As far as I know, only a couple of truly minor errors were ever discovered in the software.

The operating system supplied with the diskette accessory system was, however, another matter. That disk operating system contained a tremendous number of errors. Only when the fourth version was released did I have a usable system, and even that version contained errors. In the meantime, independent software suppliers developed and marketed corrected and enhanced versions of the disk operating system. These also had their shortcomings and errors.

These two examples illustrate that reasonably complicated software systems of high quality (that is, essentially error free) can be developed in practice, but we still revert to our old ways and turn out shoddy work (for example, the IBM 705 and 1401 Autocoder assembly programs described earlier).

INDUSTRIAL APPLICATION OF TOY COMPUTERS

When microcomputers were first introduced on a relatively wide scale in the late 1970s, the established serious manufacturers of large and minicomputers dismissed the microcomputers as toys, not to be taken seriously by their industrial and commercial customers. I was never sure whether this reaction was honestly meant or whether it was an attempt to protect themselves and their products from threatening competition. Whereas the first microcomputers certainly did have definite limitations, they also found productive and profitable applications.

The first industrially viable application of such a "toy" computer in which I was involved was a small project for a producer of metal products. The problem was to determine how to cut rods of a fixed length into shorter rods of various required lengths so that the scrap produced was minimized. A brief investigation led to the conclusion that the cost of implementing and running an appropriate program on the company's main computer system would be at least as expensive as the probable cost savings. The alternative of procuring a microcomputer just for this purpose was considered and, because such a machine was so inexpensive, the client decided that it was worth trying.

Implementing a mathematically optimum algorithm was not feasible on a microcomputer, but in the process of investigating such possibilities I discovered simple heuristics for calculating cutting plans that almost always computed an optimum cutting schedule (that was recognizable as such) and always gave better results than the previously used manual method. Comparison of the new method with cutting schedules from many actual previous production lots indicated that the new method implemented on the "toy" computer would yield non-toy results: 40 percent of the production planner's time and more than 3 percent of the production costs affected by his planning decisions would be (and later were) saved. With some trepidation I went to the first meeting with the production planner, who would become 40 percent redundant on introduction of the system. Much to my surprise he was very happy with and strongly supported my proposal because he would be able to devote much of his time to other important tasks that he had previously been forced to neglect. In fact, he wanted another program to compute cutting plans for two-dimensional plates, but that was beyond the capacity of the small microcomputer system.

Thus the myth that microcomputers were "toy" machines, not to be taken seriously by businesses, began to crumble. Again, a pragmatic balance between theory and practice led to success.

TRIAL AND ERROR—ALWAYS ERROR

After assisting a client to specify a large software system for an order-entry and processing application, the software was programmed. When the coder tried to link and load the many modules in the system, no one was really surprised at the result: the error message "MEMORY OVERFLOW." The coder then set out to define an overlay structure for the program.

Although the coder was experienced and did not just pick overlay combinations at random to try, his many attempts were not really systematic and did not lead to success. I was asked to look into the matter. It quickly became apparent that the possible number of combinations that could be tried was so large that trial and error could not be considered to be a reasonable way to approach the problem. A little more analysis showed that, in fact, no overlay combination would fit into available memory, that is, a trial-and-error approach would never lead to success. Knowing how much the memory requirements had to be reduced, we proceeded in a more goal-oriented way and determined that the memory requirement could be reduced sufficiently by redefining certain large data areas local to several modules as global data areas. The analysis of the data on the individual modules was then repeated and several satisfactory overlay structures identified. One that would minimize the reloading of overlay segments during execution was then selected.

Despite the fact that the trial-and-error method has withstood the test of time very poorly, it is still very popular among software developers.

COMPUTER PROGRAMMING FOR HIGH SCHOOL FRESHMEN

When computing courses were first introduced in high schools, I was struck by the double standard regarding the qualifications placed on the teachers and, more importantly, regarding the standards set for the students' work. Whereas teachers of other subjects such as biology, chemistry, history, social studies, languages, mathematics, and so on had all studied their subjects for several years in college, teachers of the computing class had had no contact or only brief contact with the subject in college. Although the students were expected to delve into the grammatical structure of natural languages, they were not expected to become correspondingly familiar with the syntactical rules of the programming language they were learning. Although they were expected to be able to prove the Pythagorean theorem, to prove that the square root of two is not a rational number, and to derive the quadratic formula, they were not expected to prove that the algorithms they specified and the programs they wrote did anything in particular, much less something correctly. Although they were expected to be able to organize their essays clearly and logically, they were not expected to be able to structure their programs in a similar manner. In short, significantly lower standards of quality were set for their work in computing courses than in other classes.

It seems to me that such an approach could only instill in them a corresponding attitude of lower standards regarding programming and that this attitude must carry over to their software development work later in their vocational life. I now realize that many of my fundamental attitudes toward many things were set in my early childhood and schooling, and I cannot help but believe that the same applies to other people as well. The German language has for this situation a very apt saying containing a considerable element of truth: "Was Hänschen nicht lernt, lernt Hans nimmer mehr"—loosely translated, what one does not learn as a child, one will not learn as an adult.

THE BEGINNING OF MY CONVERSION
TO REAL SOFTWARE ENGINEERING

During the 1970s an increasing number of articles and books on various mathematical aspects of programming, proving the correctness of programs, and so on came to my attention. Some were quite mathematical in nature; others, very informal. The more mathematically oriented ones seemed to contain interesting and probably useful content, but it was far from clear to me how to apply that material in day-to-day software development practice. It was also not clear which material was potentially applicable in practice and which was not. The applicability of the material in the informal works was in most cases clear, but its substance seemed to me to be rather thin or lacking. But at least some signs of a mathematical foundation for practical software development were perceivable.

I began to use the ideas in the less formal treatises in my software development work in a quite informal way. I began by using the idea of a loop invariant and found the concept to be helpful. It enabled me to write programs a bit more quickly and with much more confidence in their correctness. I noticed that the first drafts of my programs contained significantly fewer errors than before. The first program I wrote for a client using these ideas ran without error from its initial implementation.

Encouraged by such initial improvements in my programming, I decided to look more deeply into the more mathematical material on program correctness. Gradually and over a fairly long time I came to see how some of it could be recast and reformulated for practical application. Only slowly did I realize how the application of this material to practical verification and design problems could be systematized in simple, mechanistic, and easily repeatable ways. This was not an easy process and, I must say frankly, was hindered by the form in which the more theoretical material was usually presented. The theoreticians had done very good work but had not, in my opinion, communicated it satisfactorily to anyone outside their own discipline. More than once I wondered if the authors had intentionally written it in such esoteric language in order to enhance or protect their status from encroachment by lowly practitioners. As time went by, I discovered that this material was not as inherently difficult (or esoteric) as it had first appeared to be.

MY FINAL CONVERSION TO MATHEMATICALLY BASED SOFTWARE DEVELOPMENT

Soon after the success with the program mentioned in the previous paragraph, I was asked by a client to develop a management game program to be used in management seminars. After a colleague and I developed the required mathematical models of the market and of the competing firms, I set about designing the software system and writing the programs. Thinking that the loop invariant for the main loop in the highest-level control program would be so simple that I need not write it down, I began writing the program early one morning. Late that afternoon I was almost finished. The various segments and ends of the code I had written just did not fit together. I examined them again with the intent of forcing a successful fit, but it just would not work. Admitting defeat and the loss of an entire day's work (and billings and net income), I quit for the day. The next morning I started all over. In the late afternoon, I found that again the various pieces and ends of my work did not fit together. They came much closer to fitting than on the first day, but they still did not fit.

I decided that if the loop invariant was really so simple, perhaps I should write it down after all. It took me about a quarter of an hour to do so. Using the loop invariant as a checklist I then successfully wrote the control program in about three-quarters of a day, a bit less time than each of the unsuccessful prior attempts had taken. The experience gained in those first two unsuccessful attempts was of no help in solving the problem; all the assistance of value came from the loop invariant.

The loss of net income equal to two day's billings was an expensive price to pay for what should have been obvious to me by then. But I learned my lesson: for every loop a loop invariant. Only when I write a "for loop" with exactly the same structure as I have already written many times do I not write down a loop invariant first. Today I can no longer write a loop without a loop invariant, because without one, I have no idea what the initialization of the loop should do, I cannot derive the loop condition, and I cannot begin to design the body of the loop (the loop invariant is the main component in the specification of the body of the loop, proof rules W1 and W2).

That financial loss converted me to real software engineering, once and for all. I vowed that I would never risk writing a program by trial and error, fumble and stumble again. For every loop a loop invariant.

A Difficult Question

The managing director of a large company for which I had just completed a consulting assignment asked me, "Is my EDP department any good? It takes at least two years to get any new system developed and running. And then, more often than not, their systems do not really fulfill our needs. What is wrong? What should I do about it?"

This was one of the most difficult to answer questions I had ever been asked. I highlighted the shortcomings and causes underlying the problems he had mentioned and said that these were not unique to his company but were common to software development in essentially all organizations. The causes were industry-wide, perhaps society-wide, and could not be adequately explained in a short meeting. I was not satisfied with my answer and could only assume that neither was he.

I wanted to formulate a proper answer but realized that it would take quite a bit of analysis and time to do so. About the same time my wife was having great difficulty understanding how the software development industry could possibly be as incompetent and irresponsible as suggested by my probably slightly emotionally charged statements uttered in fits of frustration over the loss of my time due to bugs in the software I used. I decided to answer both my client's and my wife's questions in the form of a book, which became *Software Reflected: The Socially Responsible Programming of Our Computers.*

Uneventful Interlude

My next software development project, which involved developing several subsystems for a management game, proceeded unproblematically. I developed the main calculation routines and delivered them to my direct client, the system developer. They worked. Because I finished earlier than expected while the system developer's own staff were behind schedule, I was asked to develop several smaller parts of the system, that is, for preparing reports. The project went well and uneventfully. My loop invariants once again paid off.

"WHEN WILL YOU START TESTING?"

In the mid-1980s I was asked to develop the application software for a medical laboratory. The software was to process orders from doctors for analyses of blood and urine samples, assign the work to specific work stations within the laboratory, collect the results, and prepare reports of the results organized by patient and doctor. The system was to include an on-line communications link with an automatic analyzer, an impressive and marvelous piece of fine mechanics that analyzed tiny quantities of a number of samples simultaneously for a number of different chemicals, enzymes, and so on. A second phase, tentatively planned from the beginning, would collect billing information and generate a quarterly bill for each doctor.

After assessing the user's needs, I set about designing the application software system. The driver for the serial communications interface with the automatic analyzer was to be written by a member of the hardware supplier's staff, so he and I agreed on an interface between my application software and his driver. We agreed on an approximate installation date at the laboratory. The hardware supplier delivered the computer to my office. Every once in a while the programmer of the driver and I contacted each other with some question. The conversation usually ended with my question, "Have you started writing the driver yet?" and his reply, "Have you started testing yet?" Only after three or four of these exchanges did I realize that he believed that my testing time would be long enough for him to develop and test his driver. I warned him that this assumption was not valid, but he apparently did not believe me.

About half way through my development work we agreed with the client on a particular Monday as the concrete delivery date to the laboratory. My work continued, and the dialog between the programmer of the driver and me followed our usual pattern. As time progressed I became ever more worried about his driver, but as long as I had not started testing, he felt confident that he would have sufficient time to write the driver.

During the last week of my development work, I repeatedly asked him when he would pick up the computer from my office and suggested Friday afternoon. In response to his usual counter question, I replied that I would finish the system Thursday afternoon, test it Friday morning, and be ready for him to pick up the computer Friday afternoon. He obviously did not believe that such a software system written over a period of about a month could be tested and debugged in half a day. Late Thursday afternoon our usual dialog was repeated. Late Friday morning, much to his surprise, I informed him that I had finished my testing as planned and would like him to pick up the computer that afternoon. He agreed to inform the laboratory that we (he) would be late in delivering the system and why. When we did install the system two weeks later, the application software worked as agreed. It took two to three days to debug his driver. My loop invariants paid off again.

In daily operation the system's reliability was limited by two factors: the hardware (the disk controller tended to overheat and fail) and the serial communications link. A small addition to my subprogram communicating with the automatic analyzer provided a simple and adequate quick warm restart capability, but we never did find out what caused the communications link to disconnect occasionally (typically once or twice a week).

REINCARNATION OF AN OLD BUG

Several years later a new model of the automatic analyzer was ordered by the laboratory to replace the old one. Its communications interface was said to be upward compatible with that of the older model with one or two minor exceptions. I was asked to modify the application software I had provided earlier. The supplier provided a booklet with the technical specification of the new analyzer's communications interface.

I prepared a new version of the appropriate subprogram, which was a minor modification of the previous one, and installed it. Much to my surprise, it did not work. Investigation revealed that the specification I had been given contained one page twice. I had not noticed earlier that the two pages had the same number but different contents. I called the supplier's technical staff and was informed that one page was a revision of the other and that it was an error that my copy included both versions. I had, by Murphy's law, used the wrong version. I read the updated version of the page carefully and changed my subprogram accordingly. This time the application software worked.

The laboratory staff then tested the system, mainly the new analyzer. The supplier's technical representative insisted on testing it with a small number of samples in order to minimize wasting the expensive chemicals. The machine passed all tests. Finally my insistence on a test with a full tray of 30 samples was taken seriously. The test resulted in an error message. The analyzer complained that the number of samples for which the computer (with my software) requested analyses exceeded the allowed limit and then performed the wrong analyses on the samples for which it did accept requests. With up to 29 samples in the tray the system worked, but not with 30. It was obvious that the software in the analyzer contained an error in the termination condition of one loop. This was, of course, unsatisfactory, because the laboratory usually analyzed at least two full trays of samples each day. The technician from the analyzer's supplier agreed to contact his parent company in the United States for a new version of the software. When the corrected version arrived a couple of weeks later and after it was installed and correctly executed, the technician told me that the same error had initially been present in the software for the previous version of the analyzer several years before. I remarked that I remembered that such errors in loop counting, exiting one iteration too early or too late, were common in the 1960s but could only be considered amateurish programming in the 1980s. The testing of that software must have been rather cursory, for the testers had obviously not followed an old, simple rule: test all boundaries and limits (in this case trays with 0, 1, 29 and 30 samples and an analysis request for 31 samples in a tray). I pitied the programmers—who had obviously not yet learned the lesson of the loop invariant as I had and their other customers.

"LET'S TRY OUT THE NEW FEATURE"

After the analyzer functioned correctly, the technician asked me if a new feature in the analyzer would be of interest for this laboratory's operations. I replied that, had it been available when I designed the software, it would have facilitated my design work and I would have used it, but that it would bring no benefit now. (Another old adage of engineering dominated my thinking at this point: "If it works, don't fix it.") The technician prevailed on me to at least try it out and I agreed. I modified a copy of the relevant subprogram to use the new feature. I asked him if the analyzer would ever send a certain sequence of messages to the computer running my software, pointing out that my software would not function correctly in response to such a sequence. He assured me that the analyzer would not send such a sequence and we ran a test.

The system failed. In order to identify precisely what was going wrong, the technician attached a message display and recording computer to the communication line. It displayed a sequence of messages of precisely the type we had briefly discussed. The technician was surprised that a software developer could state unambiguously under what conditions his software would—and, even more surprisingly, would not—function correctly. But it was really quite easy: I simply looked at the precondition and the loop invariant I had included as a comment in the subprogram in question several years before. I do not know if the analyzer's software was ever modified to eliminate the possibility of sending such a sequence of messages.

"IT WORKED"

A colleague, the manager of a subsidiary of a U.S. computer equipment manufacturer in Europe, asked me to write an extension to their system software that had been requested by one of their larger and more important customers. Officially he should have requested this addition from the company's European software development staff, but he did not trust them to get the new software right and did not want to risk damaging his relationship with this important but very critical and problematic customer. Having seen the results of my work on the medical laboratory system, he asked me to develop this new software, which I did.

When I arrived at my client's offices to install the new software on their machine, they informed me that a new version of the system software had just been installed and that the interface specification had been changed. This necessitated several changes to my new software that I then made. The various preconditions and postconditions I had specified for my various subprograms enabled me to easily trace the effects of the interface modifications and identify which parts of my program would have to be altered and which not. I turned the operational system over to my client's technician, who would install it at their customer's site.

I heard nothing more about the matter for some time. In a telephone conversation with my client about another matter, I asked how their customer liked the new addition. "Fine" was the brief reply. Presuming that one can always do better, and can learn not only from mistakes but also from successes, I asked what in particular the customer liked about the new software. After a few seconds of thoughtful pause, my client replied, "it worked." My loop invariants, preconditions, and postconditions paid off again.

THE AUTHOR'S PLAGUE

Since the early 1980s I have written a number of consulting reports, articles for professional journals, speeches, four books, and a translation of one of them. In these writing endeavors I have used at least six different word-processing systems and versions. Except for the first and simplest one (Scripsit I for the Tandy TRS-80), every one has exhibited software errors that interfered noticeably with my work. More than one generated tables of contents containing a few erroneous page numbers. The error with the worst consequences caused the system to hang up when I copied a passage of text containing certain constructions to the end of the document. Ironically this happened while I was writing a consulting report on the applicability of correctness proofs to certifying software.

The word processor I am using to write this recollection has an annoying but not debilitating habit of occasionally refusing my request to save the document, complaining that it cannot write to the hard disk and suggesting that I check to see if it is write protected. When this happens, I cancel the request and immediately issue it again. So far my second request has always been accepted and carried out. I still hope and dream that someday I will have a word processor that works correctly. I am not sure whether I am just setting high standards or am naive.

Seminar on Developing Error-Free Software in Practice

After experiencing the benefits from using correctness proof ideas, concepts, and techniques, I decided in the mid-1980s to develop and present a seminar on using them in practice. Since then I have presented this seminar over 20 times in Germany, the Netherlands, Denmark, and Great Britain, and even once in Beijing, China, at the request of the Institute for Software of the Academy of Sciences (Academia Sinica).

The reaction to this seminar is, I am convinced, indicative of widespread attitudes and the potential of this material in practical application. Marketing the seminar has been difficult; potential participants appear to be skeptical of the very idea of a mathematically based approach to practical software development, even to the point of complete disbelief. A number of reasons seem to underlie this reaction, but all probably converge on the perceived (more accurately, presumed) difficulty of learning and applying these concepts.

Once the participants come to the seminar, though, the problems largely disappear. They quickly acquire the ability to use these ideas and concepts in group projects, and most recognize the potential applicability of this material. After three days they are reasonably familiar with the material and its informal to semiformal application; however, with only a few exceptions they are not in a position to use it effectively on their own. A supportive work environment and the opportunity to discuss the material with colleagues is necessary, in most cases, in order to realize the potential advantages. Additional guidance and training after accumulating some experience are also helpful.

University Courses

I have taught courses on designing error-free (that is, provably correct) software in universities. At first some had reservations about this approach, but their concerns have essentially disappeared in the last few years. Despite remaining reservations, awareness of this material and its potential applicability to software development work is growing in academia, both among faculty members and students.

But Some Errors in Software Are Commercially Desirable

A participant in one of my seminars recommended to his management that the seminar be offered on an in-house basis during the software house's annual week-long excursion to a foreign country. These excursions combined business and pleasure. Each employee participated in several days of organized seminars and training sessions. Another few days were filled with sightseeing and relaxing at the pool. I was pleased by the acceptance of my seminar that this invitation represented, as well as by the opportunity it provided for me to visit a North African country for the first time.

At our first meeting, the director of this company and I discussed the seminar, its contents, and its relationship with and possible implications for the company's business. He pointed out that although reducing the error rate in their software output was in principle of interest, their goal was not to reduce it to zero. The presence of a few residual errors ensured the opportunity to remain in contact with the customer and, in addition to correcting the errors, to add desirable new features to the programs and to develop new software, that is, to sell follow-on business. Such business was very attractive for several reasons, among them the lower business development costs. As long as their error rate was no higher than that of the competition, there was no real reason to reduce it significantly. It should be emphasized that his attitude should not be construed as irresponsible, simply pragmatic. He was honest enough to express this opinion; I suspect that many other software development managers think this way but would never admit it.

Conclusions

My career in computing began with the course 6.538 in early 1956. Now, 40 years later, it is appropriate, I believe, to reflect on what my experiences during those 40 years mean and what I can conclude from them. The following statements are my personal opinions, but they are carefully considered opinions. To some readers, my opinions may be controversial, but to me they are obvious—and unavoidable—conclusions arising out of my 40 years of experience in computing and software.

First and foremost in my view is that software development can and should be practiced as an engineering field. By "engineering" I mean a field

1. that is based on a mathematical and scientific foundation that enables the designer to calculate (in our case, in a logical rather than a quantitative sense) important characteristics of the artifact he has designed *before* it is built;

2. in which artifacts of value (normally economic) are designed, built, installed, and operated; and

3. whose practitioners take seriously their responsibility to their customers, to society in general, and to themselves.

Clearly, software fulfills criterion (2). A mathematical and scientific foundation for software development exists in the theoretical world, but it has not yet been embraced by the world of practice. Largely because of this, software development practitioners are not in a position to accept the responsibility referred to in criterion (3) as engineers in the traditional fields have long done.

The mathematical and scientific foundation for software development should be used in the design phase, not just for verification. It is both less effective and less efficient to design software in the old way and only then to attempt to verify its correctness formally.

It is apparent from the anecdotes above that I have turned to mathematics many times for help. I have done this for three reasons:

- Mathematics frequently enables me to think effectively about and solve problems I could not have come to grips with in any other way.

- As a student engineer I was conditioned in the true Pavlovian sense to turn to mathematics when working on new or difficult problems.

- The elegance and simplicity of mathematics and the elegance and simplicity that the application of mathematics imparts to the problem in question and its solution can be enjoyed in their own right.

In short, mathematics has been my genie in the wonderful, magical lamp.

In all professional fields a significant gap exists between theory and practice, but it seems to me that this gap is much larger in the software field than in any of the traditional engineering and other professional fields. Two important aspects characterize this gap in the software field: (1) Many practical problems exist for which theoreticians have not sought solutions, and (2) much potentially useful theoretical knowledge exists but has not been put into practice. Both aspects of the gap suggest to me that a different balance is called for between purely theoretical efforts and practical efforts in order to optimize the return on society's investment in computing science research. In my view, society is getting a far lower return on this investment than is possible and than it should expect and demand.

Much better communication between the theoretical community and software development practitioners is required. A necessary precondition for such an improvement is that more members of each group should concern themselves with the results and problems of the other group. In engineering fields, reorganizing, transforming, and consolidating theoretical knowledge into forms facilitating systematic application by practitioners is recognized as a legitimate activity of engineering researchers; in my observation, this is not really true in the software development field. In engineering fields, normal working engineers read technical literature with a distinct mathematical and scientific content and apply such material in their work; from experience, I know that this does not apply nearly as widely to normal working software developers.

We should realign our thinking so that working on uninvestigated or inadequately solved aspects of practically motivated problems is considered worthy of the term "research" and that applying mathematically rigorous techniques in software development and verification in practice is not looked down on as impractical and a waste of time. In short, software theoreticians should not be above communicating with software practitioners in their language and should be willing to adapt the notation, content, and structure of their messages to those practitioners. For their part, practitioners should not be afraid to learn such lessons as that of the loop invariant, from which I gained so much.

Certainly there are practical problems inappropriate for the attention of the researcher, just as there are ways of attempting to apply theoretical knowledge that are hopelessly inefficient and inappropriate in practice. But the fact that examples of inappropriate thrusts into the other area exist does not mean that all possible thrusts must be inappropriate. Expressed more mathematically, $\exists \neq \forall$.

Software developers have, over the years, produced lots of valuable stuff and have exhibited impressive creativity. Furthermore, we have done the hard part of the job well; however, we have often botched, sometimes quite badly, the easier, mechanistic, less creative part of the job: getting our software correct and free of logical errors.

Perhaps the golden key to solving the problem of error-filled software will appear when purchasers of software refuse to accept (and pay for) substandard or erroneous software. Only then will software suppliers be forced to take responsibility for their errors and for the consequences of those errors and to take effective steps to reduce their error rate to levels typical in engineering fields.

6

PURSUING PROGRESS: ACADEMIC/LABORATORY PIONEERS

The history of computing really began in research laboratories in the United States and in Europe—most were in academia, but some were in government and private industry. Considerable research had been conducted in those laboratories before the first software applications, intended to solve real problems for real customers, were actually written. This chapter contains the recollections of some of the pioneers who worked in those laboratories.

The early history of laboratory research into computers and software is best illustrated by the first of this section's software pioneers, John M. Bennett. Bennett's story begins as World War II ends. He is an Australian, and in the late 1940s, as he headed off to England as a graduate student (the first to work under that legend of early computing, Maurice Wilkes), he was caught up in the excitement and magic of this thing called the computer

Bennett's word pictures of that early era are vivid. You can almost smell the formalin from the cadavers formerly stored in what later became the Cambridge University computer room. You are let in on the prank in which the EDSAC computer printed out an April Fool's message to a particularly humorless victim, "Ease up, Ken. I've been working all night. EDSAC." You shiver with the programmers working the night shift in an unheated computer center at the British computer company Ferranti. You suffer with the unreliability of those early computers, so tenuous that adding debugging code to a program could slow it sufficiently to encounter a machine error it had not encountered before the addition. You learn that the SILLIAC computer (an Australian variant of the University of Illinois' ILLIAC) had room to cool a six-pack of beer in its heat exchangers. Truly, the pioneering days of computing were ripe for the adventurer!

Our second laboratory pioneer is Bruce I. Blum. Like Bennett, Blum found his way into the academic laboratory through private industry. (For Bennett it was England's Ferranti; for Blum it was Wolf Research and Development). Like many other pioneers, Blum began in another field, history, and stumbled into computing when Johns Hopkins University misassigned him to the computer center—he had explicitly asked to go into operations research. The shortage of software-skilled people resulted in strange bedfellows in the early days of computing.

Blum's personal stories revolve around the role of the software specification. Early in his career he was asked to produce a specification even though he had never heard of it and had no idea what it was for! Later, when he understood and supported the concept of specification, he could not reconcile his understanding with what he kept running into in practice: "The requirement's inherent fuzziness with respect to real-world needs." As he reached retirement, Blum came to the conclusion that he did not believe in the specification: "I reject its relevance." The details of that personal journey, an odyssey complicated by the deep-seated belief of his computer science colleagues that specifications were a vital and critical part of the construction of software, make Blum's story particularly fascinating. He becomes a contrarian tilting at the windmills of the computer science establishment.

Peter Denning's story tells in-depth his personal experience with the notion of virtual memory, which he calls "One of the great engineering triumphs of the computing age." His story intertwines with those of several other pioneers in this book, each of whom encountered virtual memory or the need for it in a different way.

My favorite part of Denning's story is his "Aha!" episode, when, during Christmas recess from MIT in 1966, he had an insight that led to his discovery and definition of what he called the "working set model," the key notion that allowed the pieces of virtual memory to fit together into a meaningful whole. He concludes his story, in an appendix, with a wonderful fable with the ultimate in shaggy dog endings.

The final pioneer in this chapter is Raymond C. Houghton. Houghton bases his story on his advocacy for the role of tools in software construction. The laboratories where he worked were not in academia, but rather in government: the National Security Agency (NSA) and the National Bureau of Standards (NBS, now the National Institute of Science and Technology, NIST).

Houghton spins several interesting tales:

- How he (mis-)used the early Dartmouth time-sharing system, to do what we would call email today, to communicate with a girlfriend at a distant college.

- How he found himself with four layers of management between himself and the customers for a program he was writing, making it impossible to finish the job he was assigned to do.

- How he was asked by management on a Friday afternoon to revise a design, with a deadline of the following Monday morning. He used the weekend to write his letter of resignation instead.

Here are the stories of these laboratory pioneers.

AUTOBIOGRAPHICAL SNIPPETS

John M. Bennett

INTRODUCTION
AUSTRALIA BEFORE COMPUTERS

At the end of World War II, I found myself with a degree in civil engineering and the experience of four years in Royal Australian Air Force ground radar, which included an excellent radiophysics course organized for the armed services by the University of Sydney School of Physics. As I had been under 21 when I graduated, I was entitled under the Commonwealth Reconstruction Training Scheme (CRTS) to enroll in any university course. In fact, because of my wartime experience, I chose further training in electrical engineering, physics, and mathematics.

As part of this training, I spent several months during the summer of 1946–47 attached for vocation experience to the Electrotechnology Division of the Council for Scientific and Industrial Research (CSIR, now CSIRO, Commonwealth Scientific and Industrial Research Organization). The chief of that division was David Myers, later to become Vice Chancellor of La Trobe University. David Myers was interested in computer development, both analogue and digital (my principal assignment was to cali-

---

This account is based in part on my contribution to *Computing in Australia: the development of a profession,* John M. Bennett et al. (eds), Hale and Iremonger (Sydney), in association with The Australian Computer Society, 1994. No attempt has been made to give technical details of the applications or computers discussed. These are available elsewhere in the literature.

brate a ball-and-disc integrator inherited from the Australian Army artillery where it was part of a gun-laying mechanism).

One member of the division, Ross Blunden, was experimenting with scale-of-ten ring counters as a possible part of an arithmetic unit for a future computer. (Ross eventually became Professor of Traffic Engineering at the University of New South Wales.) At that time, I also met Trevor Pearcey, a member of the CSIR Radiophysics Division, which had been set up primarily for wartime radar development. Pearcey later designed and built CSIRAC, a computer that began operation in 1950.

The typing pool of the Division of Radiophysics was once located in the room that later became my office when the university took over the CSIRO building. My office had the singular distinction of being where opera singer Dame Joan Sutherland, a one-time member of the pool, once typed.

It is interesting that Australia's first significant contact with computing dates back to before World War I. In 1913 a totalizator designed and built in Australia by a West Australian railway engineer (George, later Sir George, Julius) was installed in Auckland (it was designed originally in 1909 as a voting machine). His company (Automatic Totalisators Ltd.) continued as a major supplier of totes, a field that CDC (Control Data Corporation) entered in the late 1960s by providing a computer-based system for Australian off-course betting. Julius was one of the founders of CSIR and its first chairman.

In 1947 I was employed by the Brisbane City Electric Light Company (now part of the South East Queensland Electricity Board). One of my assignments was to carry out with a desk calculator some very repetitive calculations to plan the development of the Brisbane River Valley's power distribution network for the following decade. At that time, purely by chance, I heard a radio talk about the ACE computer being developed at the U.K. National Physical Laboratory (NPL) just outside London.

Here was a tool that would solve my computing problems and many others. The academic institution nearest to NPL of which I had heard was London University's Imperial College. So with the help of an ex-serviceman's research grant, I applied to its Electrical Engineering Department for acceptance as a research student. Fortunately for me, the head of the department, Willis Jackson, passed my application to Douglas Hartree, then chairman of the Cambridge University Mathematical Laboratory governing committee. Hartree arranged for me to become a member of the EDSAC (Electronic Delay Storage Automatic Calculator) team headed by the Laboratory's director, Maurice Wilkes. So I found myself in Cambridge in September 1947 as Wilkes's first research student.

CAMBRIDGE 1947–50

Wilkes had attended a computer summer school at the University of Pennsylvania's Moore School of Electrical Engineering in Philadelphia in 1946, and returned to Cambridge with a clear plan to build a working machine as quickly as possible. The choice of a suitable storage technique was a major problem. This was solved by the adoption of mercury delay lines, using techniques developed at the Admiralty Signals Establishment (ASE) for storing radar traces so that ground echoes could be suppressed by subtracting successive traces.

The suggestion for the use of mercury delay lines was made by Tommy Gold, who had worked at ASE during the war. Gold, who was then a member of the Cavendish Laboratory, later became director of the Center for Radiophysics and Space Research at Cornell University. Bill Renwick, an engineer who had worked on the ASE project and was familiar with the delay line technique, was recruited by Wilkes to the EDSAC team.

EDSAC, which was to become the world's first stored-program electronic computer in regular operational use, was built in part with war surplus valves purchased at an agreed figure per pound weight. The Mathematical Laboratory's professional officer who negotiated the purchases usually managed to return from his buying expeditions with several times the weight of valves that appeared on the invoices, which made him an invaluable member of the team. Most of the input/output equipment (teleprinters and uniselectors onto which the initial orders—now generally referred to as the bootstrap sequence—were wired) were provided by the Cambridge Post Office under a semi-permanent loan arrangement.

It was usual in Cambridge for a research student in his first year to provide cheap labor on a project not necessarily related to his thesis topic, and my case was no exception. In my first year I was responsible for designing, constructing, and testing the main control unit. This unit sequenced the machine through the cycle of extracting from the store and decoding instructions (orders, we called them), extracting operands, initiating individual arithmetical and logical processes, and proceeding to the next instruction. I also designed, constructed, and tested the bootstrap facility.

EDSAC was built in a room on the top floor of a building that was once the dissecting room of the Cambridge University anatomy school. This historical association brought with it an advantage and a disadvantage. The advantage came in the form of a large goods lift that had been designed to carry two cadavers. The disadvantage became apparent in the summer when the formalin (used to preserve the cadavers) that had impregnated the floorboards over the years was vaporized by the heat. The smell of formalin vapor is very penetrating!

The rest of my time at Cambridge was spent learning some mathematics and working on the computerization of various engineering computational procedures for my thesis. I devised one programming technique that was probably a first—the use of an interpretive scheme. (Actually, my *Shorter Oxford English Dictionary* did not recognize the word *interpretive*—only *interpretative*. After my first publication describing the technique, I discovered my error, and, in a later paper, tried to correct it, but too late—the term *interpretive* had been adopted by others. However, the story has a happy ending. Years later, I found that the full *Oxford English Dictionary*, a singularly permissive lexicon, allows the use of either word.)

My reason for using the interpretive technique at that time was to save space in solving a differential equation using the Runge Kutta process. EDSAC had a small store by modern standards (initially 256 36-bit words most—but not all—of the time and no backing store), so every bit was important. Among other uses, I employed interpretive techniques to develop subroutines for the Ferranti Mark 1* on the Ferranti Mark 1 (in 1950) and later while in Sydney to develop a subroutine library on SILLIAC for the Snowy Mountains Authority (SNOCOM) computer. The usual justification for adopting interpretive techniques—because it facilitates the implementation of custom-built languages—was a fortuitous by-product.

Occasionally some contacts on the EDSAC uniselectors holding the bootstrapping sequence would develop an insulating film. We soon found a quick, if empirical, cure: an appropriately aimed carbon tetrachloride stream from the department's fire extinguisher!

I remember an April Fool's day prank from that time. David Wheeler (then a fellow research student and until recently Professor of Computer Science at Cambridge) arranged a surprise for one of our colleagues, Ken Dodds, by inserting one extra hole in the paper tape containing his program. This hole had the effect of transferring control to instructions that had not been cleared from the EDSAC store. We had a problem because the queue to use the machine was particularly long that morning. However, one of us made a grand gesture and surrendered his place to ensure that the doctored program would run before noon, as was required by the April Fool's Day ritual. It worked like a charm. Our EDSAC program printed out: "Ease up Ken, I've been working all night. EDSAC." Our colleague was not amused!

My Ph.D. thesis is entitled "Some Engineering Applications of Digital Computation," and only two of the eight chapters (structural engineering stress analysis with extension to optimal design—commenced in September 1948—and the power engineering load flow problem with extension to the calculation of machine swing curves—commenced in September 1951) strictly conformed to this title. At the time, engineers approached the first of these problems by a method of successive approximations and the second by the use of an analogue machine—a network analyzer. As far as I know, my matrix-based approach in both cases, appropriate to digital computers, was the first time it had been used. This approach is standard today.

MANCHESTER 1950–53

Toward the end of 1950, after taking a close look at other employers, I accepted an offer from Ferranti Ltd in Manchester. Ferranti had won a contract, surely a record for its brevity, to construct a computer "to Professor F. C. Williams' specification" a few days after FC's successful demonstration of the Manchester MADM to Sir Ben Lockspeiser, then the U.K. government's chief scientist. MADM was a development of a test rig for the original Williams CRT store, which began operating in June 1948. One member of the team that had built it was G.E. (Tommy) Thomas, who in due course became chief of the CSIRO Division of Information Technology.

The computing industry was then not as rigidly compartmentalized as it is now, and everything one did was new and exciting. I found myself involved in a potpourri of tasks, including various marketing assignments, machine specification writing, and programming group management.

The Ferranti Mark 1, which was installed at Manchester University in 1951, was the world's first commercially manufactured machine to be delivered and had some strange features. All programming was in scale-of-32, with 0, 1, 2, 3, for example being represented by the corresponding teleprinter characters /, E, @, A; numbers were displayed least-significant digit first. Alan Turing of Turing machine fame (then a reader at Manchester University), who was one of the principal users of the Mark 1, could never understand the problems lesser mortals had with the system, since he held the scale-of-32 multiplication table in teleprinter character form in his head!

The machine had no shift instructions. All shifting was carried out by multiplication by an appropriate power of two. To enable subroutines to be brought down from the drum backing store to any section of the working store, eight registers—called B-lines because they were stored on a CRT placed between the accumulator (A) and the control (C) CRTs—were provided with the intention that they be used as base registers for adjusting subroutine instruction addresses according to a subroutine's position in the working store. They were never used for this purpose but were very useful as index registers.

The Ferranti programming group had access to the university's Mark 1 between midnight and 8 a.m.—if no one else had booked it by 5 p.m. on the previous day. This inconvenient arrangement brought with it two other problems. First, the machine was cooled by air taken into the computer room after passing through a steam heater that heated it to acceptable room temperature. The air was then passed through the machine to remove the heat generated by the components. Since the university stoker went off duty at midnight, by about 2 a.m. the room temperature in winter was that of the outside air. So programmers on the early morning shift in winter had to be well rugged up.

The second problem concerned my attempt to get the company to buy some camp beds so that programmers waiting their turn to use the machine could get some rest. I could never convince our Scottish personnel officer, jealously guarding the company's image (our team was about half male and half female), that she should agree to such a step. Eventually, I solved the problem by the judicious use of petty cash.

Because the coding system of the Mark 1 was something of a sales liability, I was asked to suggest a redesign. My proposals were accepted, and the redesigned machine was marketed as the Mark 1*. An important effect of the change in specification was that it led to a reexamination of many features of the electronic design, with a considerable improvement in reliability—an unexpected benefit.

The construction of the Mark 1* was financed by a guaranteed order from the National Research Development Corporation (NRDC). The order was initially for five machines, which Ferranti, retained by NRDC, sold on commission. This was a convenient arrangement that might well be followed by other government organizations charged with encouraging the development of new technology.

To accelerate program development on the Mark 1, I introduced in 1951 a trace routine and a routine to print out the contents of specified registers in any form required at any point of a program—probably the first use of this latter technique. Unfortunately, the mean time between machine errors was so short that the resulting slowing down of program execution made the use of these tools hazardous for large programs.

Ferranti Ltd had undertaken to display a computer at the 1951 Festival of Britain, and late in 1950 it became evident that this promise could not be fulfilled. I suggested that a machine to play the game of Nim against all comers should be constructed with a versatile display to illustrate the algorithm and programming principles involved. The design was implemented by a Ferranti engineer, Raymond Stuart-Williams, who later joined RCA.

In its simplest form, two players with several piles of, say, matches play the game of Nim. The players move alternately, each removing one or more matches from any one pile. Whoever removes the last match wins. The machine was a great success, but not quite in the way intended, as I discovered during my week as spruiker (showman) at the festival stand. Most of the public were quite happy to gawk at the flashing lights and be impressed. A few took an interest in the algorithm and even persisted to the point of beating the machine at the game. Only occasionally did we receive any evidence that our real message about the basics of programming had been understood.

We were then very concerned with devoting our efforts to outselling other computer manufacturers. We did not realize that a much greater missionary effort was required for industry to accept the radical change of thinking needed for the switch to using computers.

One curious quirk of the U.K. government procurement system is worth recounting. Ferranti machines used punched paper tape, the English Electric DEUCE (then our main competitor) used punched cards. A computer with punched paper tape input bought by a U.K. government department had to be paid for from the department's own budget, but if input was by punched cards, the computer was counted as office machinery and could be bought from Her Majesty's Stationery Office budget. We were told we lost a number of sales to English Electric for this reason.

Virtually every project we undertook at this time was new. Among these might be listed, in addition to the interpretive and diagnostic routines mentioned earlier, various matrix calculations, geodetic survey calculations, actuarial life tables, life insurance policy processing, perspex cutting strategy, and sales records. Of the list of 21 projects of which I have details, four would be classed today as program testing aids, two as clerical calculations, five as operations research, and seven as engineering calculations. Our success in these projects, working under conditions that were far from ideal, speaks highly for the quality and dedication of the team.

SALES

Vivian Bowden (later Lord Bowden of Chesterfield) and Bernard Swann (a statistician) were initially Ferranti's entire sales team. Bowden was a physicist who had taken his Ph.D. under Rutherford at Cambridge's Cavendish Laboratory. One of his first tasks with Ferranti was to integrate the work of a number of contributors into a book, *Faster than Thought*, a collection of computer articles published in 1953 to tell the world how computers came about and what they did. He had been a radar specialist during World War II (heading the IFF V-V Identification Friend or Foe) development team at TRE (Telecommunications Research Establishment) and, with Sir Robert Watson-Watt, had served as a consultant to the U.K. film industry before coming to Ferranti. He was a good showman with a well-developed sense of the serendipitous and a wide circle of contacts in the U.K. and the United States, a useful ally on any sales outing and always an entertaining companion.

Bowden wrote 8 of the 26 chapters in the book, which was first published in 1953. It had 24 contributors (I contributed 3 chapters). The book was well received—in fact, at the time it was effectively the only book on computers available, and much of it still makes good reading today, especially the sections on Babbage and Lady Ada Augusta Lovelace.

On rereading one of my contributions to the book ("Digital Computers and the Engineer"), I was reminded of its anonymous opening quatrain, which is worth repeating:

> Crinkle, crinkle little spar,
> Strained beyond the yield-point far,
> Up above the world so high;
> Boy, I'm glad that I don't fly.

Bowden was provided with much helpful material on Lady Ada by her granddaughter (Lady Wentworth), who owned a stud farm near Gatwick Airport south of London. Lady Ada's grandfather had owned a stud farm, and her daughter (married to the poet Blunt) had imported some fine Arab stud into England. At the time the book was being written, Lady Wentworth (aged 80) had been advised by her medico to stop playing squash after being hit in the eye by a squash ball!

It was typical of Bowden that one day he brought a Dutch calculating prodigy, William Klein, to the "tin hut," the prefabricated building in which the programming group was housed, to demonstrate his skills. The Dutchman's performance was very impressive. Apparently he had a twin brother, Leo (a medico), who, as a member of the resistance, had been killed in the war. They had both been calculating prodigies—but, according to Bowden, one could be upset by flashing lights in his eyes, the other by making bumbling noises!

In 1951 and again in 1953 Bowden crossed the Atlantic with a Ferranti team (including myself), the intention being to convince the Americans that they should buy Ferranti machines. Everyone we talked to was very interested in what we had to say—but of course our equipment suffered from the sales disadvantage that it was not built in the United States. Ferranti did in fact sell a Mark 1 in North America—to the University of Toronto.

Among the Mark 1 and Mark 1* sales in Europe was a machine sold to Royal Dutch Shell—their first computer. The sales negotiations went on for days, and every *i* was dotted, every *t* was crossed. During the process, we were all kept on very short commons. Then, after the contract was signed at 10:30 p.m. on the last evening, we were hosted to one of the best dinners I have ever eaten!

Ferranti sold a Mark 1* to the University of Rome—Italy's first computer—paid for with Marshall Plan money. We had been told of the possibility of a sale by an Italian count who knew that most of the funds allocated to Italy under the Marshall Plan had been spent, so it was said, on an unsuccessful attempt to win a contract to manufacture radar equipment for NATO in Italy. Only sterling was left—just enough to buy our machine! The count certainly earned his 10 percent commission. The computer was sold after three Ferranti representatives (Bowden, Swann, and myself) met the University of Rome's Professor Picone, who asked us two questions through an interpreter. The first was whether we would invert a large (for the time) matrix that was needed for a dam design stress analysis, one of his research projects. We did this. We also pointed out that we could invert larger ones if a magnetic tape unit—not developed at the time, though we did not tell him this—was ordered. It was delivered in due course and worked well! The second question was whether Ferranti would provide practical computer experience for two of his team. The answer was in the affirmative, and I stayed in touch with both of them for many years—Professor Paolo Ercoli (Rome University) and Dr. Sacerdoti, who was Italy's IFIP (International Federation of Information Processing) representative.

One of Bowden's stories will be appreciated by followers of the British TV series *Yes Minister.* As a life peer, Bowden was a member of the House of Lords. At one stage, he became Junior Minister for Air, and of course wanted—using the efforts of his team of civil servants—to make a few changes to the procedures then current. The implementation of his ideas seemed to be taking forever, and one day, while in the departmental toilet, he overheard two of his team discussing him. One complained about the changes Bowden was trying to bring about, and the other replied that, if they did not hurry matters, he would move on before the status quo was altered. This was too much for Bowden—and soon after he resigned.

Bernard Swann was someone from whom I learned much. Many of his words of wisdom have served me well in subsequent years. I remember one occasion on which Bowden was apologizing on the company's behalf for something that had gone wrong. Afterwards, Swann remarked: "Vivian always fires all his guns at once—no ammunition left for the next round." Since then, this counsel has helped me on a number of occasions.

Ferranti's basic problem in the early fifties was that its main turnover was in power transformers, sold to the stable, relatively noncompetitive power industry through a sales department on a 5 percent sales budget. This was the basis of the sales allocation for computer sales—and the programming group, which was counted as part of the sales department, had to be financed from it. As one can imagine, this constraint proved to be a severe limitation on our activities.

LONDON 1953–55

In 1953, I moved to London to join a new group, Ferranti's London Computer Laboratories (LCL). LCL was set up under the leadership of Bill Elliott (who eventually became Professor of Computing at Imperial College) in premises on Manchester Street. These premises, as it turned out, were about 100 yards from the site in Dorset Street that was once occupied by Babbage's house.

Most of Elliott's team at LCL had come with him from Elliott Bros. (no relation) because of the termination of a major Admiralty contract—an excellent mechanism for effective technology transfer, if a little painful for the individuals concerned. This team included Charles Owen, whose plug-in units were such that logical design of complete computers using them could be carried out by non-engineers—a successful approach that eventually produced PEGASUS and PERSEUS for the Ferranti stable. Owen later joined IBM (with Elliott) and was responsible for the design of the 360/30, for which he was awarded an IBM Fellowship.

While with LCL, I proposed several machine designs, three of particular interest—one with a content-addressable store in the context of the analysis of land survey calculations, one for process control, and one for the insurance industry (which eventually saw the light of day as PERSEUS, referred to earlier). During this period I learned the hard way from the market's reaction to new, custom-built designs that no organization likes, in the words of Alexander Pope, to be "the first by whom the new are tried," and much more mileage can be gained with the argument that it is undesirable to be "the last to lay the old aside."

The first PERSEUS was ordered in 1955 (on the basis of a preliminary specification only) by the South African Mutual Insurance company (SAM). I went to Capetown to work out the detailed configuration required for SAM, but before I departed I was mystified by the reasoning that had led to this purchase for a country where labor was so cheap. I discovered that apartheid regulations prevented the employment of nonwhites for clerical duties. Furthermore, black Africans were buying so much insurance that not enough white clerical staff (mainly young women between the ages of 17 and 25, at which stage they were expected to get on with the more important affairs of life) could be recruited to process the paperwork!

The second PERSEUS went to a Swedish insurance company. I remember being told that it paid for itself well before delivery because of the extra policy sales resulting from the publicity the PERSEUS purchase brought with it.

EX-RADAR STORAGE DEVICES

During my period in the U.K., I was fortunate in being associated with three types of storage used originally in connection with radar echo storage during World War II—mercury delay lines with EDSAC, CRT storage with the Ferranti Mark 1, and solid delay lines that were used with PEGASUS and PERSEUS at London Computer Laboratories.

Because of an interest in elasticity deriving from my civil engineering background, I was able to contribute to the development of the last of these devices by pointing out that pulses in solid delay lines (wires) in the torsional mode were dispersion free. This property was put to very good use in memory units designed by Gordon Scarrott, who arranged for torsional impulses to be introduced by magnetostrictive excitation.

BACK IN AUSTRALIA

At the beginning of 1956, I joined Harry Messel's School of

Physics group at the University of Sydney to head the operational side of SILLIAC. I accepted this post (from the beginning of 1956) with some trepidation as Australian university research funding was notoriously meager. At that stage, I had not met Harry Messel.

Messel, a Canadian ex-paratrooper, had come to Sydney in 1952 via the University of Adelaide, having written his Ph.D. thesis on the effects of cosmic rays at the Dublin Institute of Advanced Studies. This is not the place to itemize his achievements while head of the School of Physics (he retired in 1987): these are set out in *The Messel Era*, edited by D. D. Millar, Pergamon (Sydney) 1987. His main achievements include the following.

- Setting up the Nuclear Research Foundation (now the Science Foundation for Physics), which up to his retirement had raised in today's terms over $A100 million for research (this was Australia's first university private foundation: there are now over 40 at Sydney University alone).

- Adding five more research groups to the School of Physics (plasma physics; radio astronomy; optical astronomy; solar energy and environmental physics, which called for a vessel to investigate the social habits of crocodiles in Northern Australia).

- Organizing science schools in most years from 1958 through 1985, attended initially by about 500 teachers (1958–61) and later by over 2,500 school students (1962–85) from Australia and eight other countries.

- Organizing on short notice the writing of a school science textbook for use in New South Wales schools for a new integrated science syllabus;

- Attracting a stream of very able research students, many of whom now occupy chairs and senior positions in industry and government (one of them, now Sir Robert May, has recently been appointed chief scientist to the U.K. government). Several of them have moved to the computer field, to which they have made a number of substantial contributions.

- Most important of all from the point of view of this recollection, arranging for the funding of computers, including SILLIAC and later the English Electric KDF9 (initially for service computing), and making possible the building up of the Basser Computer Science Department. This department in due course was able to offer a full three-year sequence of courses, with an Honours year and post-graduate research and advanced course activities (see the next paragraph). With Messel's support, the department became autonomous (that is, independent of the School of Physics) in 1979. Its service function became a separate entity (no longer associated with the School of Physics) in 1972.

In 1987, at the age of 65, Messel retired as the rules of the day required. However, active as ever, he became the executive chancellor of Bond University, Australia's first private university.

SILLIAC

SILLIAC (the Sydney version of ILLIAC) was based on the design of the University of Illinois Automatic Computer and was built with funds provided by a donor, Adolph (later Sir Adolph) Basser, after whom the Department of Computer Science was named. It had been built by Brian Swire and a team that included Barry de Ferranti (now a senior Sydney IT consultant). (The connection between Barry and the U.K. Ferranti family is through Barry's great great grandfather, who was court musician to King Leopold I of Belgium and was known at the time as the Paganini of the guitar.) SILLIAC was considerably faster than any machine then available commercially.

The individual sections of SILLIAC were constructed under contract by the Sydney firm, Standard Telephone and Cables, so in a sense it was the first computer to be built by Australian industry. Brian Swire and his team later added magnetic tape units of a design that was unusual for the time: they could read and write tapes in either direction. Brian left the computer field in the early 1960s to join the School of Physics Plasma Physics Department, and in 1964 died as the result of an unfortunate electrical accident.

Brian Swire was an unusual engineer in that his interest in the machine did not cease once it became operational. His conscientious pursuit of reports of perceived machine malfunctions was exceptional and often took the form of a hunt for "dry" joints with the aid of a rubber mallet, with which he used to thump the chasses containing the electronic storage CRTs.

SILLIAC began regular operation on July 4, 1956 (appropriately enough for a U.S.-based design) and was officially launched in September with, among other demonstrations, a game of Nim. A few days after the invitations to the launching ceremony at University of Sydney had been sent, we received an invitation to attend the launching of another machine—an English Electric DEUCE (UTECOM)—at the University of New South Wales (then the University of Technology) on the day immediately preceding our launching day!

The game of Nim at the launching ceremony at the University of Sydney went well. However, I had programmed it so that a number of simultaneous games could be played on a time-sharing basis. When the program was first used in this mode, a programming error showed up. This error resulted in the record of one game being altered when changes were being made in the record of a second game being played simultaneously. These changes sometimes occurred when the machine was losing—a phenomenon that one delighted player took to be computerized cheating.

SILLIAC had two heat exchangers, one at each end of the machine. Each had a capacity just sufficient to act as cooler for six bottles of beer—a convenient arrangement that was put to good use. One other curious feature of the hardware was the point-to-point interchassis wiring. Many of these connections were several feet long and a portion of each connecting wire had been made into a helical spring, enabling the wire to be "stretched" so that maintenance engineers could replace otherwise inaccessible vacuum tubes.

The story of the background of SILLIAC is worth repeating. One of the outstanding theoreticians Messel recruited to his staff was John Blatt from the University of Illinois. A graduate from Cornell University, he made his reputation as a nuclear physicist and was co-author with Victor Weisskopf of an authoritative textbook on the subject. Messel rated him as one of the top four theoreticians in the world at the time of his recruitment—an assessment that later events continued to justify. Blatt convinced Messel that an electronic computer had become an indispensable tool for theoretical work. Messel needed little convincing since his own theoretical cosmic ray shower work was producing complex mathematics that begged for a fast computing facility. John had wide American contacts and through his close connection with Paul McDaniel, chairman of the American Atomic Energy Commission, he was able to obtain the blueprints for ILLIAC, the new computer for the AAEC being designed by the University of Illinois.

Brian Swire was sent from the University of Sydney to the University of Illinois to gain experience and on his return the university contracted with the Sydney company Standard Telephones and Cables for the construction of components for SILLIAC. Only one detail was missing: funding. The cost was estimated at £A50,000. Messel went the rounds in a campaign to raise the funds. There was no interest shown by the university nor by business; he was advised in the press by a senior industrialist to stick to his slide rule. The government did not want any part of it, saying that the computer was unnecessary. At this point, he was introduced by a new member of his yet-to-be inaugurated foundation to Adolph Basser, who owned a jewelry store. Basser did not know a thing about computers, but was very impressed with Messel's explanation of their speed, power, and usefulness. He was so impressed that when one of Basser's horses, Delta, won the 1951 Melbourne Cup, he donated the prize money—£A50,000—to Messel's new foundation, on February 12, 1954, at the council meeting of the foundation, just before its inaugural meeting. In any event, the original estimate of SILLIAC's cost was low by £A25,000 and an additional £A25,000 was needed to add a magnetic tape backing store. At the dinner to launch the foundation Adolph Basser doubled his initial gift to cover these items—so his total gift was worth over $A1.5 million in today's currency.

SILLIAC's Successors

SILLIAC's successor was the English Electric KDF9, which was about 35 times faster. The KDF9 was purchased by the university mainly with funds donated in 1962 by Dr. and Mrs. Cecil H. Green (Cecil Green was among the founders of Texas Instruments) and GSI (Geophysical Services Incorporated). A gift from IBM of a 7040 in 1966 facilitated handling IBM-compatible packages—and users developed fierce loyalties to one or other of these two machines, an interesting phenomenon.

The KDF9, which began operating in 1964, had a stack designed to overcome the mismatch between store access time and computing time. This stack permitted the use of addressless instructions and was based on the reverse Polish notation, which came to the notice of the English Electric engineers because it had been embodied in GEORGE, a programming system developed for UTECOM. GEORGE was the work of Charles Hamblin, who until his death in 1985 held the chair of philosophy at the University of New South Wales. Hamblin and I had been members of the same RAAF officer training radiophysics course in 1942.

In the mid-1960s, I arranged for SILLIAC, KDF9, and a small CDC process control machine, the CDC 1700, to be interconnected by a team headed by Chris Wallace (hardware) and John Winings (software) to form one of the world's first local area networks, with interactive input from over a dozen keyboards. One unexpected lesson this interconnection taught us was that, if interconnected computers do not have a common earthing point, damage from lightning can be expensive. Unfortunately for relations between the hardware and software groups, the lightning strike in question occurred immediately after the hardware had been thoroughly tested—and it was quite a problem for the software team to establish why their programs would not work.

In 1967, a PDP8/338 was installed as a practical work adjunct to the graphics teaching module introduced at that time. Between 1974 and 1979, the bulk of the practical work associated with undergraduate courses used the University Computing Center's CDC Cyber 72, and in 1979 the department installed a DEC VAX 11/780 to handle the bulk of this teaching load. In 1985 and 1986, Macintosh laboratories were introduced—for reasons to be discussed in the section on courses.

SERVICE COMPUTING

For about ten years of my computing career (three in Manchester, the rest in Sydney) I was responsible for building up an interface between users and a computer. This role had several functions—apart from satisfying my missionary zeal. It introduced me to a wide range of interesting specialist applications, some of which led to original (joint) publications with the users concerned—applications that otherwise I would have had no incentive to investigate.

From the late 1940s to the early 1960s the service function (i.e., using computers to carry out computing on a service basis) placed much more emphasis on getting answers to real problems, rather than helping users with the details of the latest fashionable languages. It is a pity that today this aspect of service work has been de-emphasized. One effect is that computer science departments are more and more concerned with the mechanics of using computers rather than devising algorithms as tools for solving problems. The use of computers for specialized calculations has been increasingly handed back to specialist departments, e.g., x-ray crystallographic calculations are now handled entirely by chemistry departments. Perhaps this way of introducing students to computers is a measure of the success of the computer science service function in the past. However, it inevitably reduces the amount of cross-fertilization between users.

In order to provide at short notice a demonstration of the usefulness of computers as a teaching tool for school teachers, a colleague, Bruce Chartres, and I cobbled together an interpretive scheme that eased the problems of floating point arithmetic, counting, printing, and so on. The system was called A9 because of the numbering of the sequence of University of Illinois subroutines it used, which finished at A8. It was almost user friendly and caught on in a rather embarrassing way. When the KDF9 was introduced, so many programs had been written in it that it was necessary to supply a special compiler to handle them. Moreover, a similar system was later written for the Australian Post Office NCR machine installed at North Sydney. Strange and lasting loyalties develop in the computer field!

COURSES

The courses we started at Sydney University in 1956 were not part of any degree sequences and there was always a marked falling off in numbers when examinations in credit subjects were scheduled. So in 1959 a formal postgraduate program was introduced—called, on the advice of the Dean of Science of the day (a mathematician), the Diploma in Numerical Analysis and Automatic Computing. The inclusion of "numerical analysis" in the title apparently acted in some cases as an employment disincentive and so the title was later changed to Diploma in Computer Science (with no change in content). One more example of Humpty

Dumpty's dictum: "[A word] means what I choose it to mean, neither more nor less."

My proposals for the overall design of the courses—which were accepted by the faculty—were intended to make the most of the quality of the intake of University of Sydney students—perhaps the highest in the state of New South Wales. The intention was that students intending to make a career in the computer field should have sufficient knowledge of mathematics and available numerical techniques to be capable of handling a variety of industrial problems such as those I had encountered in U.K. industry.

With a long established institution such as the University of Sydney, which has little or no control over its sources of funding and is regarded as being in a no-growth phase, acceptance of a long-term plan involving a substantial redistribution of resources was not likely. However, the existing organizational framework permitted a "little by little" approach, and this was adopted with some success. Of course, every few years, a detailed plan for the future was prepared, usually as part of the triennial planning procedure. Preparing these plans was a sort of ritual that was an excellent catharsis for the soul but otherwise an exercise in futility—because of the unwillingness of the principal funding agency, the Commonwealth government, to earmark funds and the inadequacy of the internal administrative machinery as an instrument of change. However, the system permitted short-term ad hoc adjustments. So, with the help of successive vice chancellors, who provided resources to resolve crises arising from increases in student numbers as they occurred, we did not do too badly.

The basic reason for the department's growth has been student numbers. My personal view is that universities exist for students, and in the long run resources (staff and equipment) should be provided to cater for the student needs, which usually reflect community needs (because of employment opportunities). Failure to respond to this pressure will in the long run result in reduced funding and the establishment of alternative educational institutions—a process that has already happened once in Australia with the establishment of colleges of advanced education and seems likely to repeat with an expansion of private universities.

A plausible motivation for the founding of at least one of the medieval universities (the University of Bologna) is that the copying processes of the monastic scriptoria were so costly (it is said that a year's salary of a professor of the day would buy only two legal or four medical text books) that students found it expedient to employ lecturers to dictate manuscripts to them. If the lecturers did not perform as desired, they would be fired by the students. In due course, the lecturers, with longer term associations with the organization than with the students, inevitably came to control the organization, and it was the students who were fired if they did not perform. (However, it is still not unusual for students to take notes dictated by lecturers.)

In our case, a computer science stream in the Physics Honours year was introduced as a first step towards an undergraduate sequence. Then with the expansion of the field and growing student demand a third-year course was introduced, followed in 1975 by a second-year course, and finally in 1978 by a first-year course, thereby completing a full undergraduate computer science sequence. In addition, private funding made it possible to attract for a term each year an overseas visitor specializing in some aspect of management data processing. A short course for industry starring the visitor for which a substantial charge was made helped to top up the fund.

We offered a number of optional in-depth units for our better (honours) students in their final year. Some of these—such as graphics, networking, and security (cryptography)—were popular and still continue, but one exception is worth mentioning. In the hope that some of these students might help introduce robotics into Australian manufacturing industry, one of these courses was on robotics. However, in the long run there was not sufficient staff interest to continue with it in the Computer Science Department after my retirement. All was not lost, however, as it had been attended by students from the Mechanical Engineering Department, which took it over, robot and all.

At the university's request, in 1985 we introduced a short introductory course entitled General Computing Studies. The practical work for this course was serviced by an Apple Macintosh laboratory, and the following year, with this precedent, three similar laboratories were introduced for our first-year course.

Apart from my Australian Computer Society, International Federation for Information Processing and International Council for Computer Communications activities, and various University of Sydney and consulting assignments, perhaps the most significant contribution to building up the computing profession in

Australia with which I (together with other staff members) was associated was the number of graduates from the Basser Department of Computer Science at the University of Sydney, which I headed until I retired (at the end of 1986). By that time about 2,000 students had completed the program, and an additional 4,000 students from all disciplines had completed introductory courses offered by the department. For comparison, the Graduate Careers Council of Australia's estimate of the total number of computer science majors choosing computing as a career up to and including 1986, was about 4,000 from universities and 2,000 from Colleges of Advanced Education. (These technical institutes have now been upgraded to university status.) In addition, in 1986, six holders of computer science professorships in Australia and New Zealand had come from our department. Furthermore, our 1986 enrollment of honours and Ph.D. students was the highest in Australia.

Initially, my own teaching activities emphasized programming, logical design, and numerical techniques. As the staff numbers increased, the first two topics were taken over by other staff members, and my own offerings were confined to numerical techniques and a lecture series with the title "Computing Milieu." This series consisted of a broad overview of trends in design and use of computers, with emphasis on economic data and the organization of the IT industry. In such a fast moving field, keeping the course up-to-date took more of my time than I had bargained for.

We encountered difficulty convincing the university administration of our need for funding for tutor demonstrators for tutorials and practical work. The administration viewed computer science as having funding needs similar to mathematics, instead of physics or chemistry, as we argued. In the end, an argument based on equating expenditures on computing equipment (particularly terminals) with laboratory expenditure for equipment for science departments with practical classes won the day. We were at last given sufficient funding for demonstrators to help students with their practical work difficulties.

SABBATICAL LEAVES AND RETIREMENT

The pattern of Australian academic life provides for one period of sabbatical leave every seven years. I took my first three leaves in London (ICL, London Computing Centre, and London School of

Economics) and the last in Stanford. For the first three of these, I took on specific assignments, such as giving lecture courses similar to the ones I had offered in Sydney. However, the Stanford leave (on a Fulbright Fellowship) was by far the most effective. I had no lecture or consulting commitments, and so I had time to think. A paper exploiting structure in linear programming calculations was the result.

After retiring in 1986, I made myself useful as part of a small consulting group—an activity that faded eventually, possibly because the group put too little effort into selling its expertise. I also spent about half a year at the University of Singapore (1988–89), where the Department of Information Systems and Computer Science was headed by an erstwhile Basser Computer Science Department research student, Chung Yuen. I offered a course on numerical algorithms—which I had also been giving as a post-retirement honours option course at Basser.

Shortly before my retirement, with the support of a group from industry, I was instrumental in setting up the Research Foundation for Information Technology (RFIT) at the University of Sydney. RFIT continues to hold regular luncheon meetings, and is a source of funding for the department.

RESEARCH INTERESTS

It is interesting to look back over my list of publications, technical and semi-technical, and reflect on the proportion that represented novel technical ideas at the time. By my count, these include 32 embodying computational techniques, 13 concerning software techniques, and 5 describing architectural proposals. As the years went by an increasingly high proportion of the papers I wrote described trends and social effects of computers, a typical title being: "The Future Impact of the Computer on Commerce, Education and Society."

COMPUTING SOCIETIES IN AUSTRALIA

In 1957, a group of us discussed the need for a professional computing society and decided that, although it would be premature at that stage to set up such a society, we nevertheless needed a mechanism for organizing regular computer conferences. So, with the help of the Institution of Engineers Australia (with David Myers as president), an organization called the Australian National Committee on Computation and Automatic Control (ANCCAC) was inaugurated in 1958, with myself as founding Chairman.

ANCCAC consisted initially of eight professional societies, and three other societies were later admitted. Its primary function was to organize triennial conferences; the first conference was in 1960, with 150 papers delivered to 650 attendees. The member societies acted as guarantors against losses—which in any event never occured.

State computer societies were formed in Victoria and New South Wales, and both of these societies became members of ANCCAC. I was President of the New South Wales society in 1965 and assisted with negotiations to form a joint society among the five state societies that existed at that time: South Australia, founded 1960; Victoria, founded 1961; Queensland, founded 1962; New South Wales, founded 1963; and ACT, founded 1965. As a result, the Australian Computer Society came into existence on January 1, 1966; I was elected the foundation president.

ANCCAC continued in existence as the nominal organizer of the triennial conferences (with ACS as its agent), and in March 1969 it was dissolved and its funds were transferred to ACS to support an annual award.

The five merging societies became branches of ACS. Since its formation ACS has organized regular conferences and its branches have held regular meetings (mainly monthly). It publishes a journal (*Australian Computer Journal*) and newsletters and has the usual range of professional activities, such as training courses and special interest groups.

INTERNATIONAL COMPUTER BODIES

ANCCAC was admitted to IFIP in 1962—soon after IFIP's formation. I was the ANCCAC IFIP representative in 1962–63 and became ACS representative on its admission to IFIP after ANCCAC was dissolved. I continued in that role until 1980 and served as IFIP Vice President from 1975 to 1977.

The main IFIP event to which I contributed was the 1980 IFIP Congress, held partly in Tokyo and partly in Melbourne. It was attended by about 5,000 registrants, although the number attending both halves of the conference was only about 350. The main interests of Japanese and Australian delegates were such that when representatives of each of the two countries selected sessions of most interest only one session had to be repeated in both countries.

I was elected a Governor of the International Council for Computer Communication (ICCC) in 1980 and served as Secretary General from 1983 to 1993. In this role, I played a major role in reorganizing the ICCC by-laws and in organizing several ICCC conferences.

OTHER ACTIVITIES

During my career I was a member of 12 international computer conference organizing committees, and I served as expert adviser to two Commonwealth government committees and was a member of two others. Because of my contribution to information technology, I was elected a Fellow of the Australian Academy of Technological Sciences and Engineering in 1981 and was chairman of the New South Wales Division in 1989–90. As a member of various non-IT committees I often presented IT points of view—although my membership on these committees was usually for quite other reasons.

THE MARKET

The effects of the changing nature of the computer market have received little attention in computing literature. Until about fifteen years ago, a surprising number of promising companies that at one time were leaders in their non-computing fields, entered the computer field—companies involved in electrical engineering, defense electronics, and even catering (J. Lyons & Co). Their computer activities went by the board as a result of mergers or takeovers, not because of a dearth of technical expertise in software or hardware or manufacturing. Why, then, did this occur?

The answer is that the data processing market of the 1940s, supplied by companies such as IBM in the United States and BTM (now ICL) in the U.K., consisted mainly of middle-sized firms.

Customer loyalty and the feeling that it was safer to stay with the supplier of one's current equipment made it extremely difficult for newcomers to break in to the market. So it is not surprising that irrespective of the technical attractions of their equipment and software, newcomers one by one failed to survive.

In the 1960s and 1970s in the U.K., the process of merging was encouraged by the government on the grounds that it was necessary to create a British entity strong enough to withstand U.S. competition. The creation of this entity, ICL, had the unfortunate effect of making it easier for Fujitsu to take over the whole of the U.K. computer industry in the 1990s. Shades of Alexander the Great's takeover of the Persian Empire!

However, with lowered prices, computers are now within reach of the home user and so the market is increasingly dominated by personal computer users. With the de facto standardization introduced by Intel microprocessors on which so many of today's PCs are based and the resulting interchangeability of IBM compatible software packages, both software and hardware purchases for the home have become commonplace and are even sure-fire conversational topics at suburban cocktail parties. So it is not surprising that, with the changed market, suppliers who used to dominate the market before the 1980s no longer do so. It is so much easier now for new suppliers to get into the market. For many of us whose careers started with new vendors offering equipment directed toward the pre-1960 market, it is a matter of regret that the home user market was not opening up 40 years ago! Entry to the market by newcomers would have been so much easier then.

A PERSPECTIVE

What major differences would I single out for special mention between the practices of 1950 and current practices? First, the constraints of reliability have been almost entirely removed—though this change carries with it the danger that when an error does occur, recovery can be a costly business. Second, limitations of working store size are now rarely a problem. Third, the separation between the user and the hardware-software interface has widened to the extent that accurate speed estimating for contract tendering is now a rare skill. And finally, networking—locally and worldwide—makes cooperation with someone half a world away a standard process. These are significant accomplishments. However, a major cost for most large new software projects—identifying the problem—has changed little, if at all. Nor has getting the software right, irrespective of the language used—though formal methods for specification checking (such as the language 001) are perhaps the most promising development on the horizon.

CLOSING THE CIRCLE

Bruce I. Blum

PORTRAIT OF THE PROGRAMMER AS A MIDDLE-AGED PERSON

It was 1961, I had just turned 30, and my wife told me she was pregnant with our second child. I had to get a real job. I had been working toward a Ph.D. in history and was, at the time, teaching public school and taking courses in mathematics so I could work toward a Ph.D. in mathematics. Not the kind of work suitable for a father of two. So I became serious.

A brief reminder about the early 1960s. Computers were coming out of their "giant brain" stage and invading our lives in the form of bills and tags we were warned not to "bend, mutilate, or spindle." My grandson does not even know what a spindle is. But back then I was not aware of computers. By today's standards, the technology was relatively primitive. During my job interview process, I received my first long distance telephone call from California (to New Jersey)! It was the talk of the neighborhood. I also took my first airplane flight (the seats were leather). What a brave new world I was entering.

The interviews paid off, and I was offered a real job. In June, 1962, I started at the Johns Hopkins University Applied Physics Laboratory (APL). When interviewed, I was given a choice between operations research and programming, and I chose OR.

Some of the material contained here first appeared in Bruce I. Blum, *Beyond Programming, To a New Era of Design*, University of Oxford Press, Oxford, 1996.

Of course, when I reported for work, I was assigned to the Computer Center. (The more things change, the more they stay the same.) I was taught FORTRAN II, assembly language, and the use of the APL version of the Share Operating System (APLSOS, pronounced applesauce).

Behind the big glass window was an IBM 7090 (later upgraded to a 7094) and a 1401 (later 1410). The 1410 was used to transfer data from punched cards to magnetic tape and from magnetic tape to the printer. APLSOS read the input tapes, managed priority by sorting the inputs, ran the jobs one-at-a-time until they completed (or an operator sensed a loop), and produced and sorted the output tapes. All programs and data were managed as decks of punched cards, and we learned octal so we could read the ever-present dumps. Turnaround gave us two to three runs a day, and the system was sufficiently erratic to justify rerunning a program when we could not find the problem ("maybe it will run this time," was a constant lament).

From the perspective of the 1990s, this was a very undisciplined approach; a clear cry for the software engineering that would come some 15 years later. But there was also a social context. Programmers were hard to find, and knowledge of this particular skill defined a profession. It was easy to find a new job that would pay 10 percent more than one's present position, and many followed this stairway to success until they experienced the Peter Principle (that is, they exceeded their level of competence). Nevertheless, I was content to stay at APL and learn my trade.

My first assignments involved mathematical applications. There were no specifications; the programmer served as a guru interface between the users and the computer. They told us what they wanted, we disappeared for a while, showed them our results, they disappeared for a while, and we iterated. Then I began to work with scientific databases using magnetic tape as the archive. Eventually mass storage was introduced, but it remained expensive. Typical of our technological approach, the mass storage first was appropriated for Computer Center use. The punched cards were replaced by on-line files—a revolution that frightened all of us. We were stuck with virtual card decks that we could not hold or store (or drop). Eventually, confidence grew, costs fell, and some random access memory was even made available for data. Still, we continued to design programs around serial files (virtual magnetic tapes).

After five years, I had learned to program, debug, and design information applications. It now was time for me to take my 10 percent salary increase and move on. I went to Wolf Research and Development where (under contract) I became the chief analyst for NASA's National Space Science Data Center (NSSDC). I still had never seen or heard of a specification, but I agreed to build a system to maintain and manage the processed space science data deposited by NASA's investigators. I designed some systems and gave rather detailed instructions to my small staff. I remember how they rebelled: I was giving them too much detail and taking all the fun out of programming. I do not remember how we worked it out, but we did end up with a good system.

Upon renewal, the NSSDC contract went to another bidder. I turned down the 10 percent salary increment offered by the winning contractor and elected to stay with Wolf. Soon we were invited by GE to join a team to bid on the Earth Resources Technology Satellite (ERTS, later renamed Landsat). The team won, and as Wolf's program manager I was responsible for developing the Ground Data Handling System. When I asked my GE contact how we should begin, he told me to have our team work on the specs. Here we were in the 1970s, and I still did not know what a spec was. But this was a cost-plus contract, and I knew that in order to get overhead and fee, we had to have people working on the contract. So I told the staff to start thinking about the programs. What a management style!

Bottom line, ERTS was a success, launched on time, and was supported by an effective Ground Data Handling System. I am sure that the software could have been implemented better; certainly, our documentation was massive, naive, and generally useless. Yet, as casual as we were, our software was neither better nor worse than that of the other team members. In any event, the ERTS project had come to an end, and a large team of programmers needed new assignments. Wolf was too small to manage the strain of peaks and valleys, and I now found myself a vice president charged with finding new work for my dwindling staff.

By now it should be clear that I am good at design, reasonable at implementation, and awful (that is, average) at management. So I left Wolf and went to a large aerospace contractor who had a U.S. Navy command and control contract. (No 10 percent pay increase this time; they promised I would design and not manage.) As it turned out, I was not the only one who knew nothing about U.S. Navy command and control. After a horrible year, I returned to APL (taking a 10 percent salary cut just so I could have peace of mind).

It was now 1974, and I had seen how two of the big guys did it. I also knew how a casual approach could lead to success. I had learned how to draw up a plan, to talk the talk, but not yet how to walk the walk. That is, I was a good presenter, but not a true believer. About this time, I also started to write papers, give talks, and travel to exotic places. (I gave this kind of fun a positive spin by calling it, "making my contribution.") I started working with a friend at APL on a large project in a planning and coordination role. The team was building one of the first systems to merge multiple radar tracks to produce an integrated and automated tracking system. This assignment had so many uncertainties that specifications were unfeasible; I was at home. Eventually, the project became a huge success, and the systems were deployed under the name ANS/SYS-1.

After I made my modest contributions and before the project was finished, I was offered an opportunity to do some work at the Johns Hopkins School of Medicine. APL made a small grant available to "show" the medical school how to use computers in helping patient care. The resultant Minirecord system retained a summary medical record on patients in one clinic. The system ran in batch mode on APL's computer, and a courier delivered the results to the Baltimore campus once a day. Given that the patients had scheduled visits, this was a workable approach, and the system gained acceptance.

When the director of Clinical Information Systems left for the University of California, I was asked to take his place. Thus began a seven-year interdivisional assignment to the School of Medicine. Soon after I started, I was asked to help the Oncology Center meet its computer needs. There was to be a new facility, and a very advanced clinical information system was needed. I began with a prototype in 1976 that ran in batch mode on APL's computer, moved up to a minicomputer the next year, and in 1980 began the design of the two-computer system that remains the heart of the present networked system.

As will be pointed out, the Oncology Clinical Information System (OCIS) had a critical impact on my software thinking. But before I go into that, let me provide a snapshot of computing in the late 1970s. Interactive computing and mass storage was now readily available but still very expensive. Because we could not afford a mainframe, we chose a PDP-11. It had 256K words of memory and some 50MB of hard disk space. We selected MUMPS-11 as the operating system and language because it was used in many medical applications (the "M" stood for "Massachusetts General Hospital"), it had powerful data access tools, it facilitated text manipulation, and it provided interactive support to the 12 terminals we could afford to buy.

There was not much experience in how to use computers in medicine at the time. In fact, in the mid-1970s, the half-life of a system was equal to the publication cycle. Thus, by the time one read about a system, the chances were 50–50 that the system was no longer in use. We were successful, however, and there seemed to be some interest in what we were doing. My department chairs gave me support to become active within the medical informatics community, and I also was allowed to attend and present at software conferences. In time, the Oncology computers were upgraded, new systems were implemented at Hopkins (for example, the Minirecord system became Emergency Room Core Record system), and our experience with clinical applications grew.

By 1983 I decided that medical informatics was maturing and that there were a number of young physicians who could make contributions I could never hope to match. I therefore decided to apply my experience with OCIS in the domain of software engineering. I returned to APL and ended up in the Research Center where I was supported by research grants until my retirement. (If it's research money, it must be research, no?)

PORTRAIT OF THE SOFTWARE ENGINEERING RESEARCHER AS AN OLDER PERSON

In the mid-1980s, software engineering still was wedded to the waterfall diagram. Sure, people joked about it, made fun of the approach, and sometimes even offered alternatives. But everyone seemed to agree that one first had to specify what was to be done; only then could we write programs that would be correct with respect to the specification. I found myself torn between two camps. On the one hand, even if I never wrote a real spec in my life, I bought into the essential role of specifications. Yet, on the other hand, how were we to specify what a system like OCIS was to do? Its "requirement" was "to use computers to improve the management and care of cancer patients." There was no clue as to how this should be done or how we might establish "correctness." Thus, I was plagued by the tension between the widespread acceptance of the requirement for a requirements specification and the requirement's inherent fuzziness with respect to the real-world needs. Resolving this tension was to become the central theme of my subsequent research.

This statement of the problem was not clear to me at the time, and I initially focused on programming productivity. Recall that the first PDP-11 version of OCIS was written in MUMPS-11. By the time we could afford a two-computer configuration that could support round-the-clock operations, MUMPS-11 had been replaced by Standard MUMPS (now called M). My options were to translate the MUMPS-11 programs, reprogram the entire OCIS, or do something else. The something else evolved into the development environment I called TEDIUM (a registered trademark of Tedious Enterprises, Inc.).

TEDIUM was motivated by the fact that the OCIS developers were spending a great deal of time on mechanical programming activities such as testing inputs for validity, writing help messages, formatting reports and screens, and so on. Moreover, they were not doing a very good job of these routine activities. The external formats were inconsistent, and the programs had errors of omission and commission. Thus, TEDIUM's initial task was to provide a program generator that allowed the designers to write a "minimal specification" describing only what is to be done; from this "specification" the environment could generate a complete program with all the checks, standards, and conventions included. TEDIUM worked, and productivity was improved by a factor of from 4 to 20, depending on the application.

When I reported my results, what was the computer scientists' response? "Uh huh, but we are working on some *really* difficult problems, not just simple information system applications." (Then they would use the patient-monitoring toy problem to show me the complexity of their approach.) The database people had no interest because they already had a solution at hand: SQL. And the object-oriented-anything crowd refused to believe that there was still a problem. People had their favorite technologies, and they rejected problems that would not match their solutions.

Brooks wrote a paper observing that the design problem is inherently a human and not a technological concern and therefore not subject to resolution by means of a "silver bullet." It was followed by a host of papers describing technological "silver-bullet solutions."

And so here I was: a well-paid researcher with solid backing working in a new area and destroying forests for publications that no one seemed to read or respond to. In retrospect, being ignored was the best thing that happened to me. It forced me to continue to explore and rethink what I was doing and what I wanted to say. Because I had access to the OCIS project data, I performed periodic analyses. For example, in the last (1994) analysis, I found that a million-line system was being supported by a staff of six who added functionality by increasing the system's system size by 10 percent each year. Productivity over a 14-year period averaged a production program for each effort day devoted to the project. Examination of the maintenance data showed that half the program changes were made by someone other than the original programmer. I also found that the system was deeply integrated, both structurally and temporally. In a 13-month period, about half the programs were either added, edited, or in some other way affected. Moreover, a large percentage of the programs were altered to integrate improvements installed two or more years after the program's initial implementation.

The effect of these various analyses was to make me reconsider the underlying assumptions regarding what we were doing when we developed software systems. OCIS was a large application, supporting some 400 terminals, used in making life-threatening decisions, and perceived to be reliable and error free. Yet it was maintained by a staff of six who altered half the programs in one 13-month period. Was this a project in real trouble (a conventional interpretation of such data) or a project that was using modern and more effective techniques (my view)? Which raised a bigger question: Is the model that we have traditionally used for software development appropriate? Indeed, is there some essential software process that is common to all software processes, and, if so, do the tools we use distort the actual process with respect to this essential process?

In time I came to recognize that there is an essential software process. It begins with the identification of a need and concludes with the delivery of a software product that responds to that need.

Different implementations of this essential process employ alternative techniques for describing the need and the response to it. In the traditional (waterfall) model, there is a two-step process. First one defines the requirements, then one creates an implementation that satisfies those requirements. Step one fixes the problem and its solution; step two implements that fixed solution. This is our time-honored approach to building hardware. But software is not hardware. Its problems are not fixed, and there is no technical reason for insisting on a fixed solution before implementation begins. Software development need not fit the architectural approach of first developing plans and then building according to those plans. By exploiting the unique properties of software it is possible to employ the sculptor's method of working with the materials to achieve the desired results—TEDIUM's "system sculpture."

With TEDIUM, the specifications are maintained on-line in the form of fragments (similar to the concept of chunks in a model of human memory). These fragments are managed independently at various levels of granularity, and they are self-organizing in the creation of larger fragments. The TEDIUM generator transforms the fragments into production-quality programs. These programs are then exercised, and when they exhibit the desired behavior, they are available for production installation. (This is system sculpture.) The operational system is frozen, and the evolution of the next version (or increment) of the system commences. Fragments are added, edited, and removed; programs are generated and tested; and the environment permits the designers to navigate through the system's up-to-date, comprehensive, holistic specification.

With TEDIUM there are no concepts of modules or files. Its fragment-based specification has no apparent structure. This approach to specifying is difficult to convey because we are accustomed to hierarchical presentations employing modularization. But modules (and hierarchies) are rare in nature. We introduce them to control complexity; in the process, however, they introduce their own, artificial level of complexity. Gradually I came to recognize the distortions introduced by modules, and my focus shifted from productivity (that is, generating many program lines from compact specifications) to representation (that is, specifying what we want the system to do as opposed to how it should be organized and implemented). I concluded that if we could

express what we want the system to do and automatically transform that expression into an implementation, a very different software process would emerge. To shift the process paradigm closer to the essential model, I needed a representation scheme free of the constraints of modules (and files) that would facilitate the specification of software solutions to real-world problems; I also required a method for automatically transforming descriptive specifications into implementation code.

In 1992 I decided that I would take these ideas and incorporate them into an upgraded version of TEDIUM that would be completed in five to seven years. A year later I concluded that even if I finished a revised version of TEDIUM, no one would care or learn from it. So I decided to write a book and drop out. I retired in late 1994 and finished *Beyond Programming* (Oxford University Press) some time afterward. The book contains my understanding of how software will be developed in the next century. The subtitle is *To a New Era of Design*, and its theme is that whereas we develop software today as if it were hardware (that is, in a two-step architectural process), in the next century we will be developing hardware as if it were software (that is, in a one-step sculpting process). Having explained that, there was not much more to say, and so I decided to stop talking about software. (*My Software Engineering: A Holistic View* describes how to develop applications using today's technology, and there are books on TEDIUM and OCIS. Thus, I have had a wonderful opportunity to get my licks in; I leave the assessment to the reader.)

What a strange essay. Is it about me, the changing technology of computing, or my views of software engineering and system design? I used the title "Closing the Circle" to suggest three overlapping concepts. First, there is the sense of closure with respect to our historic understanding of computing and how we match the development tools to the computer's capabilities. When I started in the field, the potential of computing was not yet clear, and programmers acted as the agents for satisfying the users' needs. Many of the first applications could be specified formally (for example, a mathematical formula or a report format); because the specification reduced ambiguity and facilitated communications within a large group, it became the logical first step in the process. The essential role of the programmer was a response to the limitations of the early technology. Today, the technology has improved, and users can purchase many of the necessary tools and often bypass programming altogether. But the off-the-shelf approach can satisfy only a small portion of the actual needs.

We still need complete, one-of-a-kind, integrated systems, and we will probably always need designers who can interface between the system's users and the equipment that will run the system. Are we developing the environments that designers will need to meet the demands of the future applications? I find little evidence that we are. In fact, we continue to treat the challenge of system development as if it were a variation of the initial programming problem. We still begin by defining a requirements specification, and we emphasize "getting it right the first time." Yet in most cases there really are no requirements; most of the problems are open. Open in the sense of not knowing what we need; open in the sense of changing once we install a new application; open in the sense of always evolving. Thus, to close this historic circle, we must shift to development environments that match the kinds of integrated, open problems that we now confront. Such a technology must be to the design problems of the twenty-first century what programming was to the relatively well-understood design problems of our earlier computer applications. *Beyond Programming*, of course, shares my speculation regarding what such a technology might be.

A second sense of closing the circle relates to the process of system design. This process begins with a need and concludes with a system response to that need. The need usually is dynamic, and the response is seldom completely satisfied. Thus, each circle is really an iteration within a continuing spiral. Notice that the response is defined by the need. Unfortunately, a misinterpreted need will not generate a satisfactory response; that is, an invalid requirement produces an invalid solution. This is as true for software engineering as it is for application development. Consequently, if we seek solutions to the wrong software engineering problems, we impose a ceiling on the potential benefits of our efforts. In my view, the current context of computer science is biased by the difficulties inherent in the earlier technology. I believe that most of the present research will not be relevant to the primary concerns of the next century. If this is true, we should first determine the kinds of software problems that we will confront in the coming decades and then define a computer science for responding to those problems. The present computer science, with its emphasis on programming-like notations, does not seem to me to be attacking the appropriate issues. A very strong statement, and the reader knows where to find the details of my argument.

Finally, there is a personal sense of closing the circle. I began my career not knowing what a specification was and feeling that it was most important to do what the user needed. I went through a period where I confused the management of a project with the problem solving that goes on within that project. For project management, the waterfall model offers an effective organizing structure; however, it is a very imperfect model of human cognition. Once I recognized this distinction, I realized that we must investigate the essential conduct of the design process independent of the means we use to manage it. I shifted to the *as-built* specification in which the specification describes what the current system design does, not what it ought to do (that is, the traditional *build-to* specification). And so the circle closes. I now know what a specification is, but I reject its relevance. A specification should evolve with the system, and it should provide an accurate description of the system's present behavior. We should never place much importance to a system design created when the designers have their poorest understanding of the problems to be solved (that is, when they write a traditional requirements specification).

So there you have it. Thirty-two years of computing from the post-giant-brain era to the pre-everyone-uses-TEDIUM era. This has been a very personal interpretation, and my understanding is not shared by many. Although I have no uncertainty regarding my conclusions, I do acknowledge that the rest of the world may be wrong—thereby failing to recognize the wisdom of my analysis. One thing we all can agree on, however, is that the technological advance has been remarkable. We have gone from the 7090 with its 64K words of memory to the PDP-11 with its 256K words of memory to my word-processor/TEDIUM-development-environment/grandchildren's-game-machine with its 16MB of memory. Success has opened new categories of problems that were inconceivable only three decades ago. These new problems demand new solutions along with new tools to support the creation and evolution of those solutions. There are exciting times ahead. But I have retired from the fray. Good luck to those of you who continue to battle for truth, justice, and simple common sense!

BEFORE MEMORY WAS VIRTUAL

Peter J. Denning

Virtual memory, long a standard feature of nearly every operating system and computer chip, is now invading the Internet through the World Wide Web. Once the subject of intense controversy, virtual memory has become so ordinary that few people think much about it. That this has happened is one of the engineering triumphs of the computer age.

Virtual memory is the simulation of a storage space so large that programmers do not need to rewrite programs, and authors do not need to rewrite documents, when the content of a program module, the capacity of a local memory, or the configuration of a network changes. The name, borrowed from optics, recalls the virtual images formed in mirrors and lenses—images that are not there but behave is if they were. The story of virtual memory, from the Atlas Computer at the University of Manchester in the 1950s to the multicomputers and World Wide Web of the 1990s, is not simply a story of automatic storage allocation, it is a story of machines helping programmers with protection of information, reuse and sharing of objects, and linking of program components.

In what follows, I will give an account of the history of virtual memory, including personal recollections of the events I witnessed and experienced. These recollections will make up a kind of photo album of technical snapshots of virtual memory from birth, through adolescence, to maturity. From these snapshots you will see that the real driver was the quest for a good programming environment; automatic storage allocation was actually a secondary concern. You will see that virtual memory's designers had deep insights about modularity, sharing, reuse, and objects a long time ago, a fact that may surprise some younger members of the

250

field. Without those insights, virtual memory would never have passed its adolescence.

I was a graduate student at MIT Project MAC during 1964–68, a time of intense debate on the principles to be incorporated into Multics, principles that would make a permanent imprint on operating systems. Automatic storage allocation and management of multiprogramming were high on the agenda. I contributed the working-set model for program behavior. The model generated a practical theory for measuring a program's dynamic memory demand and building an automatic control system that would schedule processor and memory for optimum throughput and response time. I also contributed a unified picture of virtual memory that helped to settle the controversies surrounding it.

PROGRAMMING WITH MEMORY HIERARCHIES

From their beginnings in the 1940s, electronic computers had two-level storage systems. In the 1950s, main memory was magnetic cores (today it is RAMs); the secondary memory was magnetic drums (today it is disks). The processor (CPU) could address only the main memory. A major part of a programmer's job was to devise a good way to divide a program into blocks and to schedule their moves between the levels. The blocks were called "segments" or "pages" and the movement operations "overlays" or "swaps." The designers of the first operating systems in the 1950s dreamed of relieving the programming burden by automating all this storage management.

It is easy to see how the programmer's job is significantly affected by a memory hierarchy. Consider matrix multiplication. If you create a matrix multiply algorithm straight from the definition in the textbook, you will create a program with three nested loops covering six lines of text. This program becomes *much* more complicated if you cannot fit the three matrices in main memory at the same time: you have to decide which rows or columns of which matrices you can accommodate in the space available, create a strategy for moving them into main memory, and implement that strategy by inserting additional statements into the program. You will come to several conclusions from the exercise: (1) devising an overlay strategy is time consuming, in this example more than programming the guts of the algorithm; (2) the overlay strategy depends on the amount of memory you assume is available; and (3) the size of the program increases by a factor of two or three. Many programmers reached the same conclusions for other programs that would not fit into the main memory.

Designers of operating systems in the early 1960s knew that automatic storage allocation could significantly simplify programming. The first operating system design group to accomplish this was the Atlas team at the University of Manchester who, by 1959, had produced the first working prototype of a virtual memory.[1] They called it *one-level storage system.*. At the heart of their idea was a radical innovation—a distinction between "address" and "memory location." It led them to three inventions: (1) they built hardware that automatically translated each address generated by the processor to its current memory location; (2) they devised demand paging, an interrupt mechanism triggered by the address translator that moved a missing page of data into the main memory; (3) they built a replacement algorithm, a procedure to detect and move the least useful pages back to secondary memory.

Virtual memory was adopted widely in commercial operating systems in the 1960s. The IBM 360/67, CDC 7600, Burroughs 6500, RCA Spectra/70, and GE 645 all had it. By the mid-1970s IBM 370, DEC VMS, DEC TENEX, and UNIX had it too. In all these systems, it was the backbone of multiprogramming, a stratagem for loading several programs simultaneously into main memory in order to maintain high processing efficiency. Virtual memory solved not only the storage allocation problem but the more critical memory protection problem. Much to everyone's surprise, these systems all exhibited "thrashing,"a condition of near-total performance collapse when the multiprogrammed load was too high (see Figure 1). [2] The concern to eliminate thrashing triggered a long line of experiments and models seeking effective load control systems. This was finally accomplished by the late 1970s—near-optimal throughput will result when the virtual memory guarantees each active process just enough space to hold its working set.[3]

Hardware designers also found virtual memory attractive. In 1965, Maurice Wilkes proposed the "slave memory," a small high-speed store included in the processor to hold, close at hand, a small number of the most recently used blocks of program code and data. Slave memory also used address translation, demand loading, and usage-based replacement. Wilkes said that, by eliminating many data transfers between the processor and the main memory, slave memory would allow the system to run within a few percent of the full processor speed at a cost of a few percent of the main memory.[4] The term "cache memory" replaced "slave memory" in 1968 when IBM introduced it on the 360/85 machine. Cache memory is now a standard principle of computer architecture.[5]

THRASHING SOLVED BY THE WORKING-SET MODEL

When I arrived at MIT in 1964, the debate over virtual memory was in full swing. Jack Dennis, who had written extensively and elo-

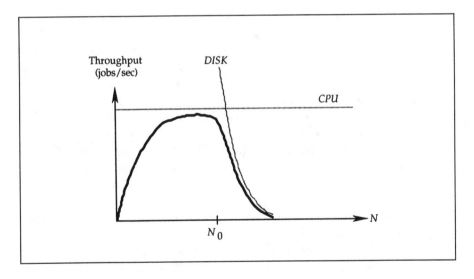

Figure 1. Thrashing was first observed in the 1960s as an unexpected, sudden drop in throughput of a multiprogrammed system when the number of programs sharing the main memory N passed a critical threshold N^o. No one knew how to calculate the threshold, which varied with the changing workload. I explained the phenomenon in 1968 and showed that a working-set memory controller would stabilize the system close to the optimal multiprogramming level. In 1975, many colleagues and I showed from queueing network models that the sudden drop was forced by saturation of the paging disk, whose limit on throughput could be calculated from disk access times and program page-fault-rate functions.

quently on the value of segmented address spaces for sharing, modularity, protection, and reusability, had won a place for segmented virtual memory in Multics. Others, such as Richard Kain, liked the elegance of the mechanism, but worried that its cost would be too high and that excessive "page turning" could kill system performance. Jerry Saltzer and Fernando Corbató took a middle ground—they sought an automatic control system that would regulate the multiprogrammed memory for optimal throughout. The ideal control would have a single "tuning knob" that would be adjusted once, like the automatic tuning system of an FM receiver.

I took it as a challenge to solve the control problem. The goal was a virtual memory system that could satisfy the programming needs of a Dennis and the performance needs of a Kain. Since fault-rates depend ultimately on the patterns by which programs reference their pages, I began to think extensively about program behavior. My quest was a single model that would account for all the individual cases (loops, nested loops, array referencing, clusters of subroutines, and so on). I came to believe that the central property of this model had to be "locality"—the tendency of programmers to write programs that address subsets of their pages over long time intervals. I purposely put the programmer into this formulation because I was convinced that human thought patterns for problem solving tended to impose structure and regularity on the dynamics of their programs; in short, locality was a universal property of programs because it is a universal property of how people think. I found many allies for this view in the virtual machine research group at IBM's Yorktown labs, especially with Les Belady, who had taken extensive measurements of programs and had found locality in every one.

After many months and many failed models for locality, late one night in the Christmas recess of 1966 I had the Aha! insight that became the working-set model. Rather than find a way to *generate* locality, all I needed was a standard way to *observe* locality. I proposed to define the working set as the set of pages referenced in a sampling window extending from the current time backward into the past (see Figure 2). The idea of sampling for used pages was not new; it appeared within usage-bit-based paging algorithms. What was new was that the window was defined in the virtual time of the program—that is, CPU time with all interrupts removed—so that the same program with the same input data

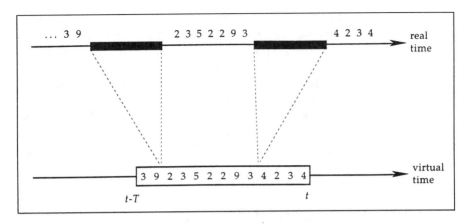

Figure 2. The working set of a program *W(t,T)* at its virtual time *t* is the distinct pages referred to by that program in the backward window of size *T*. The identities of the pages can be determined from usage bits. In this example, the page reference trace inside the window contains the distinct pages {2,3,4,5,9}, which is the working set at time *t*. At two earlier times there were page faults (because pages 2 and 4 were not present in main memory). The time intervals to service the page faults are shown in black on the real-time scale. The processing efficiency is the ratio of black to non-black intervals on the real-time scale; it improves as the window size increases.

would have the same locality measurements no matter what the memory size, multiprogramming level, or scheduler policy. This simple shift of observer made a profound difference. I called the set of pages observed in the window the "working set," a term that was already being used for the intuitive concept of the smallest set of pages required to be in main memory so that virtual memory would generate acceptable processing efficiency. The virtual-time-based definition made that precise: the larger the window, the larger the working set, the lower the probability of paging, and the greater the processing efficiency.

In the next few months I discovered that this formulation is extremely powerful. I was able to give formulas for the paging rate and size of a working-set memory policy as a function of its single parameter, window size. These basic measures could be computed from the histogram of intervals between successive references to the same page, a function that could be measured efficiently and in real time. I was able to explain in this theory what caused thrashing and how to prevent it. Although the hardware needed to measure working sets dynamically is more expensive than most designers were willing to tolerate, a number of very good approximations based on sampling usage bits were made, and they solved the problem of thrashing. A decade after the original discovery, my student Scott Graham showed experimentally that a single setting of the working-set window size would be sufficient to control the entire operating system within 5 or 10 percent of its optimum throughput. This provided the final step of the solution to Saltzer and Corbató's control problem. The basic concepts developed then are widely used today.

MEMORY MANAGEMENT THEORY

From 1967 though 1975 I worked on theories of program behavior, memory management, and system performance for computers with virtual memory.

- A program behavior model generates address traces that are statistically close to address traces measured for real programs. Within a model, a small number of parameters can be used to control locality set size, locality holding times, extent of sequential or random correlations, and the like. The model can be used to generate artificial address traces in real time, providing an input for simulators of computer systems. The model can also be used as a basis for system performance models.

- A memory management model computes the number and volume of objects moved per unit time between levels of memory for a given memory management policy.

- A system performance model computes the throughput and response time of a computer system operated under a memory management policy for a workload satisfying given program-behavior assumptions.

I had the privilege of working with many colleagues and students on the models, over 200 in all.[6] We learned many important things along the way—for example:

- The principal statistics of a working-set policy can be computed from a histogram of the lengths of intervals between repeated references to pages.

- The average duration of a locality set in a program could be estimated from Little's law applied to the working set: D = (mean working-set size)/(paging rate). D was found experimentally to be relatively insensitive to the window size of the working-set policy, giving experimental proof that locality is a real phenomenon.

- Locality in address traces derived from locality of reference in the source code of programs.

- Most programs exhibit phase-transition behavior: long intervals during which all references are restricted to a given locality set. Phases are periods of stability and predictability. Transitions between phases are chaotic.

- A simple law relates system throughput X (jobs completed per second), space-time Y (number of page-seconds of memory consumed by a job), and memory capacity M (number of pages): $M = XY$. Maximizing throughput is the same as minimizing space-time of a job, which is the objective of the memory policy.

- The reciprocal of the fault-rate function of a program gives the mean virtual time between faults; it is called the lifetime function. Allocating a program enough space to accommodate the knee of the function usually minimizes the program's space-time (see Figure 3).

- The fault-rate functions of the programs making up the workload become the parameters of a multiclass queueing network model of the computer system on which the work is run. The model allows fast computation of system throughput and response time. It also gives a direct way to compute the upper bound on throughput imposed by saturation of the paging device, giving a simple way to explain thrashing (and to avoid it).

- The working-set memory management policy is optimal: a single value of working-set window size can be tuned for the whole computer system; it need not be dynamically adjusted.

These pursuits took us through a lot of mathematics (probability and queueing theory were the most common) and experimentation (measuring systems and comparing with models). We discovered repeatedly that the stochastic models worked well

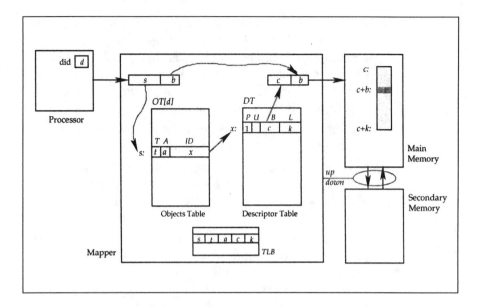

Figure 3. The lifetime curve of a program is the mean time between addressing faults as a function of the mean size of the memory space allocated to it. These functions have an overall S shape. When the size of the allocated space is close to the knee allocation, the program tends to require the minimum space-time, thus contributing to the system's capacity to deliver optimum throughput. The working-set policy can be tuned so that it operates every program close to its knee allocation.

despite the fact that their key assumptions were usually violated in practice. For example, we discovered that a queueing network model of a system would estimate throughput to within 5 percent of the value measured for that system, even though the system violated assumptions of statistical steady-state, exponential service times, and random arrivals. In 1975 I entered a collaboration with Jeffrey Buzen, who was trying to explain this phenomenon. He called the approach "operational analysis" to emphasize that models could be formulated from purely operational assumptions. Many limit theorems of queueing theory are operational laws— relationships among measurable quantities that hold for every data set.[7] Operational analysis helped us understand why the methods for measuring the statistics of "stack algorithms" and of "working-set algorithms" worked so well. (See the appendix for the results of a controversy about operational analysis.)

THE END OF THE BEGINNING

The historical thread of concern for program models, memory management, and performance models of computer systems has persisted to the present day as operating system engineers have taken the results into client-server architectures. But to help you understand the rest of the story of the maturation of virtual memory in today's operating systems, I must return to the beginning and examine more deeply the thread of concern for programming.

The literature of 1961 records a spirited debate about automatic storage allocation. By that time, FORTRAN, ALGOL, and LISP had become the first widely used high-level programming languages. These languages made storage allocation harder for the programmer because programs were larger, more machine independent, more modular, and their dynamics more dependent on their input data. Dozens of experimental studies during the 1960s sought either to affirm or deny the hypothesis that operating systems could do a better job at storage allocation than any compiler or programmer.

One by one, the technical problems were solved during the 1960s—thrashing, optimal memory management, caching, address translation for paging and for segmentation, protected subroutine calls, limited protection domains guarded by hardware. The last remaining part of the debate—whether the operating system's set of automatic overlay strategies could outperform the best programmer's manual overlay strategies—was laid to rest in 1969 by an extensive study of program locality by David Sayre's IBM research team.[8] Among other things, that team showed that the total number of pages moving up and down the memory hierarchy was consistently less with virtual memory than with manual overlays; this implied that virtual-memory-controlled multiprogramming systems would be more efficient than manual-controlled systems.

I was able to assemble a coherent picture from all the pieces and I wrote the paper "Virtual Memory," which went on to enjoy a long period of being regarded as a classic.[9] This paper celebrated the successful birth of virtual memory.

OBJECT-ORIENTED VIRTUAL MEMORY

If it ended here, this story would already have guaranteed virtual memory a place in history. But the designers of the 1960s were no less inventive than those of the 1950s. Just as the designers of the 1950s sought a solution to the problem of storage allocation, the designers of the 1960s sought solutions to two new kinds of programming problems: (1) sharable, reusable, and recompilable program modules; and (2) packages of procedures hiding the internal structure of classes of objects. The first of these led to the segmented address space, the second to the architecture that was first called capability-based addressing and later object-oriented programming.

In 1965 the designers of Multics at MIT sought systems to support large programs built from separately compiled, sharable modules linked together on demand. Jack Dennis was the leading spokesman.[10] To Dennis, virtual memory as a pure computational storage system was too restrictive; he held that modular programming would not become a reality as long as programmers had to bind together manually, by a linking loader or makefile program, the component files of an address space. Working with other designers of Multics, Dennis added a second dimension of addressing to the virtual address space, enabling it to span a large collection of linearly addressed segments. A program could refer to a variable X within a module S by the two-part name (S,X); the symbols S and X were retained by the compiler and converted to the hardware addresses by the virtual memory on first reference (a "linkage fault"). The Multics virtual memory demonstrated very sophisticated forms of sharing, reuse, access control, and protection.

What became of these innovations? The segmented address space did not survive as a recognizable entity, ostensibly because most programmers were content with one, private, linear address space and a handful of open files. The methods of address translation for segmentation were generalized by Dennis and his students into capability machines and, later, object-oriented programming. The dynamic linking mechanism did not die with Multics. It merely went into hibernation, recently reawakening in the guise of the World Wide Web, in which programs and documents contain symbolic pointers to other objects that are linked on demand.

A major turning point occurred in 1965 when Jack Dennis and his student, Earl Van Horn, worked on a paper that they called "programming semantics for multiprogrammed computations." They devised a generalization of virtual memory that allowed parallel processes in operating systems to operate in their own "spheres of protection." They replaced the concept of address with a new concept they called "capability," which was a protected pointer to an arbitrary object (see Figure 4). I was Van Horn's office mate while he worked on this project with Dennis; I remember our blackboard being filled with candidate terms like "pointer," "handle," and "generalized address," and it was some weeks before he and Dennis settled on the word "capability."

CAPABILITY MACHINES

With that extraordinary paper, Dennis and Van Horn precipitated a new line of computer architectures, the *capability machines*. They anticipated object-oriented programming: a programmer can build a manager that would create and delete objects of a class and perform operations on them. They introduced the concept called "protected entry point," a way to call a procedure and force the CPU into a new protection domain associated with that procedure. Dennis and Van Horn were especially concerned that objects be freely reusable and sharable and, at the same time, that their internal structures be accessible only to their authorized managers. Their proposal inspired others to build capability machines during the 1970s, including the Plessey 250, IBM System 38, Cambridge CAP, Intel 432, SWARD, and Hydra. In these systems, capabilities were implemented as long addresses (for example, 64 bits), which the hardware protected from alteration.[11] The RISC microprocessor, with its simplified instruction set, rendered capability-managing hardware obsolete by the mid-1980s. But software-managed capabilities, now called *handles*, are indispensable in modern object-oriented programming systems, databases, and

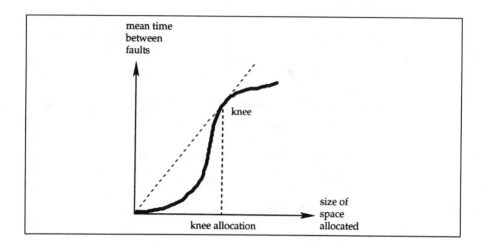

Figure 4. Two-level mapping scheme has become a universal method to translate an address to a reference to a shared object. The domain identifier register (*did*) associates the processor with an objects table that lists all the objects accessible in that domain. That table converts the local object identifier (*s*) to the global object identifier (*x*). The global identifier selects a descriptor, which in this case points to a segment of memory containing the object. A translation lookaside buffer (TLB) holds a number of most-recent paths connecting the local address to the object's location in memory; the TLB can map repeated references to the object in a small fraction of the time that the two table lookups would take. If an object is not present in main memory, the mapper will issue appropriate up and down commands to the secondary memory. With this scheme, each domain can have a (different) local identifier for the same object, facilitating sharing without prior arrangement; and the physical location of the object is recorded just once, in the descriptor, so that any relocations are effective instantly. In a large distributed system, such as Internet, the local object identifiers are the "URLs" and the global object identifiers "handles"; the main memory is on the local computer and secondary memory is a server somewhere in the network; and the up and down commands correspond to uploads and downloads performed automatically by the network protocol.

distributed operating systems.[12] The same conceptual structure has also reappeared in a proposal to manage objects and intellectual property on the Internet.[13]

You may have wondered why virtual memory, so popular in the operating systems of the 1960s and 1970s, was not present in the personal-computer operating systems of the 1980s. The pundits of the microcomputer revolution proclaimed bravely that personal computers would not succumb to the diseases of the large commercial operating systems; the personal computer would be simple, fast, and cheap. Bill Gates, who once said that no user of a personal computer would ever need more than 640K of main memory, brought out Microsoft DOS in 1982 without most of the common operating system functions, including virtual memory. Over time, however, programmers of personal computers encountered exactly the same programming problems as their predecessors in the 1950s, 1960s, and 1970s. That put pressure on the major PC operating system makers (Apple, Microsoft, and IBM) to add multiprogramming and virtual memory to their operating systems. These makers were able to respond positively because the major chip builders had never lost faith; Intel offered virtual memory and cache in its 80386 chip in 1985; and Motorola did likewise in its 68020 chip. Apple offered multiprogramming in its MultiFinder and virtual memory in its System 6 operating system. Microsoft offered multiprogramming in Windows 3.1 and virtual memory in Windows 95. IBM offered multiprogramming and virtual memory in OS/2.

A similar pattern appeared in the early development of distributed-memory multicomputers beginning in the mid-1980s. These machines allowed for a large number of computers, sharing a high-speed interconnection network, to work concurrently on a single problem. Around 1985, Intel and N-Cube introduced the first hypercube machines consisting of 128 component microcomputers. Shortly thereafter, Thinking Machines produced the first actual supercomputer of this genre, the Connection Machine, with a maximum number of 65,536 component computer chips. These machines soon challenged the traditional supercomputer by offering the same aggregate processing speed at a lower cost.[14] Their designers initially eschewed virtual memory, believing that address translation and page swapping would seriously detract from the machine's performance. But they quickly encountered new programming problems having to do with synchronizing the processes on different computers and exchanging data among them. Without a common address space, their programmers had to pass data in messages. Message operations copy the same data at least three times: first from the sender's local memory to a local kernel buffer, then across the network to a kernel buffer in the receiver, and then to the receiver's local memory. The designers of these machines began to realize that virtual memory can reduce communication costs by as much as two-thirds because it copies the data once at the time of reference. Tanenbaum describes a variety of implementations under the topic of distributed shared memory.[15]

VIRTUALIZING THE WEB

The World Wide Web extends virtual memory to the world.[16] The WWW allows an author to embed, anywhere in a document, a "uniform resource locator" (URL), which is an Internet address of a file. The WWW appeals to many people because it replaces the traditional processor-centered view of computing with a data-centered view that sees computational processes as navigators in a large space of shared objects. To avoid the problem of URLs becoming invalid when an object's owner moves it to a new machine, Kahn and Wilensky have proposed a two-level mapping scheme that first maps a URL to a handle, maps the handle to the machine hosting the object, and then downloads a copy of the object to the local machine. This scheme is structurally identical to the mapping of object-oriented virtual memory considered in the 1960s and 1970s.[17] With its Java language, Sun Microsystems has extended WWW links to address programs as well as documents;[18] when a Java interpreter encounters the URL of another Java program, it brings a copy of that program to the local machine and executes it on a Java virtual machine. These technologies, now seen as essential for the Internet, vindicate the view of the Multics designers a quarter century ago—that many large-scale computations will consist of many processes roaming a large space of shared objects.

CONCLUSION

Virtual memory is one of the great engineering triumphs of the computing age. Virtual memory systems are used to meet one or more of the following needs:

1. *Automatic Storage Allocation.*Virtual memory solves the overlay problem that arises when a program exceeds the size of the computational store available to it. It also

solves the problems of relocation and partitioning arising with multiprogramming.

2. *Protection.* Each process is given access to a limited set of objects—its protection domain. The operating system enforces the rights granted in a protection domain by restricting references to the memory regions in which objects are stored and by permitting only the types of reference stated for each object (for example, read or write). These constraints are easily checked by the hardware in parallel with address formation. These same principles are being used for efficient implementations of object-oriented programs.

3. *Modular Programs.* Programmers should be able to combine separately compiled, reusable, and sharable components into programs without prior arrangements about anything other than interfaces, and without having to link the components manually into an address space.

4. *Object-Oriented Programs.* Programmers should be able to define managers of classes of objects and be assured that only the manager can access and modify the internal structures of objects.[19] Objects should be freely sharable and reusable throughout a distributed system.[20] (This is an extension of the modular programming objective.)

5. *Data-Centered Programming.* Computations in the WWW tend to consist of many processes navigating through a space of shared, mobile objects. Objects can be bound to a computation only on demand.

6. *Parallel Computations on Multicomputers.* Scalable algorithms that can be configured at run-time for any number of processors are essential to mastery of highly parallel computations on multicomputers. Virtual memory joins the memories of the component machines into a single address space and reduces communication costs by eliminating much of the copying inherent in message passing.

From time to time over the past 40 years, various people have argued that virtual memory is not really necessary because advancing memory technology will soon permit us to have all the random-access main memory we could possibly want. Such predictions assume implicitly that the primary reason for virtual memory is automatic storage allocation of a memory hierarchy. The historical record reveals, to the contrary, that the driving force behind virtual memory has always been simplifying programs (and programming) by insulating algorithms from the parameters of the memory configuration and by allowing separately constructed objects to be shared, reused, and protected. The predictions that memory capacities would eventually be large enough to hold everything have never come true and there is little reason to believe they ever will. And even if they did, each new generation of users has discovered that its ambitions for sharing objects led it to virtual memory. Virtual memory accommodates essential patterns in the way people use computers. It will still be used when we are all gone.

APPENDIX: OPERATIONAL ANALYSIS

Operational queueing theory was simpler than regular queueing theory for basic formulas, but messier for the more sophisticated queueing systems; it was controversial among queueing theorists. A popular criticism was that the operational assumption of homogeneity—service rates of servers do not depend on system state—was nothing more than an exponential service-time assumption in disguise. That criticism was neatly dispelled by Ken Sevick and Maria Klawe, who gave an example of an operationally deterministic system whose throughput and response time were calculated accurately from classical queueing formulas but which in no sense satisfied an exponential service time assumption. Another criticism was that one cannot make predictions of a future system's performance without assuming that the present and future systems are manifestations of the same underlying stochastic process. Buzen said that stochastic processes had nothing to do with it; he argued that prediction in practice operates as a process of stating future parameter values and using a validated model to calculate future performance measures. Such small triumphs did little to assuage the critics, who believed that operational analysis denied the existence of stochastic processes.

In 1981, I witnessed a debate between Buzen and one of his critics. I was struck by the symmetry of their arguments. Each started with his domain as the ground and claimed that the other was in effect performing unneeded, error-inducing mappings to get to the same answer. They were both describing the same loop from different angles! This prompted me to write the following little fable.

> *A Tale of Two Islands*
> *Once upon a time there were two islands, Stochasia and Operatia. The citizens of Stochasia had organized their society around a revered system of mathematics for random processes. The citizens of Operatia had organized their society around a revered system for experimentation with nondeterminate physical processes. Both societies were closed. Neither would ever have known of the other's existence had it not been for the events I shall now describe.*
>
> *At a moment now lost in the mists of antiquity, a great sage of Stochasia posed this problem: Given a matrix of transition probabilities, find the corresponding equilibrium probability distribution of occupying the possible states. The sage worked out the solution, which he engraved on*

stones. Ever since, whenever the Stochasians encounter a problem in life, they phrase it in these terms and, using the stones, they find and implement its solution.

At another moment now lost in the mists of antiquity, a great sage of Operatia posed this problem: Having observed a matrix of transition frequencies, calculate the corresponding distribution of proportions of time of occupying the possible states. He worked out the solution, which he engraved on stones. Ever since, whenever the Operatians encounter a problem in life, they phrase it in these terms and, using the stones, they find and implement its solution.

In a recent time there was an anthropologist who specialized in islands. He discovered the two islands from photographs taken by an orbiting satellite. He went to visit Stochasia, where he learned the secrets of their stones. He also visited Operatia, where he learned the secrets of their stones.

Struck by the similarities of the secrets, the anthropologist asked the elders of each island to evaluate the approach used by the other island. In due course, each island's elders reached a decision.

The elders of Operatia told the anthropologist: "The Stochasians are hopelessly confused. They have developed a highly indirect approach to solving the problem posed by our great sage. First, they transform the problem into an untestable domain by a process we would call 'abstraction.' Using their stones, they find the abstract answer corresponding to the abstract problem. Finally, they equate the abstract answer with the real world by a process we would call 'interpretation.' They make the audacious claim that their result is useful, even though the two key steps, abstraction and interpretation, cannot be tested for accuracy. Indeed, these two steps cannot be tested even in principle! Our stones tell us elegantly how to calculate the real result directly from the real data. No extra steps are needed, and nothing untestable is ever used."

The elders of Stochasia told the anthropologist: "The Operatians are hopelessly confused. They have developed a highly indirect approach to solving the problem posed by our great sage. First, they restrict the problem to a single case by a process we would call 'estimation.' Using their stones, they estimate the answer corresponding to their estimate of the problem. Finally, they equate the estimated answer with the real world by a process we would call 'induction.' They make the audacious claim that their result is useful, even though the two key steps, estimation and induction, are not error free. Indeed, these two steps cannot be accurate even in principle! Our stones tell us elegantly how to calculate the general answer directly from the parameters. No extra steps are needed, and nothing inaccurate is ever used."

The anthropologist believed both these arguments and was confused. So he went away and searched for new islands.

Some years later, the anthropologist discovered a third island called Determia. Its citizens believe randomness is an illusion. They are certain that all things can be completely explained if all the facts are known. On studying the stones of Stochasia and Operatia, the elders of Determia told the anthropologist: "The Stochasians and Operatians are both hopelessly confused. Neither's approach is valid. All you have to do is look at the real world and you can see for yourself whether or not each state is occupied. There is nothing uncertain about it: each state is or is not occupied at any given time. It is completely determined."

Later, the anthropologist told this to a Stochasian, who laughed: "That's nonsense. It is well known that deterministic behavior occurs with probability zero. Therefore, it is of no importance. How did you find their island at all?" Still later, he told this to an Operatian, who laughed: "I don't know how to respond. We have not observed such behavior. Therefore it is of no importance. How did you find their island at all?"

The anthropologist believed all these arguments and was profoundly confused. So he went away and searched for yet another new island. I don't know what became of him, but I heard he discovered Noman. (Noman is an island.)

ENDNOTES

1. J. Fotheringham, "Dynamic Storage Allocation in the Atlas Computer, Including an Automatic Use of a Backing Store," ACM Communications, Vol. 4, No. 10, Oct. 1961, pp. 435–436; and T. Kilburn, D.B.G. Edwards, M.J. Lanigan, and F.H. Sumner, "One-Level Storage System," *IRE Transactions EC-11*, Vol. 2, Apr. 1962, pp. 223–235.

2. P.J. Denning, "Thrashing: Its Causes and Prevention," *Proc. AFIPS FJCC 33*, 1968, pp. 915–922.

3. P.J. Denning, "Working Sets Past and Present," *IEEE Trans. on Software Engineering SE-6*, Vol. 1, Jan., 1980, pp. 64–84.

4. M.V. Wilkes, "Slave Memories and Dynamic Storage Allocation," *IEEE Trans. EC-14*, Apr. 1965, pp. 270–271.

5. J. Hennessey and D. Patterson, *Computer Architecture: A Quantitative Approach*, Morgan-Kaufmann, 1990.

6. Denning, "Working sets past and present."

7. P.J. Denning and J. Buzen, "Operation Analysis of Queueing Network Models," *ACM Computing Surveys*, Vol. 10, No. 3, Sept. 1978

8. D. Sayre, "Is Automatic Folding of Programs Efficient Enough to Displace Manual?" *ACM Communications*, Vol. 12, No. 12, Dec. 1969, pp. 656–660.

9. P.J. Denning, "Virtual Memory," *ACM Computing Surveys*, Vol. 2, No. 3, Sept. 1970, pp. 153–189.

10. J.B. Dennis, "Segmentation and the Design of Multiprogrammed Computer Systems," *JACM*, Vol. 12, No. 4, Oct. 1965, pp. 589–602; and E.I. Organick, *The Multics System: An Examination of Its Structure*, MIT Press, Cambridge, Mass., 1972.

11. R.S. Fabry, "Capability-based Addressing," *ACM Communications*, Vol. 17, No. 7, July 1974, pp. 403–412; G.J. Myers, *Advances in Computer Architecture*, 2nd ed, Wiley, //AU: CITY?// 1982; and M.V. Wilkes and R. Needham,. *The Cambridge CAP Computer and Its Operating System*, North-Holland, //AU: CITY?// 1979.

12. J.S. Chase, H.M. Levy, M.J. Feeley, and E.D. Lazowska, "Sharing and Protection in a Single-Address-Space Operating System," *ACM TOCS*, Vol. 12, No. 4, Nov. 1994, pp. 271–307.

13. Kahn & Wilensky 1995. "A Framework for Shared Digital Objects." A web paper, available from http://cnri.reston.va.us.

14. P.J. Denning and W.F. Tichy, "Highly Parallel Computation," *Science*, No. 250, Nov. 30, 1990, pp. 1217–1222.

15. A.S. Tanenbaum, *Distributed Operating Systems*, Prentice-Hall, Englewood Cliffs, N.J., 1995.

16. T. Berners-Lee, "The World Wide Web," *Technology Review*, June 1996. See also T. Berners-Lee, "WWW: Past, Present, and Future," *IEEE Computer*, Vol. 29, No. 10, Oct. 1996, pp. 69–77.

17. J.B. Dennis and E. Van Horn, "Programming Semantics for Multiprogrammed Computations," *ACM Communications*, Vol. 9, No. 3, Mar. 1966, pp. 143–155; and Fabry, "Capability-based Addressing."

18. G. Gilder, "The Coming Software Shift," *Forbes ASAP*, Aug. 5, 1995.

19. Myers, *Advances in Computer Architecture.*

20. Chase et al., "Sharing and Protection in a Single-Address-Space Operating System"; and Tanenbaum, *Distributed Operating Systems.*

GROWING UP WITH SOFTWARE TOOLS

Raymond C. Houghton

Like most software pioneers, I first started developing software with tools that were very crude. Early cave people used cutting tools to carve communications on trees and on cave walls. To communicate with the computer, I also used cutting tools and trees. But unlike cave people, my trees were beat to a pulp and formed into the shape of cards and paper tape. The cutting tools that I used punched little rectangular holes in the cards or little asterisk-shaped holes in paper tape.

Although paper tape was a more compact way to handle my communications with the computer, unrolling and rolling the paper tape was a painful process I usually tried to avoid. The computer easily read paper tape faster than one could maintain the growing pile on the other side of the tape reader. After reading a long tape, I would usually end up with a tangled pile of paper tape that resembled a dish of spaghetti.[1]

To avoid this spaghetti mess, my usual medium for communicating with the computer was with cards. Cards were less messy then paper tape, but they had their perils, also. The greatest fear was the *dropped* deck. A dropped deck would likely have cards out of order that would cause unpredictable results if read by the computer. There was a place for sequence numbers on cards, but only the paranoid programmer punched sequence numbers. The rest of us trusted rubber bands and boxes to keep our cards in order.

The most common problem with cards was the *mangled* card. Mangled cards were created by the card reader seemingly at random, but more often according to Murphy's laws. A mangled card usually brought all processing to a complete standstill until the

mangled card was replaced with a fresh duplicate. An important skill of a software pioneer was making exact duplicates of mangled cards, quickly.

The computer that I first used was at Norwich University around 1966. At Norwich, I was on the computer center staff working part-time while completing my undergraduate degree. At that time, Norwich had an IBM 1620, a computer that holds a unique place in computer history because it was a decimal-based computer that did arithmetic by looking up answers in a table. Most computers today are binary-based, with arithmetic done by combinational logic. Since this was the first computer that I ever worked on, I thought this was the norm—little did I know. The reference sheet that I used for the IBM 1620 is shown in Figure 1.

Like most early computers, the 1620 did not have an operating system. Instead, it had a monitor that performed basic tasks such as loading and executing programs. Programs could be developed in 1620 machine language or in a high-level language

INSTRUCTIONS FOR NORWICH UNIVERSITY IBM 1620 COMPUTER

Mnemonic	Code	Instruction
A	21	Add
AM	11	Add (I)
B	49	Branch
BB	42	Branch Back
BD	43	Branch on Digit
BI	46	Branch on Indicator
BNF	44	Branch No Flag
BNI	47	Branch No Indicator
BNR	45	Branch No Record Mark
BT	27	Branch and Transmit
BTM	17	Branch and Transmit (I)
C	24	Compare
CF	33	Clear Flag
CM	14	Compare (I)
DN	35	Dump Numerically
H	48	Halt
K	34	Control
M	23	Multiply
MM	13	Multiply (I)
NOP	41	No OPeration
RA	37	Read Alphamerically
RN	36	Read Numerically
S	22	Subtract
SF	32	Set Flag
SM	12	Subtract (I)
TD	25	Transmit Digit
TDM	15	Transmit Digit (I)
TF	26	Transmit Field
TFM	16	Transmit Field (I)
TR	31	Transmit Record
WA	39	Write Alphamerically
WN	38	Write Numerically

(I) means Immediate

Switch and Indicator Codes

Q_8	Q_9	
0	1	Program switch 1
0	2	Program switch 2
0	3	Program switch 3
0	4	Program switch 4
0	6	Read Check Indicator*
0	7	Write Check Indicator*
1	1	High-Positive Indicator
1	2	Equal-Zero Indicator
1	3	High-Positive or Equal-Zero Indicator
1	4	Overflow Check Indicator
1	6	MBR-Even Check Indicator*
1	7	MBR-Odd Check Indicator*
1	9	Any Data Check

*Will cause 19 to be ON

Alphameric and Paper Tape Code

00	b	000x0.000
03	.	0xx0x.0xx
04	)	0xxxx.x00
10	+	0xxx0.000
13	$	0x0xx.0xx
14	*	0x00x.x00
20	–	0x000.000
21	/	00xx0.0x0
23	,	00xxx.0xx
24	(	00x0x.x00
33	=	0000x.0xx
34	@	000xx.x00
41	A	0xx00.00x
42	B	0xx00.0x0
43	C	0xxx0.0xx
44	D	0xx00.x00
45	E	0xxx0.x0x
46	F	0xxx0.xx0
47	G	0xx00.xxx
48	H	0xx0x.000
49	I	0xxxx.00x
‡0		
51	J	0x0x0.00x
52	K	0x0x0.0x0
53	L	0x000.0xx
54	M	0x0x0.x00
55	N	0x000.x0x
56	O	0x000.xx0
57	P	0x0x0.xxx
58	Q	0x0xx.000
59	R	0x00x.00x
62	S	00xx0.0x0
63	T	00x00.0xx
64	U	00xx0.x00
65	V	00x00.x0x
66	W	00x00.xx0
67	X	00xx0.xxx
68	Y	00xxx.000
69	Z	00x0x.00x
70	0	00x00.000
71	1	00000.00x
72	2	00000.0x0
73	3	000x0.0xx
74	4	00000.x00
75	5	000x0.x0x
76	6	000x0.xx0
77	7	00000.xxx
78	8	0000x.000
79	9	000xx.00x
⊕or ‡		00x0x.0x0
	EL	x0000.000
Tape Feed		0xxxx.xxx

$\overline{1}$ through $\overline{9}$ are punched like J to R

$\overline{0}$ appears like – on 1624 punch, but like + on 1901 punch.

Figure 1. Machine instructions for Norwich University's IBM 1620

such as FORTRAN. But using FORTRAN was an involved process that often created many mangled cards. These cards usually did not come from the FORTRAN deck itself but from the large decks that surrounded the process of precompiling, compiling, loading, and executing programs. Figure 2 is the instruction sheet for this process. The precompiler was a two-inch thick deck that scanned for errors. [2] Then there was the four-inch processor (compiler) deck that was needed to translate the FORTRAN program to 1620 machine language and produce the object deck from the card punch. The object deck always seemed to have a width of at least one-inch, even for two-line FORTRAN programs. Finally, there was the three-inch subroutine deck that contained the FORTRAN library, not to mention the data deck. It was no wonder that my first goal as a software pioneer was to find ways to avoid compiling programs.

AVOIDING THE COMPILER

I avoided the compiler by using a new teletype that had arrived at the Norwich computer center. The teletype, which was remotely connected to Dartmouth College, allowed users to program in a language called BASIC using a timesharing system that was being pioneered by John Kemeny and Thomas Kurtz. Because BASIC programs were interpreted, their system not only avoided the compiler but one could edit and store programs on their magnetic drum—someone had finally invented a system that did not require the programmer to carry around a box of cards.

Dartmouth's system was best used for *quick and dirty* programs. Because disk space was at a premium, it was not useful for data-processing applications and most scientific applications. Dartmouth would not allow remote users to store programs or data on their system for long periods of time, and with the teletype as the only input/output device, it was really not practical for reusing programs.[3] Furthermore, BASIC was purportedly slow because statements in loops had to be interpreted over and over again.

For certain situations, however, I was not convinced that interpretation was slow even with loops. I had observed that in processing data at Norwich, the card reader was the bottleneck, and not because of mangled cards. Even under normal circumstances,

<u>INSTRUCTIONS FOR USING FORTRAN WITH FORMAT PROCESSING</u>
<u>using the 1620</u>

<u>"CARD SYSTEM"</u>

I. Clear the memory
   a) Set "parity" & "I/O" switches to program. OFLOW switch to program.
   b) Push RESET, INSERT, type 310000300002, push RELEASE, START
   c) Wait 3 seconds, push INSTANT STOP, RESET
   d) Set "parity" & "I/O" switches to "stop"

2. Sense Switch (SSW) I & 3 on, 2 & 4 off (SSW 4 on to type out program

3. Load the precompiler into the card reader hopper (right side of reader)

4. Press the LOAD button on the card reader, and the cards will be read in. When "Reader No Feed" lights up, push READER START on the card reader until the light goes out.*

5. Load your source program into the card reader -- push START on the computer, "Reader No Feed" lights up, push READER START on the card reader.

6. If any error messages are printed, refer to "Error codes for card program" sheet which is kept near the computer.

7. a) To run another program, push START on the computer, go to Instruction 5.
   b) To process, clear the memory (see Instruction I)

8. Load the processor deck in the card reader hopper, and push LOAD on the card reader. SSW I on type out program, SSW 2, 3, 4, off. <u>Push PUNCH START on card reader.</u> "(SSW 2 on for trace)"

9. Load your source program, push START on computer, push READER START on card reader. Computer types "prog Sw1 on for symbol table, push start"
           you put SSW I off, push START on computer
   Computer types "Sw1 off to ignore subroutines, push start"
           you put SSW I off, push START on computer
   Wait until "Processing complete" is typed out

10. a) If any error messages are printed--refer to page 8 of IBM fortran w/ format book
    b) Lift the deck of blank cards from the punch side of the card reader (left hand side) and push NON-PROCESS RUN OUT on card reader. Remove your object program from left hand hopper, discard blank cards (last 2 cards of deck).

11. Load your object program and press LOAD on the card reader. "(SSW 4 on for trace)"

12. Load the subroutine deck, push START on the computer, READER START on card reader.

13. Load your data deck, push START on computer, READER START on card reader.

14. More than one set of data may be run by pushing INSERT, typing 4908300, RELEASE START.

15. If all else fails, <u>READ THE INSTRUCTIONS AGAIN.</u>
    *Follow this procedure every time "Reader No Feed" lights up. (Unless the card reader is still operating.)

Figure 2. Instructions for compiling a program

the 1620 spent most of its time waiting for the card reader to get another card. I speculated that for these applications, interpretation might actually make the 1620 more efficient. One could not only avoid the ten inches of card decks needed for compiling, but the CPU would have something to do between each read card.

To test my hypothesis, I designed and implemented a simple programming language that included features from FORTRAN but was interpreted like BASIC. Figure 3 is a page from the

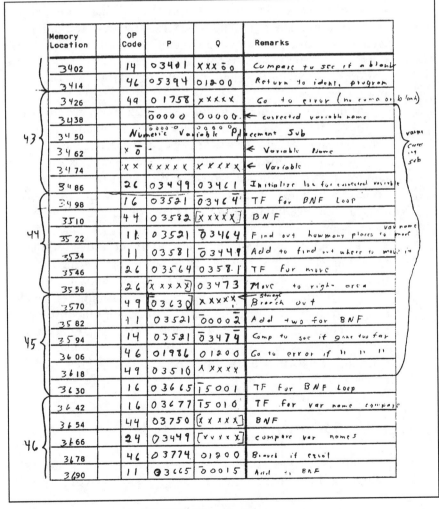

Figure 3. A page from the HOWTRAN interpreter

machine language, interpreter program. The 1620's decimal-based operation greatly simplified this task. The resulting language, nicknamed HOWTRAN by the computer systems staff, did improve information processing applications. But thanks to the growing popularity of magnetic tape, the language had a very short life-span of only a couple years. It quickly joined the programming language graveyard, along with the thousands of other languages whose special application was destroyed by new technology.

Although I had achieved minor successes in avoiding the compiler for information processing applications, I was still looking for ways to avoid it in scientific applications. I had observed that one could avoid recompiling a program by hand-compiling the changes and then *patching* those changes directly into the object deck. This eliminated recompiles once syntax errors were removed, as long as the changes in the FORTRAN program were not major.

After Norwich, this patching method actually became quite useful when my career turned to industry. As a maintenance programmer still working with cards at General Electric (GE), I could only get two job turnarounds per day, and compiling a program and testing a program were considered two separate jobs. If a program required just a couple corrections to get it up and running, this patching technique would complete the program a full workday sooner.

Although using this technique classed me with the hot-shot programmers at GE, it was clearly software engineering malpractice. Making corrections at higher levels without introducing errors is hard enough, but opening the possibility of making errors in hand compilation and introducing inconsistencies between high-level and machine language created additional risk. I did survive this stray from software engineering principals, but I learned, by necessity, to maintain programs with great care and much precision.

SPAGHETTI DESIGN

My time as a maintenance programmer left me longing for experience on the other, more creative, end of software development—requirements analysis and software design. An opportunity arose in the Washington, D.C., area at Computer Sciences Corporations (CSC). They had recently won a satellite command and control contract from NASA, and they needed software designers for this effort. Prior to this time I had no software analysis and design experience, but I had taken several graduate-level computer science courses, and apparently that was good enough.

My time in analysis and design at CSC was to be short-lived, partly because of circumstances beyond my control. When I started working at CSC, they had just completed the design and development of a system for off-track betting in New York. The system was supposed to allow people to remotely bet on horses at race tracks in different geographical areas, but the project's introduction failed miserably. CSC had not anticipated the load that would be created by the heavy initial use of the system. To make matters worse, CSC's miscalculation was right under the nose of a very observant Wall Street. CSC's stock plummeted from the mid-30s down to single digits.

As a result, NASA grew very skeptical about CSC's ability to deliver their satellite control system, and it affected communications between client and customer. When I started working at CSC, I enjoyed direct contact with NASA engineers, but within about a month's period, four layers of management were inserted in between. Questions that I had about the operation of the satellite's on-board computer, its peripherals, and sensors had to filter up CSC's chain of command and down NASA's. The responses had to come back by the same route. These circumstances reminded me of the childhood game where a message is verbally passed secretly around a room and the result is a final message that bears no resemblance to the initial message. In my case, I often found that this review process overgeneralized my questions to the point where, like the game, I did not recognize my own questions or the responses to them. Given the importance of understanding the customer's requirements for a software system, these layers of management were not helping the software design process at all.

Despite the lack of information, I charged ahead with my part of the design based on what I did know and understand. CSC had a design method called Threads that we used, but the software tools that went with the method were not accessible from our location. So all our designs had to be drawn and documented by hand. I do believe this situation encouraged us to be more defensive of our design than we might have been otherwise. Any change, even a minor one, caused the design to be completely redrawn and redocumented.

When it finally came time for a review with the customer, I found that communications had not improved. I remember presenting my part of the design to a capacity crowd. I did not recognize any of the people in my audience except for my immediate management. My presentation was made without interruption and there were no questions during or after the presentation. Thinking that "no news was good news," I was surprised several weeks later when the feedback came in, page after typewritten page. Some comments were helpful, some were extremely negative, and many were in conflict with each other. Talk about spaghetti code—this had to be spaghetti design!

It was about this time that I received word that a security clearance for a position that I had applied for nearly a year earlier at National Security Agency (NSA) had been approved. I had assumed long ago that this position had vanished when I accepted the position at CSC. Although I was very tempted by this offer, I decided that I needed to at least try to clean up my part of the design and follow it through development. I declined the offer but was informed that the position would remain open for six months anyway—the temptation would not go away.

I continued to work on my design, but things were not getting better. All around me personnel changes were taking place—new managers and new designers were replacing existing personnel or were being added to the project. CSC was obviously breaking several of Brooks' laws, in particular,

> *Adding manpower to a late software project makes it later.*[4]

I found myself spending a lot of time going over old territory with new management and bringing new designers up to speed. I also found myself spending a lot of time redrawing and redocumenting my design to suit my new management's taste. On one Friday, I was told to completely redo a part of my design and submit it, *first thing* Monday morning. Instead, that weekend, I wrote my letter of resignation. I had had enough.

I did learn a lot about software engineering during these early years of my career. Most importantly, I learned that

Not having the right tools for the job leads to software engineering malpractice.

Collecting Tools

In 1974, I took the lessons I had learned at CSC with me to NSA.[5] I worked as a computer scientist in the Computer Security Division of the Office of COMSEC (communications security) Applications. Our division participated in computer security efforts on several communications systems and in COMSEC equipment.

Around this same time, the Advance Research Project Agency (ARPA) of the Department of Defense was funding investigations by tiger teams to show that computer systems, operating systems in particular, were not secure. These tiger teams clearly showed that the developers of operating systems, IBM, Honeywell, UNIVAC, and so on, were more interested in developing a product that would provide basic input/output services rather than protecting the system from either destructive users or those who wanted to gain access to information that they were not privy to.[6] What security they did provide was not provided consistently throughout the system, leaving them only as secure as their weakest link.

At NSA, it was our division's job to verify that good software engineering and computer security principals were being applied in software. To do this, we would provide advice and guidance during the initial analysis and design phases of a system and independently test and analyze the software during the implementation phase. Fortunately for us, these systems relied heavily on physical security, so the security provided by the software did not have to survive the scrutiny of a tiger team.

One of my first assignments at NSA was to investigate software tools and to acquire those that were needed to do this job. The goal of this project, which would later be called DECKBOY, was to create a toolbox, one that would contain a compatible set of tools for the analysis and testing of software. To create this toolbox, we would enlist the efforts of several software pioneers who were among the leading *toolsmiths* of the time:

- Douglas Webb from Lawrence Livermore Laboratory (LLL)—He was a member of LLL's tiger team and led the development of several tools for analyzing assembly language programs. Where most members of tiger teams were primarily interested in breaking systems, Webb's interests were broader than just a break-in. He wanted to understand the weaknesses that made the break-in possible.

- L.M. Culpepper from the Naval Ship Research and Development Center—He led the development of a tool called AUDIT that analyzed a FORTRAN program to ensure that it conformed to a set of programming standards. L.M. Culpepper reminded me of a wise old navy captain who was using this tool to keep his software *ship-shape*.

- Lee Osterweil from the University of Colorado—He, along with Lloyd D. Fosdick, led the development of a tool called DAVE, which analyzed FORTRAN programs for errors in variable referencing. Osterweil seemed to downplay the importance of DAVE because it found errors that were correctable by encouraging either better structure in FORTRAN programs or by using a more structured language like Pascal. But DAVE helped us understand many errors related to computer security because it was often errors in referencing that allowed a person to break the security of a system.

- Gordon Lyon of the National Bureau of Standards (NBS)—He, along with Rona B. Stillman and Donald Orser, led the development of early prototypes for measuring the frequency of statement use in FORTRAN programs. Lyon was a true researcher at NBS, inspired by Donald E. Knuth's early work in this area.

- Bob Glass of Boeing Computer Services (BCS)—Glass was involved in the early stages of a tool development contract between BCS and NSA. Even in those early days of tool development, Glass was a contrarian. He rightly pointed out that many of us were developing and *hyping* tools for the sake of developing tools and hyping tools. We were not keeping tools in perspective with our overall goals of improving the quality of software.

- Richard (Dick) Maitlen of TRW—He led the development of a tool called NODAL (Node Determination and

Analysis Program) for NSA. NODAL provided various measurements of testing coverage of FORTRAN programs. Maitlen was a no-nonsense, white-shirted, software engineer. He maintained excellent control over the customers (NSA's) wishes and the contractors (TRW's) ability to respond to those wishes. The result was a high-quality software product that in later years was updated to FORTRAN-77 by TRW for NBS.

- Tom McCabe of NSA—Although McCabe worked in a different part of NSA, he was asked to be a technical consultant for the development of a tool by TRW that measured the complexity of FORTRAN and Pascal programs using cyclomatic complexity.[7] McCabe was, in many ways, the antithesis of Maitlen. Where Maitlen's feet were on the ground, firmly committed to delivering a software tool that met our defined requirements, McCabe's were not. Instead, he was off dreaming about his wishes and desires for the application of cyclomatic complexity. I often felt like a referee in our contractual review meetings trying to balance McCabe's liberal interpretation of the requirements and Maitlen's very conservative interpretation.

Once we had our toolbox established, we applied the tools in projects where security measures were implemented in software. I came away from these projects with a very high degree of confidence that the software was correct and would work properly. I also gained a tremendous respect for what I felt was a very powerful set of tools. It was clear to me that our toolbox would not only assist NSA projects but would also be useful in other government agencies and in the public sector as well, particularly those tools we had developed under contract.

I put together a report on DECKBOY and proposed that it be submitted for publication in a trade journal or presented at a conference. The proposal, however, was not looked upon very favorably—NSA has never liked drawing attention to itself. Instead, it was suggested that I establish communications privately with other government agencies.

One of the most logical government agencies to contact was the National Bureau of Standards (NBS).[8] NBS had ongoing projects in the software tool area and was responsible for providing advice, guidance, and standards for software. At this time, however, the relationship between NSA and NBS was somewhat strained. Several former NSAers were already working for NBS. One person, Dennis Branstad, was leading the DES (Data Encryption Standard) project, an area that touched near and dear to NSA's heart.

As a result of my contacts at NBS, my relationship with NSA management also became strained. Whenever I got an outside phone call, my immediate supervisor would listen-in on the conversation—not in a sneaky way, mind you; he would get up from his desk and stand right next to me during the entire conversation. After such a call, I was expected to brief him about the part of the conversation that he could not hear. He was no doubt a very conscientious supervisor—staying on top of my situation at all times.

Eventually, I did get management approval to turn over parts of the DECKBOY toolbox to NBS, but I decided that I wanted to go with the tools. I talked to higher management about my desires and, to my surprise, they were very supportive. I guess I had become a bigger headache than I had thought. Without requesting it, I was given a very complimentary letter of recommendation from NSA addressed "To whom it may concern." The letter described the work that I had accomplished while working at NSA, something that I knew was rarely done. I felt honored. So, I packed my toolbag and my letter of recommendation and I was off to NBS.

PUTTING SOFTWARE TOOLS IN THEIR CLASS

My time at NBS was by far the most rewarding time that I have ever spent in my career. There were many pioneers there:

- Frances (Betty) Holberton—Holberton has often been called the first computer programmer. In a keynote address at the ACM SIGPLAN History of Programming Languages Conference, Grace Hopper said, "I think the first step to tell us that we could actually use a compiler to write programs was Betty Holberton's Sort-Merge Generator." [9] I remember Holberton admitting to me one time, "We should have called it a translator, not a compiler." She was a true pioneer.

- Al Neumann—Neuman was Mr. Documentation. He oversaw standards development for software documentation, but subsequent to this, he worked at the Eckert-Mauchly Computer Corporation on the UNIVAC. Neuman was very pessimistic about software tools, and I had to spend quite a bit of time with him, but over time, he became supportive. Regardless, he always made sure that my feet stayed on the ground.

- ABC (Rick Adrion, Marty Branstad and John Cherniavsky)—As a team, they not only nailed down the importance of validation, verification, and testing of computer software, but they also led NBS's efforts in the development of guidelines and standards for the process and products of software engineering.[10] At different times, Adrion and Branstad were my immediate supervisors, and I truly enjoyed their leadership and support.

At NBS, I became leader of the Tools and Technology Project, and my first assignment was to assess the current state of the art.[11] Under contract, I enlisted help from two other software pioneers: Don Reifer and Herb Hecht. Reifer and Hecht had already published several reports on related areas of software engineering. Reifer was one of the leading advocates for the use of tools in software development, but his greatest talent was bringing order out of chaos, a talent he applied well in classifying software tools. Give him a tool and he would classify it—it was an editor, a compiler, a cross referencer, a coverage analyzer, and so forth.

I did have a problem with his method of classification, however, because it emphasized single functionality of tools. I wanted to see a way of classifying tools that supported single tools with multiple functionality such as that being proposed for software development environments. So with Reifer and Hecht's help and the support of others in the software community, we *inverted* the tool classes and created a taxonomy of software tool features. Instead of classifying a tool into a category, we would classify the tool according to the features that it provided. For example, a programming environment might have the features of editing, translating, optimization, instrumentation, cross-referencing, error checking, and tracing.[12] By classifying tools this way, one could compare the features of one tool with those of another. This taxonomy would eventually become a Federal Information Processing Standard (FIPS 99), the structure of which is shown on the cover of the FIPS in Figure 4. The taxonomy also became the basis of a survey paper on software tools published in *IEEE Computer.*[13]

Not only did the taxonomy show the features that a tool had, it also showed the features that a tool did not have. For a short time, I took the taxonomy on the road for a two-city tour in California at conferences sponsored by the Data Processing Management Association (DPMA). My talk was called "Key Features of the Ada Programming Support Environment (APSE)." In my presentation, however, I also presented what I considered key features that were not part of the three Ada environments currently under development within DoD. In the receptions following these conferences, I was often asked, usually tongue-in-cheek, but not always, if I could somehow cutout that part of my presentation.

THE DOG AND PONY SHOWS

Two documents published in the early 1980s helped to propel software tools into the limelight. A study by the General Accounting Office (GAO) found that software tools could offer the government better management and control of software development, but more importantly, they used the magic words, "lower cost."[14] The other document was a book published by Barry Boehm that clearly showed, right on the cover, that software tools were a significant factor in improving software productivity.[15]

It was decided at an organizational meeting for the 5th International Conference on Software Engineering (ICSE5) that, in addition to the usual paper and panel presentations, there would also be a forum for presenting tools. Leon Stucki from Boeing Computer Services would become the conceptual leader of this effort, and Gerry Estrin from UCLA would become the spiritual leader. Thanks to Seymour Jeffrey, who was general chair of the conference and my boss's boss's boss, I would put aside just about everything else I was working on for the next year and make this "tool fair" a reality.

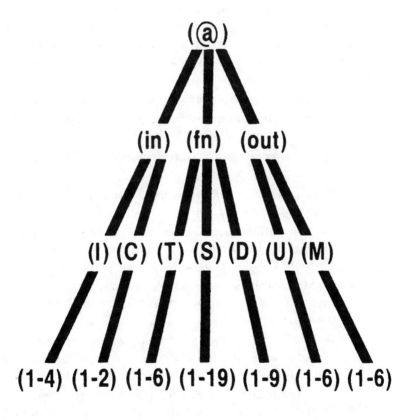

Figure 4. Tool taxonomy structure

We wanted the tool fair to be an educational forum. Our goals were to preview tools currently in research, to increase knowledge of what was currently available, and to demonstrate how tools are used in software engineering. Our most important goal was to do this in a professional, nonsales manner. We envisioned small, classroom-sized demonstrations of tools that were integrated and scheduled with the rest of the conference. We would also ask for presentation proposals that would be reviewed and approved by committee.

The staff of IEEE, on the other hand, had different ideas. They saw the tool fair as a revenue generating exhibition where demonstrators would pay for a booth and hawk their tools to conference attendees. Their position was that this educational forum idea came too late in the planning process and would not be supported by conference fees. Eventually, a compromise was reached, but it took monetary support from NBS to obtain it.

In the end, the tool fair was a major success. We had over 33 tools demonstrated at the fair, and many novel ideas, including the following, were introduced for the first time to attendees:

- Nicholas Wirth, the father of Pascal, demonstrated a tool called Lilith that worked on a personal computer using a *high resolution* display and a *mouse*.

- Robert Fenchel from UCLA demonstrated a tool that included integral contextual help.

- Debbie Scherrer from Lawrence Berkeley Laboratory demonstrated a portable version of UNIX.

- Jon Chris Miller from the Catalyst Corporation demonstrated a tool that *magically* introduced structure into spaghetti COBOL programs.

- Ed Miller from Software Research Associates demonstrated a tool that measured his trademark C1 level of testing coverage.

- Tom Gilb from Norway charismatically demonstrated a tool that supported automated design by objectives. By the end of the conference, he had created a cult following.

- Mark Overgaard from Softech Microsystems demonstrated the first programming environment for Pascal, the UCSD p-System.

NDNOTES

1. I have often wondered if this is where the term *spaghetti code* really came from.

2. All measurements are based on my recollection and, I hope, not exaggerated—like the fish that got away.

3. In truth, I did make use of Dartmouth's system for other purposes besides quick and dirty programs. By allowing different geographic locations to use their facility, they had inadvertently created a facility for exchanging email. I made very practical use of this capability by communicating with a girlfriend at Colby Junior College.

4. F.P. Brooks, Jr., *The Mythical Man-Month*, Addison-Wesley, Reading, Mass., 1995.

5. My father thought I went to NASA.

6. It is sad that these security lessons were not learned by those developing systems for microcomputers. As I write this recollection on my computer, I have an underlying fear that a virus is about to destroy this text.

7. "A Complexity Measure," *IEEE Trans. on Software Engineering*, Vol. SE-2, No. 4, 1976.

8. Today, NBS is known as National Institute for Standards and Technology (NIST).

9. June 1, 1978.

10 W. Richards Adrion, Martha A. Branstad, and John C. Cherniavsky, "Validation, Verification, and Testing of Computer Software," *ACM Computing Surveys*, June 1982.

11. This, of course, was the first assignment for every government project.

12 In Betty Holberton's honor.

13. Raymond C. Houghton, Jr., "Software Development Tools," *IEEE Computer*, Vol. 16, No. 5, May 1983, p. 63.

14. General Accounting Office, "Wider Use of Better Computer Software Technology Can Improve Management Control and Reduce Costs," Report No. FGMSD-80-38, April 1980.

15. Barry W. Boehm, *Software Engineering Economics*, Prentice-Hall, Englewood Cliffs, N.J., 1981.

- John Barkley and Pat Powell from NBS demo
  FORTRAN 77 Analyzer that had made its way
  to NSA then to NBS and eventually would ma
  back to TRW.[16]
- And not to be left out of all the fun, I demon
  tool for finding out about software tools, "Th
  Software Tools Database."

The success of the tool fair at ICSE5 spawned two
especially devoted to software tools: SoftFair, held in
D.C., in 1983, was chaired by Leon Stucki and myself;
II, held in San Francisco in 1985, was chaired by Ma
SoftFair was eventually dropped by IEEE so that it wo
pete with ICSE, which had been scheduled to occu
quently.

Tools Today

Today, the individual tools of the past are regularly int
the systems we use to develop software. Just like the
sor that I am currently using—which has a tool
includes a spell checker, a grammar checker, a thesau
ation, a word counter, and more—we expect the syst
use to develop software to similarly have all the tools
do the job. Design systems must support both graph
descriptions of a system, they must have a database
track of the products of design, and they must have
that automatically take the design to lower-levels of
tion. Programming systems must not just compile pro
must also support editing, testing, and debugging, as
vide support for gradually building programs and exan
structure during the building process.

My interest in software tools continues to this toda
often fascinated by their capabilities. I sometimes find
ing with them for hours, discovering their strengths
nesses and applying them to various applications. At
some days, I look back at the *real* work that I have ac
and wonder if I should return to my goals of the 1960
software tools.

16. Barry Boehm and Maria Penedo, "A Software Development Environment for Improving Productivity," *IEEE Computer*, Vol. 17, No. 6, June 1984,

7

AFTER THE BEGINNING: CONCLUSIONS

Just north of Indianapolis lies an unusual, tiny settlement. Conner Prairie is a historical museum, a re-creation of a village in 1836, lying amidst the cornfields of an Indiana countryside, and among the burgeoning houses of an ever-expanding mini-megalopolis.

Conner Prairie settlement is more than simply a historical museum in village form—there is something special about the place. Let me take you for a walk through it.

As we approach the settlement, the sign at the entrance offers a clue to its special character: "Welcome to Conner Prairie. It is 1836." Over there, under the sign "Golden Eagle Inn," is a place to spend the night. Let's step in and see what the inn of 1836 was like.

"Howdy," says a large, red-faced woman, wearing a long dress of the era. "Welcome to the Golden Eagle. Beds are twelve-and-a-half cents a night, and you share with whoever comes in."

As you continue conversing, you begin to realize something strange is happening. The conversation appears to be happening in 1836, and—try as you might—you cannot shake the feeling that your own end of the conversation is occurring in 1836 as well. You examine the room, check out the kitchen, and talk about whether you want to spend the night. You are being transformed, almost unwittingly, into a vintage 1836 person.

You visit other buildings, and the same thing happens. The school teacher asks where you are from, and when you name a western state he says, "There is no such state." (It has not joined the Union yet here in 1836). The local doctor explains that he is more interested in land speculation than in doctoring, and launches into a discussion of how, during this slave era, states must be paired—slave and nonslave—in order to enter the Union. The storekeeper explains how he is stocking up on liquor because an election is coming up and the politicians provide free liquor in front of his store—the polling place—to encourage voters to turn out. And through it all, you are feeling more and more 1836ish. Conner Prairie settlement is, in other words, participatory theater. The people in the buildings, the actors, perform on a very flexible stage, and you inevitably join in their play. Through this means, history comes alive.

In this book, I have attempted to create a sort of Conner Prairie settlement, allowing you, the reader, to wander through the lives of the pioneers of software development and to experience what it was like in those historic early days of computing. But the performers on this book's stage are not actors, they are the real thing, the people who actually played the roles they describe. Their recollections are not contrived, they are real and as fresh as the fond memories that obviously remain alive in their minds.

It has been my goal in this book to capture those very special memories before they are gone. I hope you have enjoyed wandering through the pages of our stage!

APPENDIX:
BIOGRAPHICAL SKETCHES

ROBERT L. BABER

Robert L. Baber was born in Los Angeles, California, in 1937. He received his S.B. and S.M. in electrical engineering from the Massachusetts Institute of Technology in 1959. This course of study included several practical semesters at IBM laboratories in Poughkeepsie and Binghamton, New York; he was in the first group of MIT students participating in this cooperative program. He also studied nuclear engineering. In 1962 he received his S.M. in industrial management from MIT. Baber served as a programmer analyst from 1962 until 1964 in the Signal Corps of the U.S. Army, mostly in a computer center in an atomic bombproof installation in the middle of a rock mountain not too far from Washington, D.C. He moved to Germany in 1964, where he was employed by Control Data in technical sales support. From 1966 until 1970 he was a consultant in the Diebold Research Program, which investigated many aspects of applying EDP systems in business and similar organizations. Subsequently he was a senior consultant with the Frankfurt branch of the management consulting firm Harbridge House. From 1975 until 1996 he was an independent management consultant specializing in conceiving, planning, and implementing computing systems for business, administrative, and technical applications.

Baber developed a seminar on designing provably correct software that he presented in several European countries and, on the invitation of the Institute for Software of the Chinese Academy of Sciences, in Beijing. He has written four books on various aspects of designing error-free software. He developed and instructed courses on this subject as an external lecturer in the Computing Science Department of the Johann Wolfgang Goethe University, Frankfurt/Main, Germany. In 1994 he received his doctorate in computing science from the Technische Hochschule Darmstadt, Germany.

In 1996 Baber was appointed visiting professor in the Department of Computer Science at the University of the Witwatersrand, Johannesburg, South Africa. His primary teaching and research interests are in the areas of designing error-free software and transforming software development into a true engineering discipline.

Baber is a Chartered Engineer and a Fellow of the British Computer Society, a Senior Member of the IEEE and its Computer Society and a member of the German Society for Computing Science. He was a cofounder and first chairman of the Computer Chapter of the German Section of the IEEE. He is also a member of the German Association of Engineers (VDI) and of the German Society of Electrical Engineers (VDE). He is registered as a European Engineer (Eur. Ing.) in the European Federation of Engineering Associations (FEANI).

JOHN M. BENNETT

John M. Bennett, A.O., B.E. (civil), B.E. (mechanical and electrical), B.Sc. (Qld), Ph.D. (Camb); his affiliations include FTSE, FACS, FBCS, FIEAust, FIMA, FIEE, FRSS. After four years in RAAF ground radar, he entered the computer field in 1947 as a Ph.D. student with the Cambridge University EDSAC team. After obtaining his doctorate he spent 1950 to 1955 with Ferranti Ltd in Manchester and London. He returned to Australia in 1956 as senior numerical analyst at the University of Sydney, with responsibility for the management of the university's first computer, SIL-LIAC, and the organization of associated courses. In 1961, he was appointed Professor of Physics (Electronic Computing). In 1981, the title of the chair was changed to computer science. He has been president of the Sydney Association of University Teachers (1964–65); Chairman of the University of Sydney Appointments Board (1970–74); Fellow of the University of Sydney Senate (1976–77, 1980–84); and President of the Sydney University Association of Professors (1977–78). He retired from the

University of Sydney at the end of 1986 with the title of Professor Emeritus.

From 1959 to 1963, he was foundation Chairman of the Australian National Committee for Computation and Automatic Control (ANCCAC). He was President of the NSW Computer Society in 1965. In 1966, he became foundation president of the Australian Computer Society (ACS). He is an honorary life member of ACS, and in 1980 was the recipient of an ACS Chips Award. He was co-editor of *Computing in Australia*—the history of ACS's first 25 years. He was Vice-President of the International Federation for Information Processing (1975–78), and Trustee (1974–75, 1978–80). In 1981, he was elected a Governor of the International Council for Computer Communications (ICCC), of which, from 1988 to 1993, he was the Secretary-General. In 1981, he was elected a Fellow of the Australian Academy of Technological Sciences and Engineering, and in 1983, became a member of the Council of that academy. From 1989 to 1990, he was Chairman of the NSW Division. In 1982, he received the Officer of the Order of Australia (AO) award. In 1985, he was awarded the 1984 ACS ANCCAC Prize.

He has served on the boards of two computer companies and has acted as a consultant on various computer matters to a number of companies and universities and to government and UN agencies. He was a member of the Australian Government Committee on the Computerization of Legal Data (1973) and the Committee on Privacy (1973). He visited the United Kingdom in 1966 as a British Council Distinguished University Scholar and in 1975 as a Commonwealth Visiting Professor. In 1981, he visited Stanford University as an Australian-American Educational Foundation Senior Scholar. In 1988–89, he spent a term with the National University of Singapore as a Visiting Professor. At various times, he has been invited to lecture in Hong Kong, India, New Zealand, the People's Republic of China, South Africa, the United Kingdom, the United States, and the former Soviet Union.

He has published over 150 papers and technical reports on various aspects of computing and associated social effects. Recently, his interests have been concerned with the manipulation of sparse matrices arising in linear programming and in structural and electrical networks, certain aspects of computer networks, information retrieval, and workforce and privacy implications of computer use.

BRUCE I. BLUM

There is a certain symmetry to Bruce I. Blum's life. He spent his first 30-some years finding a profession, the next 30-some working in that profession, and now is engaged in what he hopes will be 30-some years of active retirement. To start at the beginning: After an aborted academic career in history, he studied mathematics and took a job in what he thought would be operations research. Fortunately, in 1962 programmers were needed, and that is what he became.

He started working with computers at the Applied Physics Laboratory (APL) of Johns Hopkins University and left for industry after five years. He spent the next seven years with Wolf Research and Development, where he became a vice president. He did not like that job, so he worked for TRW for a year and then returned to APL in 1974. He became a full-time faculty member in the Johns Hopkins School of Medicine in 1975. He returned to APL in 1983 to devote himself to research in software engineering.

During the period of his commercial work, he designed scientific information systems: for navy submarine data, for the first Landsat, for the National Space Science Data Center, and for Navy command and control. After he joined the school of medicine, he became active in medical informatics. He developed several clinical information systems, the largest of which is still in operation. He also initiated the Springer-Verlag series Computers and Medicine, wrote *Clinical Information Systems,* and organized several conferences.

When he returned to APL, he concentrated on the development of open systems, that is, systems whose requirements evolve as the product is implemented and used. He has written three books on the subject, the last of which (*Beyond Programming*) presents his view of how systems will be designed in the twenty-first century. Having solved the central problem of software engineering, he gave up his email account and retired. He now devotes himself to photography and the search for a "profession" that will take him through the next 30 years.

BARRY W. BOEHM

Barry W. Boehm was born May 16, 1935. He received his B.A. degree from Harvard University in 1957, and his M.S. and Ph.D. from UCLA in 1961 and 1964, all in mathematics. He is currently TRW Professor of Software Engineering, Computer Science Department, University of Southern California; and director of the USC Center for Software Engineering.

Between 1989 and 1992, he served within the U.S. Department of Defense (DoD) as Director of the DARPA Information Science and Technology Office and as director of the DDR&E Software and Computer Technology Office. He worked at TRW from 1973 to 1989, culminating as chief scientist of the Defense Systems Group, and at the Rand Corporation from 1959 to 1973, culminating as head of the Information Sciences Department.

His contributions to the field include the Constructive Cost Model (COCOMO), the Spiral Model of the software process, and two advanced software engineering environments: the TRW Software Productivity System and Quantum Leap Environment. He has served on editorial boards of several scientific journals, and as a member of the governing board of the IEEE Computer Society. He currently chairs the Information Processing Panel of the Air Force Scientific Advisory Board and the Board of Visitors of the Software Engineering Institute.

His honors include being a guest lecturer of the USSR Academy of Sciences (1970); and receiving the AIAA Information Systems Award (1979), the J.D. Warnier Prize for Excellence in Information Sciences (1984), the ISPA Freiman Award for Parametric Analysis (1988), the NSIA Grace Murray Hopper Award (1989), the ASQC Lifetime Achievement Award (1994), and the ACM Distinguished Research Award in Software Engineering (1997). He is an ACM fellow, an AIAA fellow, and an IEEE fellow and a member of the National Academy of Engineering (1996).

ROBERT N. BRITCHER

Robert N. Britcher is retired from IBM. He teaches system architecture, design and integration, and software management at Johns Hopkins University and, occasionally, writes about software.

His work on the automation of air traffic control began in the 1960s and continues today with Lockheed Martin.

He lives and works near Washington, D.C.

Peter J. Denning

Peter J. Denning is Vice Provost for Continuing Professional Education at George Mason University. He served as associate dean for computing and chair of the Computer Science Department in the School of Information Technology and Engineering at George Mason University (1991–1996).

He was the founding director of the Research Institute for Advanced Computer Science (RIACS) at the NASA Ames Research Center in Mountain View, Calif. He served in that capacity from 1983 to 1990, when he stepped down and became research fellow until 1991.

Before accepting the RIACS assignment, Denning was head of the Computer Sciences Department at Purdue University, where he was a professor of computer sciences (1975-1984) and an associate professor (1972-1975). He was an assistant professor of electrical engineering at Princeton University (1968-1972). Denning was one of the four founders of the CSNET, which evolved into the first fully self-supporting community network; CSNET is a precursor of the NSFNET and the NREN. He has worked closely with NASA on computational science and on the high-performance computing and communications program.

Denning's primary research interests are computer systems architecture, parallel computation, operating systems, performance modeling, hyperlearning systems, and organizational informatics. He has published over 260 papers and articles since 1967. His work on virtual memory systems helped make virtual memory a permanent part of modern operating systems. His book with E.G. Coffman, Jr., *Operating Systems Theory*, was published by Prentice-Hall in 1973 and is still widely used today. His book with Jack Dennis and Joseph Qualitz, *Machines, Language, and Computation*, was published by Prentice-Hall in 1978. His edited collection, *Computers Under Attack: Intruders, Worms, and Viruses*, published by Addison-Wesley in 1990, was a best-seller. His book, *Beyond Calculation: The Next 50 Yeras of Computing* (Bob Metcalfe, co-editor) was published by Copernicus Press in 1997 and was praised for "astonishing intellectual breadth" in *The New York Times.*

Denning was president of the Association for Computing Machinery (1980–82). He has held leadership posts in the ACM continuously since 1968, including 20 years on the ACM council. He served as chairman of the Task Force on the Core of Computer Science (1986–88), as chair of the ACM Editorial Committee, and member of the publications board (1986–92). He was elected chair of the publications board in 1992, and has led the development and implementation of the ACM digital library.

Denning served as editor-in-chief of *Communications of the ACM* (1983–92), which under his guidance has become the leading technical magazine in computing. During this period, he radically altered the character of the journal from a research publication to an up-to-date communication for practitioners. He continues as a contributing editor of *Communications.* He is an associate editor of *Acta Informatica.* He was consulting editor for computer science for the MIT Press, editor-in-chief of ACM's *Computing Surveys,* and editor of the Elsevier/North Holland series on *Operating and Programming Systems.* He wrote the column "The Science of Computing" in *American Scientist* from 1985 through 1993.

Denning holds two best-paper awards, a teaching award, a career accomplishment award, three Society fellowships (AAAS, ACM, IEEE), and distinguished service awards from both ACM and CRA (Computing Research Association). He was named the recipient of the ACM 1996 Karl Karlstrom Outstanding Educator Award for his efforts in developing a scientific core for operating systems, in formulating a core curriculum for computing, and in elucidating computer science to the broader scientific community.

ROBERT L. GLASS

Robert L. Glass is president of Computing Trends, publishers of *The Software Practitioner.* He has been active in the field of computing and software for over 40 years, largely in industry (1954–82 and 1988–present) but also as an academic (1982–88). In industry (North American Aviation, Aerojet-General Corp., and Boeing), he has managed both development and acquisition projects, built and maintained software for most application domains, and engaged in research and development. In academia, he taught for five years in the software engineering graduate program at Seattle University and spent a year as a visiting staff member at the Software Engineering Institute.

He is the author of 20 books and 60 published papers on computing and software, editor of the *Journal of Systems and Software,* publisher and editor of *The Software Practitioner,* and was for 15 years a lecturer for the Association for Computing Machinery. He received an honorary Ph.D. from Linkoping University, Sweden, in 1995.

HAROLD JOSEPH HIGHLAND

Harold Joseph Highland, FICS, FACM, is a dinosaur who was graduated from the university and received his commission as a second lieutenant in 1938. In 1981 he retired with the academic rank of distinguished teaching professor from the State University of New York's Technical College at Farmingdale. Upon retiring he founded *Computers & Security* and served as editor-in-chief for a decade. *Computers & Security* in 1983 became the official journal of the International Federation of Information Processing's Technical Committee on infosec [IFIP/TC11].

As editor-in-chief emeritus, he continues to write his column, "Bits & Bytes," and serves as counsel to the Computer Security Technical Committee of the Chinese Computer Federation (Beijing, People's Republic of China) and to other government agencies in the United States and overseas.

He has written several hundred technical articles and papers as well as 27 books, several of which have been translated into Japanese, German, French, Italian, Dutch, Russian, and Finnish. He was the first recipient of the IFIP Kristian Beckman Award made in public recognition of an individual who has significantly contributed to the development of international information security. He also received the IFIP Outstanding Service Award, ISSA's Thomas Fitzgerald Award, the Distinguished Service Award from the Institute of Management Sciences College of Simulation and the Special Recognition Award from the board of directors of the Winter Simulation Conference, and the ACM/SIGSIM Award for Special Service.

He is the only American fellow of the Irish Computer Society (ICS), and he is also a fellow of the Association for Computer

Machinery (ACM). He is a member of the New York Academy of Sciences (NYAS), American Association for the Advancement of Science (AAAS), American Cryptographic Association (ACA), the Internet Society (ISOC), IEEE's Computer Society (IEEE/CS1), Information Systems Security Association (ISSA), and the Association for Corporate Computing Technical Professionals.

RAYMOND C. HOUGHTON, JR.

Raymond C. Houghton, Jr., began his computing career in 1966 as a computer operator at Norwich University while completing a B.S. degree in mathematics. After graduating in 1969, he worked in industry as a programmer for General Electric and later on the technical staff at Computer Sciences Corporation. In 1974, his career turned to the government when he began working as a computer security analyst for the National Security Agency and later as the leader of the Software Tools and Technology Project at the National Bureau of Standards.

While working in the Washington, D.C., area, Houghton's career started a turn toward academics. In 1975, he completed an M.S. in computer science at George Washington University, and in 1980, an M.S. in Electrical Engineering at Johns Hopkins University. In 1984, he turned to academics on a full-time basis when he began working on a Ph.D. at Duke University. While completing his research, Houghton began teaching part-time at Augusta College, a member of the University System of Georgia. In 1991, Houghton completed his Ph.D. at Duke and accepted a full-time position at Augusta College where he eventually reached the level of associate professor. In 1993, he accepted a teaching position at Skidmore College where he taught part-time prior to opening his own business in 1995. Today, Houghton is the owner and president of Cyber Haus Computer Learning Centers, Delmar, New York.

Throughout his career, Houghton has been an active writer and speaker. His writings have appeared in *Computer, Communications of the ACM*, Auerbach Publications, and numerous government reports and conference proceedings. Besides his activities with tool fairs during the 1980s, he also chaired sessions at the International Conference of Software Engineering and participated in program development for the 1983 and 1985 SoftFairs.

He has been honored with Certificates of Appreciation and Recognition from the IEEE Computer Society and the Department of Commerce.

WATTS S. HUMPHREY

Watts S. Humphrey is currently an SEI fellow at the Software Engineering Institute of Carnegie Mellon University. He joined the SEI after his retirement from IBM in 1986. While at the SEI, he established the Process Program, led the initial development of the Software Capability Maturity Model, and introduced the concepts of Software Process Assessment, Software Capability Evaluation, and, most recently, the Personal Software Process (PSP).

Prior to joining the SEI, he spent 27 years with IBM in various technical executive positions, including the management of all IBM commercial software development. This included the first 19 releases of OS/360. Most recently, he was IBM's director of programming quality and process.

Humphrey holds graduate degrees in physics from the Illinois Institute of Technology and in business administration from the University of Chicago. He is an SEI fellow, a member of the ACM, an IEEE fellow, and a past member of the Malcolm Baldrige National Quality Award Board of Examiners. He was awarded the American Institute of Aeronautics and Astronautics Software Engineering Award for 1993, and the SEI Leadership Award in 1987. His publications include many technical papers and six books. His most recent books are: *Managing the Software Process* (1989), *A Discipline for Software Engineering* (1995), *Managing Technical People* (1996), and *Introduction to the Personal Software Process* (1997). He holds five U.S. patents.

FRANK LAND

Frank Land, a refugee from Nazi Germany, studied economics at the London School of Economics (1947–50), and after doing research in economics joined the U.K.'s leading food and catering enterprise, J. Lyons, as a management trainee in 1951. J. Lyons had by then embarked on their pioneering venture to build a computer called LEO (Lyons Electronic Office), capable of assisting the company with its data processing. In 1952 he attended a one-week comprehension course for LEO and as a result was invited to join the LEO team as a programmer. The success of LEO led to J. Lyons setting up a subsidiary company to manufacture and sell business computers. Frank Land worked for LEO until 1967, as an application systems programmer, systems analyst, and consultant, rising to the position of chief consultant.

In 1967 the National Computer Centre of the U.K. granted the London School of Economics the sum of £30,000 to establish a post for teaching and research into computer-based business systems. Land was elected for this post. At the London School of Economics he set up a successful graduate program at the masters and Ph.D. levels, and became involved in a number of major research initiatives. In 1982 he was awarded the first chair of systems analysis in the U.K. In 1996 he was invited to come to the London Business School as professor of information management. During his academic career Frank Land has accepted invitations to act as visiting professor at the Wharton School, University of Pennsylvania, Sydney University, Curtin University, Bond University, University of Cairo, and at the Indian Institute of Management. He formally retired in 1991 but was invited to return to the London School of Economics as visiting professor of information management to continue his research work and supervision of Ph.D. students. In 1995 he was further invited to act as visiting professor at the School of Management, University of Bath. Land has published many papers and books, including his latest, *User-Driven Innovation: The World's First Business Computer,* with colleagues from LEO days, David Caminer, John Aris, and Peter Hermon, published by McGraw-Hill in 1996.

BEN G. MATLEY

Ben G. Matley worked in the computer industry for 15 years and then left industry to teach computing at higher education institutions. While in industry, he taught at local colleges as adjunct faculty. Subsequently, he accepted tenure track positions both at community colleges and at universities. He established initial vocational computer curricula at two community colleges, and assisted in establishing degree programs in computing at two universities.

Matley is the author of numerous journal articles and conference papers on computing, education, and mathematics. Most of his publications address the social aspects of computing, but he is also the senior author of a book on national computer policies, and sole author of a textbook on Algebra, among other works. He was named Distinguished Visitor for the IEEE Computer Society, and he is listed in Marquis' *Who's Who in the West.*

Matley earned his A.B. general degree in physics and mathematics at San Diego State University; his M.B.A. in management at the University of Southern California; a Certificate in Data Processing awarded jointly by UCLA and UCLA Extension; and his Ed.D. degree in curriculum development at Nova University in Ft. Lauderdale, Florida. He is also a holder of the CDP professional designation in computing. He is presently professor of mathematics at Ventura College, Ventura, California.

DAVID MYERS

David Myers, B.Sc., D.Sc. Eng., was born on June 5, 1911, in Sydney, Australia, and received his scientific education at the University of Sydney, 1928–33. He spent the next three years alternating between Metropolitan-Vickers Electrical Co. in Manchester and Oxford University. On returning to Australia in 1936, he became the first chief of the Division of Electrotechnology, CSIRO, and from 1948, professor of electrical engineering at the University of Sydney. He was president of the Institution of Engineers, Australia, 1958–59. He accepted appointment in 1960 as dean of applied science at the University of British Columbia until he returned in 1965 to Australia as the foundation vice-chancellor of La Trobe University in Melbourne, from which he retired in 1976.

DONALD J. REIFER

Donald J. Reifer's career in both industry and government spans almost 30 years. Reifer started in the business right out of college as a programmer with Hughes Aircraft Company in the days of fixed-point computers and drum memories. After several years, he took on management responsibilities for a number of weapon system and factory automation projects. He left Hughes in the mid-1970s to join the Aerospace Corporation. At Aerospace, he managed all of the software activities for the space transportation system in support of the U.S. Air Force. In the late 1970s, Reifer joined TRW where he was deputy program manager for the Global Positioning Satellite System. When opportunity presented itself, Reifer left TRW and formed RCI, the firm he still is affiliated with as its President.

During the 1980s and early 1990s, Reifer and RCI specialized in helping clients harness evolving software engineering technology. Using quantitative techniques, he helped clients develop the business cases executives needed to substantiate change. In 1993, Reifer joined the Department of Defense (DoD) under an Intergovernmental Personnel Act agreement with the Defense Information Systems Agency (DISA). For about two years, he led the DoD Software Reuse Initiative and the Ada Joint Program Office as the chief of the DoD Software Initiatives Office.

Some of Reifer's honors include the Secretary of Defense Medal for Outstanding Public Service (1996), the DISA Outstanding Service Award (1995), the Defense Mapping Agency Appreciation Award (1995), the Freiman Award for Outstanding Contributions to Parametric Estimating (1991), and the NASA Distinguished Service Medal (1985). Reifer is a member of Omicron Delta Kappa and Eta Kappa Nu honor societies and is listed in *Who's Who*.

Norman F. Schneidewind

Since 1971, Norman F. Schneidewind has been a professor of information sciences and director of the Software Metrics Research Center in the Information Systems Group at the Naval Postgraduate School, where he teaches and performs research in software engineering and computer networks. He is the developer of the Schneidewind software reliability model, which is used by NASA to assist in the prediction of software reliability of the NASA Space Shuttle, by the Naval Surface Warfare Center for Trident and Aegis software reliability prediction, and by the Marine Corps

Tactical Systems Support Activity for multifunction distributed system software reliability assessment. The model has been recommended by the American Institute of Aeronautics and Astronautics and the American National Standards Institute's Recommended Practice for Software Reliability. The model is also implemented in the Statistical Modeling and Estimation of Reliability Functions for Software (SMERFS) software reliability modeling tool. Schneidewind is a fellow of the IEEE, elected for "contributions to software measurement models in reliability and metrics, and for leadership in advancing the field of software maintenance." He was awarded a certificate for outstanding research achievements in 1992 by the Naval Postgraduate School. He is listed in *Who's Who in Engineering.*

Schneidewind is a member of the Department of Defense Software Engineering Institute Measurement Steering Committee. He was chairman of the working group that produced the IEEE Standard for a Software Quality Metrics Methodology, which was published in March 1993. In 1993 he was given the IEEE Computer Society's Outstanding Contribution Award "for work leading to the establishment of IEEE Standard 1061-1992, Standard for a Software Quality Metrics Methodology." He was elected to and serves as a member of the IEEE Software Engineering Standards Committee Management Board. Also, he chairs the IEEE Standards Software Reliability Planning Committee. He is past chair, IEEE Technical Committee on Simulation. He has served in a number of additional officer positions on IEEE and ACM software engineering councils and boards. Schneidewind organized the first Conference on Software Maintenance in 1983. He was the general chair for the International Conference on Software Maintenance, 1996. He was the general chair of the International Symposium for Software Reliability Engineering, 1994; program chair of the 9th International Conference on Distributed Computing Systems, 1989; editor of the IEEE Computer Standards Department; and associate editor, *IEEE Transactions on Software Engineering.*

Prior to joining the Naval Postgraduate School, from 1951 to 1971 Schneidewind held several technical management positions in the computer industry where he directed a number of projects, including the National Marine Data Program, Executive Office of the President; National Traffic Data Center, U.S. Department of Transportation; studies on information systems for the Library of

Congress; Bay Area Rapid Transit System computer control system; Navy Submarine Logistics project; and Marin County data processing study. He also managed the development of a 100 million–record title company tax-and-lien application and was the manager of a 60-person computer center that processed these applications. He had his start in the commercial computer field as an engineer for UNIVAC. For his service on an outside panel that made a comprehensive review of U.S. Customs activities and plans in data processing, he received the Commissioner's Award of the U.S. Bureau of Customs for "Contributions to the Data Processing Advisory Panel."

He has a B.S.E.E., University of California (Berkeley); a M.S.E.E. and a M.S.C.S., San Jose State University; a M.S.O.R. (engineering), and a doctorate with a major in operations research, University of Southern California. He is a member of Eta Kappa Nu, Tau Beta Pi, and Alpha Pi Mu Engineering Honor Societies; and Sigma Xi Research Society. He also holds the Certificate in Data Processing (CDP) from the Institute for Certification of Computer Professionals.

INDEX

IEEE

COMPUTER SOCIETY

Press Activities Board

Vice President:
I. Mark Haas
Managing Partner
Haas Associates
P.O. Box 451177
Garland, TX 75045-1177
m.haas@computer.org

Jon T. Butler, Naval Postgraduate School
James J. Farrell III, Motorola
Mohamed E. Fayad, University of Nevada
I. Mark Haas, Haas Associates
Ronald G. Hoelzeman, University of Pittsburgh
Gene F. Hoffnagle, IBM Corporation
John R. Nicol, GTE Laboratories
Yale N. Patt, University of Michigan
Benjamin W. Wah, University of Illinois
Ronald D. Williams, University of Virginia

Editor-in-Chief
Advances in Computer Science and Engineering Board
Pradip Srimani
Colorado State University
Dept. of Computer Science
601 South Hows Lane
Fort Collins, CO 80525
Phone: 970-491-5862 FAX: 970-491-2466
srimani@cs.colostate.edu

Editor-in-Chief
Practices in Computer Science and Engineering Board
Mohamed E. Fayad
Computer Science, MS/171
Bldg. LME, Room 308
University of Nevada
Reno, NV 89557
Phone: 702-784-4356 FAX: 702-784-1833
fayad@cs.unr.edu

IEEE Computer Society Executive Staff
T. Michael Elliott, Executive Director
Matthew S. Loeb, Publisher

IEEE Computer Society Publications

The world-renowned Computer Society publishes, promotes, and distributes a wide variety of authoritative computer science and engineering texts. These books are available in two formats: 100 percent original material by authors preeminent in their field who focus on relevant topics and cutting-edge research, and reprint collections consisting of carefully selected groups of previously published papers with accompanying original introductory and explanatory text.

Submission of proposals: For guidelines and information on Computer Society books, send e-mail to cs.books@computer.org or write to the Acquisitions Editor, IEEE Computer Society, P.O. Box 3014, 10662 Los Vaqueros Circle, Los Alamitos, CA 90720-1314. Telephone +1 714-821-8380. FAX +1 714-761-1784.

IEEE Computer Society Proceedings

The Computer Society also produces and actively promotes the proceedings of more than 130 acclaimed international conferences each year in multimedia formats that include hard and softcover books, CD-ROMs, videos, and on-line publications.

For information on Computer Society proceedings, send e-mail to cs.books@computer.org or write to Proceedings, IEEE Computer Society, P.O. Box 3014, 10662 Los Vaqueros Circle, Los Alamitos, CA 90720-1314. Telephone +1 714-821-8380. FAX +1 714-761-1784.

Additional information regarding the Computer Society, conferences and proceedings, CD-ROMs, videos, and books can also be accessed from our web site at http://computer.org/cspress

4/15/97